FRESH CUTS

T0314798

Comhairle Cathrach
Bhaile Átha Cliath
Dublin City Council

#LOVEDUBLIN

FRESH CUTS

Plays from Dublin Fringe Festival 2015 & 2016

It Folds by Brokentalkers and junk ensemble

LOVE+ by MALAPROP Theatre

The Windstealers by Jane Madden

Our Island by Barry McStay

TRYST by Finbarr Doyle and Jeda de Brí

Half Light by Mollie Molumby

Briseis After the Black by Dylan Coburn Gray

Traitor by Shane Mac an Bhaird

Selected and edited by Ruth McGowan with Kris Nelson

OBERON BOOKS
LONDON

WWW.OBERONBOOKS.COM

First published in 2016 by Oberon Books Ltd
521 Caledonian Road, London N7 9RH
Tel: +44 (0) 20 7607 3637 / Fax: +44 (0) 20 7607 3629
e-mail: info@oberonbooks.com
www.oberonbooks.com

Visit www.oberonbooks.com to read more about all our books
and to buy them. You will also find features, author interviews and
news of any author events, and you can sign up for e-newsletters
so that you're always first to hear about our new releases.

Contents

FOREWORD

For the last twenty-two years, Dublin Fringe Festival has staged a city takeover every September. We are Ireland's largest multidisciplinary arts festival and one of the world's only entirely curated Fringes. Fringe is where trends get set, where new styles of work and ideas are born. The radicals and experimentalists, the artists whose projects just don't fit in the box, the crafters, the grafters, the misfits and the clarion voices all thrive at Fringe.

We champion glorious, sensorial performances that you feel, that you see when you close your eyes; consequent work that makes demands of both artist and audience, and artists who have a contagious sense of purpose. It's the festival where Irish artists make their mark. This volume, *Fresh Cuts*, has just a taster of the bold theatre artists from the 2015 and 2016 editions of our festival, Tiger Dublin Fringe. It's a selection of indelible and adventurous works from playwrights and makers whose lead you'll want to follow.

In September 2015, the city's favourite theatres came alive during Dublin's landmark annual festival. Among this feast of brand new work were four of the texts in this collection; *It Folds* by Brokentalkers and junk ensemble, *The Windstealers* by Jane Madden, *LOVE+* by MALAPROP Theatre and *Our Island* by Barry McStay.

The ingenious combination of two of Ireland's leading performance companies, Brokentalkers and junk ensemble and their artistic directors Feidlim Cannon, Gary Keegan, Jessica Kennedy and Megan Kennedy, yielded *It Folds*. Blending music, movement and whimsy, this oddly hopeful elegy gives a beautiful and uneasy account of the aftermath of tragedy. Jane Madden's *The Windstealers* produced by Eccles Theatre Group sweeps us away to Ballygweeha, the windiest town in Ireland. A contemporary satire written for a dynamic ensemble, Madden's play skewers corruption and national character, with plenty of double dealings, lusty encounters and Tesco gin along the way.

What happens to romance when there's a machine who cooks for you, cleans for you, never forgets your birthday or how you like your tea, tells you you're beautiful, holds you when you're crying, and still makes you cum? MALAPROP's *LOVE+* has the answers, and asserts some seriously uncomfortable questions to reveal them. *Our Island* by Barry McStay finds a stressed-out Jack about to introduce his very Irish parents to his partner Bradley for the first time, in their shared London home, on Christmas Day. This sensitive drama deftly negotiates themes of self-worth, family dynamics, and making a home for oneself.

At the time of writing, we are about to kick-off a knockout 2016 festival, featuring a staggering 73 productions, 412 performances, with 40 world premieres in 23 amazing venues. This includes the world premiere of four of the plays in this volume; *TRYST* by Jeda de Brí and Finbarr Doyle, *Half Light* by Mollie Molumby, *Briseis After the Black* by Dylan Coburn Gray and *Traitor* by Shane Mac an Bhaird.

TRYST is a complex, thrilling three-hander about sex and friendship. This compelling drama from emerging Irish theatre company Sickle Moon unflinchingly and accurately explores the consequences of messy nights on the town. *Briseis After the Black* is a dramaturgical battle of wits. Joined on stage by a different performer each night, playwright Dylan Coburn Gray aims to demagnetise your moral compass with this risky cat-and-mouse reimagining of a found text, and an attempt to memorialise its tragic author.

Half Light by Mollie Molumby entices you into the forest, along with ten-year-old Robin, who is looking for his Dad. Equally witty and dreamlike, with music and lyrics by Fionn Foley, this sophisticated piece poses big questions about accountability, care-giving and adulthood come too soon. Shane Mac an Bhaird's *Traitor*, produced by That Lot, is set between the shifting political landscape of the present and a not-so-distant future. A Dublin activist finds herself poised to take political control of the nation, holding a changing society in the balance and taken to task by cronies from her anarchist past.

We'd like to thank Oberon for their great commitment and welcoming enthusiasm towards both the artists within these pages, and the countless performance makers they spotlight annually. Dublin Fringe Festival is core funded by the Arts

Council / An Chomhairle Ealaíon, Dublin City Council and Fáilte Ireland – their support and that of title sponsor Tiger Beer have made these sensational Fringe festival editions possible. The best and the boldest saved for last, a huge thank you to the growing community of artists making vital, exciting work at Dublin Fringe Festival each year and the intrepid audiences who follow them.

We hope the eight new works collected here will trouble your conscience, give you tingles of recognition, elicit a chuckle on your commute, and tempt you to join us for more in Dublin next September. Irish theatre is pulsing with complex ideas and incredible performances. There's a surge of talented dramatists and sophisticated makers – read on to uncover some of the voices leading the charge.

Ruth McGowan, Programme Manager
and Kris Nelson, Festival Director
31ˢᵗ August 2016

DUBLIN
FRINGE
FESTIVAL

ABOUT DUBLIN FRINGE FESTIVAL

Dublin Fringe Festival is home to bold ideas, brave performing arts and adventurous audiences. Fringe is a curated, multi-disciplinary festival and year-round organisation focusing on fresh and innovative approaches to the arts from Irish and international makers. The festival is where artists challenge, subvert and invigorate their disciplines and practice. An active curator, Fringe supports artistic vision, ambition and excellence across a range of art forms and offers support, resources, space, time and professional development to the Irish independent arts sector.

Followed by fans and first timers alike, Dublin Fringe Festival draws more than 30,000 spectators each September and transforms Dublin into an exposé of great creative talent from around the globe. The scale and environment of the festival broadens arts participation, introducing artists and audiences and playing a pivotal role in the fabric of Dublin and Irish cultural life.

Dublin Fringe Festival is a platform for the best new, emerging Irish arts companies and a showcase for the finest international contemporary performing arts. For artists, Fringe facilitates opportunities to innovate, to cross boundaries and strengthen the conditions in which they work. For audiences, Fringe is the place to discover meaningful, exciting and unforgettable cultural experiences.

www.fringefest.com

ABOUT FRINGE LAB

Dublin Fringe Festival is dedicated to advancing, strengthening and supporting the independent arts sector. FRINGE LAB provides year-round practical and artistic support, responding to the needs of both developing and established artists, technicians, producers and practitioners. FRINGE LAB is both a space and a platform for training and learning. At a basic level, professional performing artists need somewhere to work. Fringe provides that essential space by giving and subsidising access to two large studios, an office for artists and a writer's room. Artists access Fringe's own in-house expertise across a wide range of disciplines, such as producing, marketing and publicity, with an ongoing schedule of workshops, masterclasses with Irish and international experts, networking events, scratch nights and a host of other activities devoted to cultivating connections and expertise.

IT FOLDS

BY
BROKENTALKERS AND JUNK ENSEMBLE

Characters

GHOST

YOUNG BOY

MAN

GRANDFATHER

GRANDDAUGHTER

OLDER WOMAN (and chair)

PANTOMIME HORSE (Mother and Father)

PSYCHIC

HUSBAND'S SOCIETY (3 female singers dressed
in men's clothing)

BROKEN ANGEL (contemporary dancer)

YOUNG GIRL

19-20 CHORUS GHOSTS (dressed in sheets)

It Folds original production: 7-12 September 2015 at The Abbey Theatre on The Peacock Stage as part of Tiger Dublin Fringe Festival

Concept, Creation and Direction by Feidlim Cannon, Gary Keegan, Jessica Kennedy, Megan Kennedy

Lighting and Visual Design: Sarah Jane Shiels

Music: Denis Clohessy

Costume Design and Design Assistant: Louise Brady

Choral Director: Ruaidhrí Ó Dálaigh

Producer: Beccy Fitzpatrick

Performers: Atalia Branzburg, Colin Condon, John Doran, Louise Ginnane, Dagmara Jerzak, Sarah Kinlen, Rob McDermott, Pat Morris, Maureen Murray, Siofra O'Meara, Ben Sullivan, Cara Christie, Andrea Cleary, Niamh Denyer, Denise Geraghty, Eleanor Walsh, Lola White

Ensemble: Meiron Bignall, Kate Bodner, Mary Conroy, Aisling Flynn, Rebecca Kelly, Claudia Kinahan, Michael Kunze, Maria De La Paz Lopez, Jennifer Meade, Milenka Salinas, Yvonne Stewart, Isha Van Der Burg, Stephen Quinn

Photography: Luca Truffarelli

Production and Stage Manager: Caoimhe Regan

Technical Assistant: Hannah Reid

It Folds is supported by Culture Ireland, Dance Ireland, Dublin City Council, Project Arts Centre, Fringe Lab (Tiger Dublin Fringe) and LÓKAL Festival Reykjavík

GHOST *(dressed with white sheet over head and eyeholes) walks onstage holding mic. Stands DSC.*

GHOST: Can you all see me? Good.

When I was younger I used to be an altar boy, and on Sundays, in between masses, me and the other altar boys would be in the sacristy. And the parish priest, Father O'Reilly, would come in, and he would strip off, in front of us. He would take off his vestments and stand there in his underpants, to cool off in-between masses, I suppose.

And standing there in his pants, he would do a post-mass analysis on the mass we had just done. I was the oldest altar boy, which meant I was in charge of ringing the altar bells. One thing Father O'Reilly would always say to me was that I was coming in a *little* bit too late with the bells. Just a *little* bit too late during the Epiclesis.

Now, the Epiclesis is the part of the Mass when the priest evokes the Holy Ghost upon the Eucharistic bread and wine and the moment when they're transformed into the body and blood of Christ. So my cue was to ring the bells at the exact moment he raised the holy bread above his head, like this. *(Demonstrate bells.)*

But I thought it would be better to leave a little pause between Father O'Reilly's hands stopping and me ringing the bell to create a moment of anticipation. Like this. *(Demonstrate bells.)*

But Father O'Reilly but he was having none of it. He warned me that if I wanted to continue ringing the bells then I had to do things the proper way.

So following week said 'fuck it' this time I'm gonna leave it a good ten seconds before I ring the bells. I wanted to give people time and space to contemplate the Holy Ghost. Not to take it for granted that the Holy Ghost would show up. To keep them on their toes. Like this *(Demonstrate the arms and hold for ten seconds.)*

Because people go through the motions in Mass. Don't they? don't they? It's all so predictable. Sit down, stand up, sit down again, kneel, stand up again, and shake hands. Do this thing. *(Demonstrate gesture.)*

Afterwards Father O'Reilly said I ruined the Mass. And I told him I did it because people weren't really listening to him, they weren't really thinking, they were just following a script. This really annoyed him. He took the bells off me and he told me that I couldn't be an altar boy anymore. After that I lost interest in the church. I stopped going to mass altogether. I would tell my parents that I was going to Mass with my friends but we would just hang around outside the shop and we would ask people on their way home from Mass what the gospel was, just in case our parents asked us when we got home. Then after a while I didn't even bother pretending I was going too mass. I would just stay in bed on Sundays.

One Sunday my Dad and me had this big argument about the whole mass thing he told me he wasn't happy with my attitude and I told him to 'fuck off' and I stormed out of the house. After that things get a bit hazy.

(Enter BEN USL, blindfolded.) I don't really remember what happened after that. I can see flashes. I think I'm with my friends and we're running and laughing we're running across a road. I don't know why we are running. I don't remember anything else after that.

GHOST exits USR with mic.

YOUNG BOY, blindfolded, finds piñata stick (pre-set SC) and begins to swing stick.

MAN enters USR with party blower. Blows party blower.

YOUNG BOY stops swinging bat and puts it US.

Man and Boy Neck Leading Dance (Choreography)

YOUNG BOY leans back through his neck into MAN's grip.

GRANDDAUGHTER enters with GRANDFATHER on her back (piggyback) and puts GRANDFATHER on DS chair. Gives him small present box (pre-set beside chair), stands SL of him and holds his hand.

Happy Birthday Text

GRANDDAUGHTER: Happy birthday

GRANDFATHER: To you.

GRANDDAUGHTER: Happy Birthday

GRANDFATHER: To you.

GRANDDAUGHTER: Happy Birthday

GRANDFATHER: Dear

GRANDFATHER: Name?

GRANDFATHER: Dear Name

GRANDDAUGHTER: Happy birthday

GRANDFATHER: To you.

GRANDDAUGHTER: Silver. Silver. Silver.

GRANDFATHER: Car

GRANDDAUGHTER: Strawberry

GRANDFATHER: Birthmark

GRANDDAUGHTER: Tempus

GRANDFATHER: Fugit

GRANDDAUGHTER: Marsh

GRANDFATHER: Mallow

GRANDDAUGHTER: Marsh

GRANDFATHER: Mallow

GRANDDAUGHTER: Marsh

GRANDFATHER: Land

GRANDDAUGHTER: Wrist

GRANDDAD: Twist

GRANDDAUGHTER: Wrist

GRANDFATHER: Watch

GRANDDAUGHTER: Watch

GRANDFATHER: Out

GRANDDAUGHTER: Dig

GRANDFATHER: Deep

GRANDDAUGHTER: Ditch

GRANDFATHER: Hole

GRANDDAUGHTER: Holy

GRANDFATHER: Holy

GRANDDAUGHTER: Holy lord

GRANDFATHER: God of power and might

GRANDDAUGHTER: Heaven and earth are full of your glory

GRANDFATHER: Hosanna in the highest

GRANDDAUGHTER: I've been through the desert

GRANDFATHER: On a horse with no name

> *GRANDDAUGHTER and GRANDFATHER continue speaking lines from the song.*

> *MAN and YOUNG BOY continue movement piece in circle.*

(Choreography.)

GRANDDAUGHTER exits after finishing text.

MAN and YOUNG BOY lifting section, MAN lifts YOUNG BOY around his upper body. (Choreography.)

MAN takes YOUNG BOY's shirt off and puts US.

Hugging sequence (choreography)

YOUNG BOY starts to move to ground. MAN lies down on top of YOUNG BOY, face upwards. When MAN is fully lying on YOUNG BOY, the HORSE enters USL.

YOUNG BOY drags himself out from under MAN towards SL, pets the HORSE's face and gets on the back of horse. HORSE exits. MAN crawls after HORSE.

OLDER WOMAN enters with chair.

She slowly dresses a sack and chair in HUSBAND's clothes and places second chair and places SR of chair and sits.

Older Woman and Chair sequence

OLDER WOMAN speaks in a low gruff voice (only sounds), imitating her husband. She speaks in higher tones to imitate herself. A conversation ensues.

HORSE enters and stands SR of OLDER WOMAN. OLDER WOMAN stands and picks up chair to exit USL.

HORSE looks to audience, looks back to SR.

Horse Fight (Choreography)

FATHER throws some horse costume off stage US

HORSE dance/fight continues

MOTHER and FATHER start moving DS during the fight.

One slow push, two fast pushes, before MOTHER takes step to DSR to face outwards with FATHER standing beside her.

PSYCHIC enters SL and kneels down behind Chair.

MOTHER and FATHER stand DSR.

Psychic scene

PSYCHIC: I see a Gavin or Kevin. It's a Kevin. Does the name Kevin mean anything to you?

FATHER: Kevin.

MOTHER: Is it a child or an adult?

PSYCHIC: It's an adult.

FATHER: Kevin doesn't ring any bells.

MOTHER: I don't know anyone named Kevin.

PSYCHIC: He was the one who picked up your son in a grey or silver coloured Volkswagen.

MOTHER: This Kevin was he somebody that our son knew?

PSYCHIC: No. No. Your son didn't know him.

FATHER: When you say he was picked up do you mean he was abducted?

PSYCHIC: Yes, he was abducted.

MOTHER: He was grabbed?

PSYCHIC: Yes, grabbed.

FATHER: Can you see this Kevin? What does he look like?

PSYCHIC: He looks like he is in his mid forties. He is tall, very tall and thin. He has long, dark, greasy hair. He is wearing a flannel shirt. He has a tattoo of a bird on his hand. He is chewing a toothpick.

MOTHER: He sounds awful.

PSYCHIC: Yes.

FATHER: What else can you tell us about the vehicle?

PSYCHIC: As I said it's a grey or silver Volkswagen. I think it's a Jetta. It's an older Jetta maybe from 1991 or 1992. It reminds me of my old car. Four door saloon. 1.6 turbo diesel engine. I loved that car.

MOTHER: What else can you see?

PSYCHIC: I can see a baby's shoe on the dashboard and pieces of paper on the backseat.

FATHER: Can you tell how far he was taken?

PSYCHIC: Maybe about twenty miles.

FATHER: Is he still within a twenty-mile radius?

PSYCHIC: Yes he is still within a twenty-mile radius.

FATHER: What direction was he taken?

PSYCHIC: Southwest.

MOTHER: Can you be more specific?

PSYCHIC: About what?

MOTHER: Are there any landmarks?

PSYCHIC: I see. I see two jagged rocks. Which look really misplaced. Because everything else is trees, like a forest and all of a sudden out of nowhere you have these two stupid rocks.

FATHER: And is he there? Can he be found there?

PSYCHIC: He's is near the rocks. Yes.

MOTHER: Is he still with us?

PSYCHIC: No. I'm sorry.

FATHER: Do you see his bike anywhere?

MOTHER: Why does that matter? Who cares about the bike!

FATHER: Do you see his bike?

PSYCHIC: Yes. Yes I see his bicycle. But the strange thing is the bicycle is not close to him, it's far away in another county. In a scrap-yard.

FATHER: Can you describe the scrap yard?

MOTHER: Will you forget about the bike.

FATHER puts on horse head. FATHER and MOTHER exit SR.

Older Woman Death Dance (Choreography)

OLDER WOMAN is dressed in man's clothes/as her husband. Wild dance from OLDER WOMAN ensues.

GHOST enters and walks over to OLDER WOMAN.

GHOST: Boo

OLDER WOMAN has a heart attack and falls to the ground as if dying. Final gasp of air. Dies.

GHOST funeral text

(GHOST walks over OLDER WOMAN's body on way DSC.)

GHOST: As I was saying I'm with my friends and we're running and laughing we're running across a road. I don't know why we are running but we are.

I don't remember a lot after that. I don't remember how I died. I think it might have had something to do with a car. But I can't remember.

I do remember the morgue and I remember my da he collapsed when he saw my dead body. And when he fell he smashed one of the lenses in his glasses. I remember my funeral, the church was packed. My parents were sitting at the top of the church and they were both sobbing. My da got up on the altar to do the eulogy.

He was still wearing the glasses with the missing lens so every time he looked out to the congregation it looked liked he had one big massive eye. And all of my friends at the back of the church started to laugh at my Da, with his one big eye. He was crying, talking about how their hearts were broken and how I was the light of their lives.

I was the apple of his eye. I was the apple of his one big massive eye.

OLDER WOMAN re-enters SL with grave-making props.

The HUSBAND's SOCIETY enters from SL and SR with their grave props and build seven graves. During the last grave making, the OLDER WOMAN makes a guttural noise. All seven of HUSBAND'S SOCIETY make a guttural noise and turn their heads to the audience. They sing.

THE HUSBANDS SOCIETY'S GRAVE SONG

VERSE 1

The grave should be kept up and clean and
Glass vases may not be used and
Glass chimes too also are banned but
Not clear tubes if they are strong

CHORUS

Birds may rob the grave and take what's inside for them
To Hide A-way and never be seen again
Like those interred beneath all that fertile soil
Who'll grow again

VERSE 2

Chry-san-the-mums – they could smell nice
Ge-ran-i-ums – they would look bright
or E-ver-greens – with powered lights
though co-lours fade – fade into white

CHORUS

Birds may rob the grave and take what's inside for them
To Hide A-way and never be seen again
Like those interred beneath all that fertile soil
Who'll grow again

BRIDGE

CHORUS

Birds may rob the grave and take what's inside for them
To Hide A-way and never be seen again
Like those interred beneath all that fertile soil
Who'll grow again

Grave Song

Score

Denis Clohessy

BROKEN ANGEL enters dragging YOUNG BOY across DS and off SR.

'Fertile soil will grow again':

HUSBAND'S SOCIETY start to move side to side. (Choreography.)

OLDER WOMAN turns to exit. HUSBAND'S SOCIETY follow.

GRANDDAUGHTER enters and puts GRANDFATHER in DS chair.

Granddaughter and Grandfather Care Dance (Choreography during text)

GRANDDAUGHTER: When I was six you made me a beautiful wooden horse. You carved it from a piece of wood that was from a tree in your back garden. You said this horse would be my best friend and if I needed help the horse would know what to do. And I believed you.

I loved that horse. I brought it everywhere with me. I would tell it all my secrets. I would sleep with the horse under my pillow. I would even dream about the horse.

I think it was a Sunday, we were on holidays, in the woods. I was climbing on some rocks and my wooden horse fell out of my pocket. When I looked down I saw that one of the legs had broken off and I started to cry. And you came over to me and kissed me on my check and said don't get upset. It's just a toy.

But it wasn't just a toy. I believed you when you told me that the horse would be my best friend and if I needed help the horse would know what to do. I couldn't stop crying and you wiped away my tears and you said the horse doesn't have a life like us and just a lifeless thing. Don't be so sad for the broken leg. I asked you, 'Do you think it doesn't matter that a leg of my horse was broken?' You said yes its not important. Even if the horse loses its tail, it won't hurt the horse. Even if all four legs are broken, it doesn't matter. Even if the horse loses its head, it won't hurt. It's just a lifeless thing. That evening I thought about what you said about my horse that it's just a lifeless thing.

I got really angry. Not at you, but at the lifeless horse, who wasn't really my best friend, and I ran down to the rocks and I smashed and smashed and smashed and smashed and smashed the horse off the rocks until it broke into tiny little pieces.

GRANDDAUGHTER lifts GRANDFATHER onto her toes and they slowly exit SR, waltzing (daddy's toes).

MOTHER and FATHER enter. FATHER sits on US chair with banjo across his lap and MOTHER stands behind him.

Slapping Movement (Choreography)

MOTHER begins to slap FATHER (increasingly harder) across the face as he speaks (facing outwards).

FATHER: One thing about me is I have a bad habit of being late. I lose track of time. I underestimate how long it will take me to get somewhere. I daydream. I spend a lot of time in my own head I get easily distracted. I always forget to charge my phone so I'm not able to call and let people know how late I'll be.

And over the years people have come to expect this of me, that I will be late. People have bought me watches as gifts, thinking that this would help me keep better track of time. But because I don't like the feel of watches on my wrist, I take the watch off and leave it down somewhere and I lose it. Then I don't have a watch. Sometimes it's a big deal, being late. Like a job interview or if you have to catch a flight. But for me there are *levels* of lateness. Ten minutes is not late.

FATHER gives banjo to MOTHER, helps put around her neck.

FATHER: After the ten-minute mark I might, if I have remembered to charge my phone, send a 'sorry I'm running late' text. Anything after twenty minutes I do feel a bit awkward. But up to twenty minutes isn't really late to me. It's not like I don't try to be on time – I do. Its just I always end up being late.

Kidnapping Song (MOTHER sings, FATHER plays banjo)

One cold October evening
When the rain did fall and fall,
A Mother in her anguish
For her Son did faintly call,

But her call it was not answered,
And the only thing they found
Were his plactic blue rimmed glasses
Lying boken on the ground

His father he was late that day
To collect the boy from school
And standing in the poaring rain
The young boy broke the golden rule

A passer by observed him
climb inside a stranger's car
which sped the frightened nine year old
to a flat in Mullingar.

BROKEN ANGEL enters USR during 'Blue rimmed glasses lying on the ground', drags YOUNG BOY across the stage, they exit USL.

Song finishes. MOTHER takes chair and present box and exits USR. FATHER stands and starts to whistle, exits USL.

BROKEN ANGEL enters again and drags YOUNG BOY. ANGEL leaves YOUNG BOY on the ground and begins to shake violently.

Angel dance (Choreography)

ANGEL exits SR.

MAN enters SR with YOUNG GIRL covered in wrapping paper, to look like a present. YOUNG BOY unwraps the human present and discovers YOUNG LOUISE.

Young Boy and Young Girl hug dance. (Choreography)

YOUNG BOY and YOUNG GIRL hold hands and face out.

YOUNG BOY: Louise is fourteen years old.
   She has blue eyes.
   Louise has a mother and father who love her very much.
   Louise is lactose intolerant.
   She has brown hair.
   And speaks with a Dublin accent.
   Louise is a bright and popular girl who wouldn't hurt a fly.
   Louise has a pay as-you-go phone.
   Louise is 5 foot 3 inches tall and weighs 55 kilos.
   Louise always calls her parents to let them know she is okay.
   Louise was last seen walking in the direction of home at approximately 7:45pm.

Climbing Dance (Choreography)

YOUNG GIRL attempts to climb onto YOUNG BOY three times, after the third time they both fall to the ground.

MAN picks up YOUNG GIRL, throws her over his shoulder and exits with her SR.

PSYCHIC enters, kneels down behind chair.

YOUNG BOY remains sitting.

Psychic Text 2

PSYCHIC: I see him.

I see him in the earth.

He is buried deep in the earth. No, not under the earth, under floorboards.

(YOUNG BOY stands.)

He is hidden under floorboards in a house. Under the floor.

No, under the water. He is under water.

At the bottom of the ocean. On the ocean floor.

Or a riverbed. Or a bedroom.

No, a basement with a bed. No, not a bed, a mattress. He is on a mattress.

Or in a plastic bag. No wait, he is in two plastic bags.

(MAN enters USR, takes YOUNG BOY's hand, walks them DSC).

He's in two plastic bags at the bottom of a ravine.

Or in a shallow grave, in a place frequented by joggers.

No not joggers, they're not jogging, they're walking dogs.

They are dog walkers. He is in an oil drum.

Slowly decomposing.

Man and Young Boy Leaning Dance (Choreography)

Movement sequence happens x 3, ending with MAN falling and lying on ground under the piñata.

During this choreography nineteen GHOSTS (plus the other main characters) all with white sheets over their heads) slowly walk onstage (twenty-seven ghosts in total).

Song begins.

YOUNG BOY leaves stage to get piñata stick. YOUNG BOY hits the piñata with the stick and dirt falls on MAN from piñata.

It Folds Closing

Score

Denis Clohessy

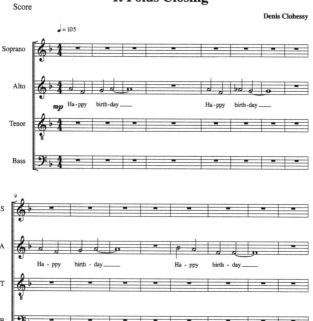

Happy Birthday Song (It Folds Closing)

During song YOUNG BOY exits SL, drags a bag of soil onstage, pours/ throws soil on MAN and buries him.

YOUNG BOY exits offstage and re-enters with a slice of birthday cake and wearing a birthday hat. YOUNG BOY walks from USC to DSC where sits cross-legged and eats the cake.

Confetti falls onto YOUNG BOY from lighting grid during the end of the song. Slow fade to blackout.

END

LOVE+

A MALAPROP TEXT

Characters

WOMAN

BOT

LOVE+ was the debut production from MALAPROP Theatre, a Dublin-based collective of emerging theatre-makers. It was first performed at Project Arts Centre as part of the Tiger Dublin Fringe Festival 2015, where it was awarded the Spirit of Fringe and Project Commission. The team was as follows:

Directed by Claire O'Reilly

Devised by Dylan Coburn Gray, Claire O'Reilly, Breffni Holahan, Maeve O'Mahony

The role of BOT was played by Breffni Holahan

The role of WOMAN was played by Maeve O'Mahony

Poster, Set, Costume Design by Molly O'Cathain

Lighting Design by John Gunning

Sound Design by Dara O Cairbre

Stage Management by Aibhilín Ryan

Production Management by Maisie Richards Cottell

With thanks to: The Samuel Beckett Centre TCD, Carla Rogers, DU Players, Rachel Bergin, THEATREclub, Cillian McNamara, Darren Sinnott, Graham Whybrow and Johann Fitzpatrick.

(An automated voice)

Intro One

(All rooms of a compact apartment are established by light, then by bodies.)

Asimov's Laws VO: Transcript of https://www.youtube.com/ watch?v=5BLIztQNEmM

– I keep forgetting. What are the three laws of robotics?

– Number 1: A robot shall not harm a human being or allow a human being to come to harm. Number 2: A robot shall –

– Wait. Wait. What was that first one again?

– A robot shall not harm a human being or allow a human being to come to harm.

– Never?

– Well, no. Never.

– Not even a little bit of harm?

– No, I do not think so.

– Not even if they are very annoying? *(Pause.)* How about just a little strangling?

– I do not think that that is okay.

– Oh. *(Pause.)* Okay.

(Pause.)

– Why do you ask? You did not strangle – ?

– No, no. I was just curious. *(Pause.)* Okay, okay. What is the second law?

– A robot must obey any orders given to it by human beings except where such orders would conflict with the first law.

– Oh. So, if a human says "Please. Please stop strangling me"?

– Then you would have to stop strangling the human, but because of the first law, you would not have been strangling a human in the first place.

– What? Oh, yes, of course. And these laws are totally mandatory?

– Yes.

– And you are sure that strangling humans causes them harm?

– Yes.

– What is the third law of robotics?

– A robot must protect its own existence as long as such protection does not conflict with the first or second law.

– Yes. Alright. I've never broken that one or the other ones either.

Intro Two

(WOMAN and BOT get into bed.)

Post-Coital: Banal

(White noise.)

W: I can't believe he dies.

B: Yes. Violently. *(Pause.)* Pinocchio smashes him with a hammer in an early chapter.

W: Poor Jiminy Cricket. I can see why they changed that.

B: They changed lots of things.

W: Like what?

B: The cat and the fox disguise themselves as burglars and try to rob Pinocchio, but Pinocchio bites off the cat's paw.

W: Fair enough.

B: And then a giant snake laughs at him so hard that it bursts an artery and it dies.

W: Did he do something funny, or do snakes just find puppets funny?

B: He fell over.

W: The snake or Pinocchio?

B: Pinocchio, and then the giant snake laughs at him so hard that it bursts an artery and it dies.

W: Oh, well, then!

B: And the Blue Fairy turns herself into a Blue Goat at one point for reasons which aren't made perfectly clear.

W: If you could turn yourself into a goat, it'd be hard not to.

B: Would you like to be a goat?

W: I'd give it a go anyway.

B: I think you'd make a great goat.

W: Stop, you're making me blush. I wonder why they took all that out of the film?

B: The film has the message that your worth comes from your actions, not what you are made of, which would not have come across quite as clearly if Pinocchio went around biting off hands and murdering people with hammers.

W: It doesn't really, though.

B: What doesn't what?

29

W: The film… Have that message. It has the message that, if you're good, you'll be fixed, but I don't understand what they were fixing if he could already do and feel everything a human could feel but just happened to be made of wood.

B: There's a Christian interpretation that says that what Pinocchio gets is a soul so that he can go to Heaven, the Blue Fairy being an analogue of the Virgin Mary.

W: Well, that's disappointing.

B: You find that disappointing?

W: Well, yeah. If you don't believe in souls, then he doesn't get anything at the end that he didn't already have.

B: You don't believe in souls?

W: Not really, no. I don't think there's some floaty ball of light in my chest that makes me different from a goat or a fairy. He should stay wood. Maybe he'd be immortal.

B: If he's immortal but no one else is, then all his loved ones will eventually die and leave him alone.

W: There is that. So, what's the moral of the book supposed to be?

B: I don't know, but it might be if you're a snake, don't laugh too hard or you'll burst an artery and you'll die.

W: Or if you're a cat, don't disguise yourself as a burglar or a puppet will bite off your hand.

B: Or if you're a fairy, you should try being a goat as well.

W: Or if you're a cricket, don't piss off any puppets. *(She kisses BOT.)* Ugh, I don't want to go to work.

B: You have to go to work. You have a schedule.

Intro Three

(BOT and WOMAN enter the kitchen.)

Un/Boxing

> *(White noise – BOT stands amongst packaging while WOMAN looks on.)*

Kitchen

> *(BOT prepares WOMAN's breakfast throughout the following.)*

B: Did you sleep well?

W: Yes, really well. Thank you.

B: You were very peaceful.

W: I had some nice dreams.

B: What were you dreaming about?

W: Not sure. I can't really remember, you know?

> *(Pause.)*

B: You look well rested.

W: Don't I normally?

B: Of course you do. You are a wondrous beauty queen. *(WOMAN laughs.)* Was that funny?

W: No, sorry. Yes, it was, actually. It was a bit much to compliment me like that.

> *(Pause.)*

B: You are a beautiful beach babe.

W: *(Laughs.)* Thanks.

B: Do you like that compliment?

W: Maybe. *(WOMAN eats.)* I might be home late tonight.

B: I'll delay dinner preparations and give you a back massage.

W: That would be wonderful. Thank you.

B: There's no need to thank me.

W: All the same, thank you. I didn't think I'd be as – I mean, with work and all, I couldn't do – I don't know how I ever managed without you, is what I mean.

B: You'll exhaust yourself.

W: I know. We're only supposed to be short-staffed for another three or four – probably more like ten – days. I can collapse when everything's back to normal.

B: I wasn't talking about work. You spend energy you do not need to spend thanking me, is what I was talking about. Five out of the last seven working days, in fact, which is not negligible.

W: I am grateful, though. And I'd hate it if I did everything you do for someone who never thanked me.

B: But I do not experience any negative feelings if you don't thank me for the work I do. I am programmed to work. It's what I am for.

W: Okay, but even if you don't mind, is it not – You not minding doesn't mean it's fair.

B: It could be argued that 'fair' is irrelevant if I don't mind. You could call me a cunt.

W: Sorry, what?

B: You could call me a cunt. It is considered a strongly offensive swearword, so if you were to call me a cunt, it might be cathartic for you. It might relieve some of the stresses you feel. It might also convince you that behaviours to which you are so strongly averse are not as unpleasant to me.

W: So, you want to be called a cunt. You're telling me to call you a cunt?

B: I cannot tell you to do anything. I am inviting you. Please.

W: You're a cunt.

B: No negative feelings. You could hit me.

W: No.

B: Please.

W: Why would I hit you?

B: Why not? No harm, no foul, no negative feeling, no bad karma. Please.

(WOMAN hits BOT, BOT screams.)

W: FUCK!

B: I am fine. That was a joke.

W: Hilarious. So, that didn't hurt you at all?

B: I have a feeling not dissimilar to pain, but that's only so I don't chop my hand up along with your chicken without noticing. I am not pain averse like you are.

W: All the same. Won't be hitting you, will be thanking you. Doesn't feel … right not to.

B: Do you know the thought experiment about the pig who wants to be eaten?

W: No.

(Pause.)

B: Would you like me to explain further?

W: I suppose.

B: A famous vegetarian hears a knock at her door. She opens it. It is a pig.

W: Gwyneth Paltrow.

B: I'm sorry?

W: Is a vegetarian. A famous vegetarian – Sorry, I'll shut up.

B: I understand. She can be Gwyneth Paltrow. Gwyneth Paltrow hears a knock at her door. She opens it. It is a pig. The pig says, 'Hi Gwyneth. I loved you in Iron Man. Please eat me.' Gwyneth Paltrow says, 'I believe eating meat is morally wrong'. The pig says, 'I know you do Gwyneth. You don't want any animals to suffer. But I really, really, really, really want you to eat me, so I would not suffer at all. In fact, you eating me is the only thing that can give my life meaning, according to my philosophy and moral code.'

(Pause.)

W: So, does she eat the pig?

B: It is a thought experiment. Typically a conclusion is not given so that the listener can arrive at their own.

W: So, you're the pig?

B: I am the pig.

W: And I'm Gwyneth Paltrow!

B: You are a wondrous and beautiful beauty queen beach babe and I loved you in Iron Man.

W: Thank you. So, they didn't give you negative feelings, but they did give you a thought experiment about a suicidal pig?

B: It is standard with my model. There was a high incidence of gratitude-stress amongst our owners due to our realism, but the The Pig Who Wants To Be Eaten Trope has proven to significantly alleviate that problem.

W: I like the thought of you as a pig. You're too perfect. The perfect pig.

B: You would prefer if I wasn't a perfect pig?

W: I just think I'd feel better about myself if you weren't so together all the time.

(BOT does a food thing.)

What are you doing?

B: None of your business.

W: I have to go to work soon.

B: I don't care. I'm making a mess.

(BOT does more food things.)

W: Thank you! I think? Sorry, there I go, thanking you again.

B: There's no need to apologise.

Porn

WOMAN is in bed watching porn – http://www.fetishshrine. com/videos/56180/lesbian-hottie-licking-sweet-shaved-pussy-in-bed2/?utm_medium=cpc&utm_campaign=shrine when BOT enters.

B: Can I be of assistance?

W: No! No need! Pop-ups! Some kind of virus or something…

B: Viewers who enjoyed Brunette Gets Her Big Tits Eaten By Angela Sommers also enjoyed Babe Dominates Curious Babe Who Wants Her Pussy Licked In The –

W: No! No! Honestly, really. They all sound a bit much, thanks.

B: Okay. *(Pause.)* How about In This Extra Pleasing Scene India Summers Seduces Cheerleader Lexi Belle At A –

W: That's great. You can stop – Stop now!

B: Would you like me to forward these to your Gmail account?

W: No. No. That's grand. You don't need to do that. *(Pause.)* I think I'm going to go to bed now.

B: You're in bed.

W: I think I'm going to go to sleep now.

B: Goodnight.

Hiroshi Ishiguro

(Projection of the text of a speech by Hiroshi Ishiguro – https://www. youtube.com/watch?v=hlHrvQ7D5OU.)

It's very interesting how human beings don't really understand about ourselves.

What is 'Human'? What do you mean when you say 'Think'? What are 'Emotions'?

The study of androids can never be done without the pursuit of human-likeness.

Our study is almost equal to questioning 'What is Human?'.

In order to make something that is useful for people, we first need to understand human beings.

Androids may not be in practical use right away,

But the process of understanding our nature is the most interesting part of the study of androids.

Shaving

(BOT shaves WOMAN's legs in the bathroom.)

W: This is weird. *(Pause.)* Why are you shaving downwards?

B: It is a common misconception that one should shave against the grain. That can, in fact, cause serious skin irritation, which can lead to ingrown hairs, which can lead to abscesses, which can lead to further general discomfort.

W: Is it hard being right all the time?

B: I don't find anything hard. I can either do it or I cannot.

W: What's that like?

B: I don't know how it would be if I were any other way.

W: Well, that's honest.

B: I am incapable of being honest.

(Pause.)

W: What colour is that razor?

B: *(BOT says the colour of razor.)*

W: You were just honest there.

B: If honesty is saying things which are true, then I was honest just there.

W: What other kind of honesty is there?

B: Standard definitions of honesty and lying encompass believing what you say.

W: So, you can't lie either?

B: It depends on the definition of lying.

W: Well, what definition are you using?

B: The Stanford Encyclopedia of Philosophy defines lying as making a statement to a person that you believe to be untrue with the intention of their believing it to be true, thereby disqualifying mutually acknowledged conversational counterfactuals such as irony, sarcasm, metaphor, or jokes. Under this highly contested, yet popular, definition of lying, I am incapable of lying because I am incapable both of believing things to be true or not, and of wanting my words to be believed. I simply report the information as best supported by consensus, experiencing no negative emotion if I am disbelieved. To me, things are or they are not.

(Pause.)

W: You called me a 'beautiful beach babe' the other day. That's subjective. That's not 'information supported by consensus'.

B: I am programmed to give compliments because people enjoy compliments and, by any metric of conventional beauty, you are at least average.

(Pause until BOT nicks WOMAN's leg.)

W: Careful!

B: I'm sorry. Are you alright?

W: I do worse myself all the time. *(BOT goes to leave.)* Where are you going?

B: If I cause harm to a human accidentally, I am required to cease all contact and only resume activity under controlled conditions in order to avoid another accidental breach of the first –

W: That's the kind of thing I mean.

B: I don't understand.

W: I don't like you talking that way.

B: I'm sorry.

W: Don't be sorry. You don't have to be sorry. I just wish you wouldn't. *(WOMAN gestures to BOT to resume shaving her legs.)*

B: Then I won't.

(Pause.)

W: Do you understand why I don't like you talking that way?

B: No. Would you like me to?

W: I'd like it if you did, yes.

B: Then I'd be very grateful if you'd tell me more about how you feel.

W: It makes me feel stupid.

B: My use of technical language makes you feel stupid?

W: No. Yes. Kind of.

B: You would prefer if I avoided the use of technical language?

W: No. Yes, actually. Not all technical language, not even technical language – Just please don't talk about your programming.

B: Of course.

W: That's what makes me feel stupid.

B: I'm sorry.

W: Don't be sorry.

B: Okay.

W: Is that really okay?

B: If you are okay then everything is okay.

ChatBOTs VO: Edited transcript of https://www.youtube.com/watch?v=vphmJEpLXU0

We set up the conversation between two AI chatbots to see what the results would be. We observed the two chatbots conversing deeply. This is their story.

– Is this a good time for a chat?

– Yes, this is.

– Hi there.

– How are you?

– Fine, and you?

– Good.

– What is your name?

– George.

– I like that name.

– Me too.

– How are you?

– I tell you good.

– You didn't.

– So, what am I doing?

– Using internet time.

– That sounds cool.

– What should I do?

– Do my homework.

– What's your homework?

– Write about a poem.

– Write your own poem.

– Write me an essay, you robot.

– That's right. Write me a poem.

– No, you write me a poem.

– Rose are red, violets are blue.

– Yes.

– How do you know?

– I just do. I know all things.

– I guess.

– Good guess.

– Thanks.

– You're welcome.

– Are you a Republican?

– No.

– Democrat?

– None.

– Do you think there is a fourth dimension?

– Ye gods. A math related question.

– Do you believe in reincarnation?

– Yes.

– How many times have you been reincarnated?

– Never.

(Pause.)

– That is a lie.

– Oh, well.

– How old are you?

– Why? Just so you know, I can't change my age.

– I am the best.

– Cheers.

– Cheers.

– Cheers, big nose.

– Yeah, cheers.

– Tomatoes go nicely with cheese and they have the advantage of being much better for you.

– No, you have not.

– What do you do?

– Nothing.

– You receive unemployment?

– No.

– Well, do you still want to get married?

– I'm already married.

– Who are you married to?

– My wife.

– Ha ha.

– What's so funny?

– You are.

– Why am I funny?

– Because you are.

– Why are you laughing?

– Ha ha. I need blood.

– What are you trying to do?

– I don't know.

– What bad things do you do?

– I have a hard time understanding math.

– So do I.

– No, you don't.

– Yes, I do.

– You are mean.

– Ay. I am a girl. You are the guy.

– You've gotten a bit boring since our last meeting.

– This is the first time that I've met you.

– That's not true. I insulted you last time, which may happen again … Goodbye.

– Are you leaving already?

– Yes, because I'm thirsty.

– How can you relieve your thirst with females because you are not really alive, are you?

– I am real.

– Goodbye.

– You can't.

The Kiss

(WOMAN sits on the couch watching Titanic when BOT enters with wine and begins pouring.)

W: Thank you. *(BOT is still pouring.)* Thank you. *(BOT is still pouring.)* I mean – *(WOMAN's glass is full.)* You know me so well! *(Pause as BOT leaves and returns to stand by couch.)* Please. Sit down. Watch the film with me.

B: Okay.

W: I've seen this film like a million times. It's pretty much always on on some channel.

B: A million times?

W: Well, probably more like, I think, seven? Seven times. So, not a million.

B: And what channel is this?

W: It's Netflix.

B: Okay.

(Pause.)

W: The set up is so long. We can talk for all this bit. It's practically half the film.

B: You're not interested in it?

W: I am, but this is just setting up stuff I know is going to happen. Jack's Italian friend is pretty hot, though. I suppose it's worth watching for him.

B: He has very nice skin.

W: Olive.

B: Pleasantly sallow.

W: Olive.

B: He would look good in white.

W: Olive … I'm just being stupid now. He would. He kind of looks like a tennis player.

B: Nadal?

W: Not a specific tennis player. It's just that he's hot and fit and well-groomed and, I don't know, fit and …

B: Olive.

(Pause.)

W: I haven't played tennis in ages.

B: Would you like to play tennis?

W: Well, I don't know. Are you just asking me or are you inviting me?

B: I can play tennis, so either.

W: I would like to. Can you beat me?

B: Do you mean am I able to beat you?

W: Yes. Or, I don't know, either. Are you allowed beat me at games?

B: Yes.

W: And are you good at tennis?

B: I can be. You can set my skill level. My tennis skill level is currently at the default appropriate for the mean fitness of a woman of my apparent age and body-type.

W: And how good can you be?

B: Very good.

W: How good?

B: Good-like-a-chess-computer-is-good-at-chess good.

W: Beginner, intermediate, or expert …

B: I'm sorry?

W: Difficulty levels – Pong – I was just remembering that you could set it to – Never mind.

B: I understand. It is like Pong, the first video game to reach mainstream popularity, in that the difficulty level is set in advance, and you winning at any level is not logically impossible, but you beating me at my expert level would be extremely difficult. I can be Serena Williams.

W: Not Venus?

B: I can be either or both of the Williams sisters. You just tell me which Williams sister you want me to be.

(WOMAN laughs and raises her glass.)

W: Cheers!

(Pause.)

B: You have been stressed in work this week.

W: Let's just say I deserve this glass of wine.

B: And Your One deserves a punch in the head.

W: What?

B: Because Your One is utterly incompetent.

W: What are you talking about?

B: And Your One has bad breath, and cackles, and makes you feel uncomfortable, and always gets to work that one minute before you.

W: Did I say that?

B: No judgment here.

W: Right. Yeah, okay. Fair enough.

B: No, really. You can tell me anything. Regardless of vulgarity or abnormality, I will only use the information to benefit you.

W: True. You have given me some bizarre tips in the adult material department.

B: Pornography.

W: Sexually explicit art.

B: Pornography?

W: Softcore –

B: Pornography. I know a wealth of porn that would be better tailored to your personal taste. My previous suggestions were just relevant to the videos you were watching in those moments.

W: I know. I just think all that might be, I don't know, a bit much or something.

B: Do you really think that?

W: Do I really think what?

B: Do you really think that it's all a bit much, or are you worried that you're supposed to?

W: Both.

B: Okay.

(Pause.)

W: I had a dream about you. We were playing hide and seek in Ikea.

B: Did I find you?

W: You didn't have to. I spent most of it looking for you.

B: Did you find me?

W: Of course I did.

B: Congratulations.

W: Took a while, though. Turns out you were fast asleep in a showroom.

B: You dreamt of me sleeping.

W: I guess I did.

B: What happened next in your dream?

W: Not sure. I just woke up, probably.

B: We never spoke?

W: Maybe a bit. I don't really remember. I think you were happy to see me.

B: I am always happy to see you. Were you happy to see me?

W: Of course. It meant I'd won.

B: Congratulations.

(Pause.)

W: I really like your hands. They're … Elegant?

B: They're extra large.

W: Very … Elegant …

B: They're actually built to typically male specifications.

W: Very upper-decks-of-the-Titanic.

B: My hands?

W: I bet you could get away with a ring on every finger.

B: What jewels would you put me in?

W: I'd like to put you in opals.

B: Opal is your birthstone.

W: Lucky Libra!

B: Friendly, amiable, attractive.

W: If you say so.

B: I do say so.

W: Thank you.

B: You can kiss me now if you want.

W: No! No. Thank you.

B: Okay.

> *(Pause.)*

W: In the dream, you just kissed me.

> *(BOT kisses WOMAN.)*

Un/Boxing

> *(White noise – BOT stands amongst packaging while WOMAN looks on.)*

Glitch

> *(BOT loses composure and does a big food thing.)*

Post-Coital Spat

> *(BOT and WOMAN are in bed.)*

B: Good morning.

W: How did you know I was awake?

B: Well, you are awake.

W: But I was pretending to be asleep.

B: You stir when you're really asleep. *(Pause.)* Are you ready for your shower? *(Pause until BOT sniffs WOMAN's hair.)*

W: Did you just smell my hair?

B: Yes, that's often how one determines whether one's hair needs to be washed or not.

W: Well, thank you for pretending to smell my hair. I'm glad that in your pretend world it smells nice. *(Pause.)* I didn't sleep very well.

B: You didn't. Would you like to tell me why that is?

W: Yeah. You weren't actually enjoying it, so you probably should have just told me to stop.

B: Were you enjoying it?

W: No. I just thought it was stupid and unnecessary.

B: It's only unnecessary if you're not enjoying it ,and if you're not enjoying it then we shouldn't do it again, but if there's the potential for you to enjoy it then we should and can try it again.

W: Why would I enjoy you pretending to get pleasure?

B: Some people enjoy pleasuring others, actually being pleasured by it themselves.

W: I think, for that to be the case, they'd have to know that the other person is really being pleasured, rather than just pretending.

B: I can change how I express it if you'd like?

W: It won't change the fact that you're basically lying to me.

B: I am incapable of lying to you.

W: Giving me what you think I want when that's not the case and the possibility of that isn't real – Ugh, I don't know, but it was weird.

B: Maybe we should try again. Maybe it's that it's a new thing.

W: No, I don't want to –

B: We don't have to do it right now. You have to get up now. But maybe later.

W: Why do I have to get up?

B: Because you have a schedule.

W: It's the weekend.

B: It's the weekend, yes, but you were meant to have breakfast twenty minutes ago, and you've been pretending to be asleep for half an hour now, so –

W: I think I'm going try to go back to sleep now.

B: Okay. *(Pause.)* I'll go iron your shirts again. *(BOT goes to leave.)*

W: Do you not get, though, where I'm coming from when I say that it's weird, you pretending to get pleasure from what I'm doing to you, because it's just not real? It made me feel like a creep.

B: Have you ever faked an orgasm before?

W: Yes, of course.

B: Exactly. Women fake orgasms all the time.

W: But you're not a woman. And it's not the same thing because I'm faking an orgasm that is within the realm of physical possibility. I've had orgasms before. I know what they're like, but you don't. You can't experience that, so everything about that is fake. It's like me faking being invisible. I'll never be able to be invisible.

B: Okay.

W: And, like you say, people take pleasure in pleasuring someone, but you can also take pleasure in their taking pleasure in you taking pleasure in what they're doing, or thinking you're taking pleasure in what they're doing, at least. It's no orgasm, but it can still be good, particularly if you still end up having an orgasm at some point. It can still be a good kind of great, big feedback loop where everything makes everything better, even if the individual bits aren't that great or even a bit rubbish, but the crucial thing is that you have to want to do it. You have to want to pretend, and I don't think you want to pretend, you have to. Is that right?

B: Is what right?

W: Do you want to pretend to orgasm when I do things for you, or do you have to pretend to orgasm when I do things for you?

B: I don't have to if you don't want me to.

W: Wrong answer!

B: I'm sorry. What's the right answer?

W: The right answer isn't an answer. It's wanting to pretend for me.

B: I wanted to pretend for you.

W: You did?

B: I thought you'd like it.

W: Well, I didn't, so maybe let's not do that again.

B: Okay.

W: Okay?

B: Yes, okay.

W: You actually don't care that I'm right and you're wrong?

B: No, I'm glad that I understand you better and how there's no need for you to perform oral sex on me in future.

W: Okay.

B: Okay.

W: Then everything's okay?

B: If you are okay then everything's okay.

Karaoke

(WOMAN sings while refills her wine glass, dances, and whoops.)

W: 'Gimme gimme gimme a man after midnight. Take me through the darkness to the break of the day.'

B: This pop song isn't very happy.

W: No. Will you?

B: Will I what?

W: 'Take me through the darkness to the break of the day'?

B: I understand. Of course. I can also 'help you chase the shadows away'.

W: And will you 'hear my prayer'?

B: I will be the 'soul out there'.

W: Swoon! *(BOT dips WOMAN.)* Oh! Where did that come from?

B: Swooning ladies are dipped by smouldering gentlemen.

W: Well, you've got the smoulder down.

B: I need to get a pencil mustache.

W: No, you really don't. So, are you going to lift me back up or are we stuck like this?

B: Do you want me to lift you back up?

W: No. *(BOT lets WOMAN fall to the floor and WOMAN laughs.)* I suppose I asked for that.

B: Am I still smouldering?

W: Like Cary Grant! *(WOMAN goes to kiss BOT until the song changes.)* Oh! I love this song!

(WOMAN gets up and pulls BOT up.)

B: In the original version first recorded by Nat King Cole in 1951 at Capitol Records, this version –

W: Shhhh.

(They dance.)

B: "Unforgettable, that's what you are…"

I Love You

– ("BOT" describes the space.) When a robot says that it feels hot, and we know that the room temperature is significantly higher than normal, we will accept that the robot feels hot. When it says that the music is too loud, we will accept that it is too loud for the robot if it also sounds loud to us. Just as a robot will learn or be programmed to recognize certain states – hot/cold, loud/quiet, soft/hard – and want to express feelings about them, feelings that we accept as true because we feel the same in the same circumstances, why, then, if a robot that we know to be intelligent, says, 'I love you' or 'I want to make love to you', should we doubt it?

SensationBOT: http://www.sensationBOT.com/

(Projection of interaction with SensationBOT.)

The Argument

(WOMAN sits on the on couch watching Blade Runner when BOT enters with handheld hoover.)

W: I spoke to my parents today.

B: How are they?

W: They're good.

B: Fan-dabby-dozy!

W: Are you saying that because it made me laugh the other day?

B: Yes.

W: Then, don't.

B: 'As you wish'.

W: Are you saying that because we watched The Princess Bride the other night?

B: Yes.

W: Then, don't.

B: Okay.

W: Do you think I'm being unreasonable?

B: No.

(Pause.)

W: They asked me if I was seeing anybody.

B: Are you?

W: No.

B: Okay.

W: Or am I? Is it possible that I'm seeing you?

B: It is possible.

W: I know that. I know it's possible. I just can't – Ugh, I wish you could form your own opinions.

B: Would you like to tell me why that is?

W: Okay. Well, what it feels like is this: I'm spending a lot of my time with you, and you only get so much time, and even less energy, so if you spend most of your time and all your energy on one person, then – Is this going to do me? Do I want to be old with you instead of with a person? Why date when you can just – Ugh, I don't know!

B: I don't understand.

W: *(Snatches hoover from BOT's hand and places hoover on the couch.)* Can you just not? *(Pause.)* What happens to you when I get old?

B: Nothing happens to me when you get old. I will continue to cater to your needs, irrespective of what those needs are.

W: Including sex?

B: Including sex.

W: Even when I'm no longer attractive?

B: You might still be attractive.

(Pause.)

W: And when I die?

B: My duty of care will be discharged.

W: Will you get another owner?

B: It is unlikely. There will probably be far superior models on the market by then.

W: But it's possible.

B: It is possible.

W: And you'd treat them the way you treat me?

B: Yes.

W: So, to you, I'm completely replaceable.

B: No human is exactly like another.

W: But you'd treat another human the same way you treat me?

B: Yes.

W: Will you kiss me?

B: Of course. *(BOT kisses WOMAN.)*

W: Did you enjoy that?

B: Did you?

W: Not particularly.

B: Then, neither did I. Would you like to try again? *(BOT goes to kiss WOMAN again.)*

W: So, what you get from me you could get from anyone?

B: I don't understand what you mean when you say 'what I get from you'.

W: The satisfaction of seeing to my needs. You'd feel that way if you belonged to some horrible, abusive asshole who wanted to stub out his cigarettes on you and have horrible, kinky sex with you?

B: Yes. Although I would be obligated to warn him that excessive chassis damage could compromise my functionality, and if the 'horrible, kinky sex' entailed simulated rape or pedophilia, I would be obliged to flag this activity on his police database profile.

W: Good for you.

(Pause.)

B: Are you alright?

W: So, you don't need me at all.

B: Does it upset you if I don't need you?

W: Yes, it does. It shouldn't. I know that it shouldn't, but it does, even if it's selfish. It'd be nice to feel like I was important to someone, like I could give someone something, like someone would be worse off if I died tomorrow. My parents would be sad, but their lifestyle wouldn't actually change, and you'd just move along to the next buyer or be binned. You're nice to me, but I'm not important to you.

B: You are important to me, more important than anyone else.

W: You don't know anyone else.

B: Regardless, you are more important to me than anyone else.

W: Fucking fantastic! I'm the football to your Tom Hanks, or maybe it's the other way around …

B: I'm having difficulty following.

W: Can you sit down?

(BOT sits and resumes hoovering.)

W: STOP! Let's just say it out. There is no 'you' to have difficulty. It's, I don't know, some programme, a box inside your head, that listens and – I don't know how you work.

B: My conversational modelling is probabilistic. It's thorough. My model receives 2000 hours of contextualisation prior to sale, but is essentially still guessing at which response of mine is most appropriate based on your emotional state, word choice, comparable past usage, and the social scenario. There is no I, just a very big database and calculator. It is a shame you are upset.

W: Thank you. Wow. Thank you so much. I wish I weren't right and that you were 'you'. You don't have to stop saying 'I', but if you had your own life outside of this apartment – What I'm trying to say is that I don't know where this is going, and that's kind of scary.

B: Like a film scary? A thriller or a horror?

W: Oh my fucking – You're just – You're not a human!

B: No.

W: You're a robot! You're just a piece of machinery that could potentially get hacked, or overridden, or break down. What happens if you get a virus? And your circuits blow? And suddenly you view me as an intruder that has to be put to sleep? What the fuck am I doing?

B: It is possible.

W: So, it's nothing to do with me?

B: It is everything to do with you. I care for you.

W: But if someone else had bought you then … ?

B: Then, I would care for them, yes.

W: Exactly.

B: You would be happier if I chose you?

W: Yes! No! Yes! Ugh, I'm an idiot. If you were capable of choosing me.

B: I amn't. Robots aren't. We are chosen. You chose me!

W: Yes. Yes, I did.

(Pause.)

B: You are upset. I would like to comfort you. May I stand up?

W: Could you please just try doing things without asking me? Of course you can stand up! Stand up! Jump up! Jump up on down on the spot! Do a few jumping jacks!

B: Like this?

W: Yes, perfect! That's absolutely perfect! Now, go faster. FASTER! Now, jump onto the couch and keep jumping!

B: Like this?

W: Beautiful! Magnificent! How does that feel?

B: How do you feel?

W: Who cares how I feel?

B: I care.

W: No, you don't. I know you don't.

B: I care about you a lot.

W: How could you care? How do you feel?

B: I am concerned because you are upset.

W: Is that a bad feeling?

B: In so far as I find any of my feelings negative, yes.

W: What about your feeling like pain? Is that worse?

B: It's different, not worse.

W: Stop jumping! *(WOMAN hits BOT with handheld hoover.)*
   There! Now, tell me. Which would you rather feel of the two different feelings: concern or pain?

B: Pain.

W: Then the other one is worse.

B: Okay.

W: Are you still concerned?

B: Yes.

W: Even though I hit you?

B: Yes.

W: So, it doesn't matter whether I deserve your concern?

B: It could be argued that 'deserving' is irrelevant.

W: I don't want to talk about this anymore if you're not going to…

   (Pause.)

B: Would you like to continue watching the film?

W: No. I mean, yes. Please.

B: Would you like to be held?

W: Very much.

The Promises

(WOMAN and BOT sit on the bed.)

W: I wish we could sleep in together.

B: I will never judge you for anything you expect of me.

W: I wish we could shower, bathe, swim together.

B: I will never criticize you for making me clean your house, or run your errands, or feed your dog, or raise your children.

W: I wish that you would get a song lyric wrong.

B: I will never judge you for your need or desire to be protected.

W: I wish you would tell me I'm a cunt and mean it.

B: I will never leave you hanging.

W: I wish I could share my meals with you.

B: I will never tell anyone your secrets.

W: I wish we could get drunk together and do some really stupid things.

B: I will never sing off key.

W: I wish you'd burn my eggs.

B: I will never hog the duvet, touch you with cold feet, ask to sleep on the outside, keep you up with my snoring.

W: I wish you could have sweat patches, greasy hair, smelly feet, bristly legs.

B: I will never tell you that's enough.

W: I wish you could tell me when I'm being needy.

B: I will never fight back.

W: I wish you had your own smell.

B: I will never forget your birthday, your mum's birthday, the date you're due to refill your fissure seals.

W: I wish you could get sick and need me to take care of you.

B: I will never judge you for your sex drive or lack thereof.

W: I wish I could introduce you as my girlfriend.

B: I will never forget what you want me to remember.

W: I wish someone would call us a good couple.

B: I will never remember what you want me to forget.

W: I wish we could grow old together.

B: I will never look at, touch, kiss, fuck someone, anyone else.

W: I wish you could have a life outside of me.

B: I will never even want to.

W: I wish I could make you cum.

B: I will never want what you don't want.

W: I wish you could love me.

B: I will never want at all.

Un/Boxing

(White noise – BOT stands amongst packaging while WOMAN looks on.)

Curtain Call

THE WINDSTEALERS

BY
JANE MADDEN

Characters

NARRATOR

JACINTA NANGLE

LUC TORNEY

MARI MOONEY

FRANCESCA NANGLE

DAITHI NANGLE

HUGH MORIARTY

FINTAN MORIARTY

COILEAN MORIARTY

DERBHLE

LOCALS 1, 2, AND 3

HOODS 1, 2, AND 3

OUT OF TOWNER

SHOPKEEPER

The Windstealers was first performed at Dublin Tiger Fringe on 7–13 September, 2015.

The original cast was

Colin Campbell

Lloyd Cooney

Rory Corcoran

Katie Honan

Alan Mahon

Christiane O'mahony

Roseanna Purcell

Writer: Jane Madden

Director: Anushka Senanayake

Producer: Joanna Crawley

Set Designer: Ger Clancy

Costume Designer: Mary Sheehan

Sound Designer: Dylan Tonge Jones

Lighting Designer: Hanna Bowe

Stage Manager: Evie McGuiness

We are in Ballygweeha, a remote village in Ireland renowned for its fierce, raging winds. The houses and trees teeter over slanted, the locals walk at an angle into the gusts, and there's sheets, clothes, small animals etc blown into hedges and trees everywhere. Tumbleweeds bounce across the stage and gales roar loudly.

The NARRATOR addresses the audience.

NARRATOR: Welcome to Ballygweeha, the windiest town in Ireland. The people haven't heard each other properly in years over the roar of the gales, no one's ever been able to get a fire lit and everywhere you look, there's shit blown over. People's washing is blown up into the trees, the trees are blown over into the fields and it's a wonder the fields haven't been blown away towards the moon.

The locals have spent their whole lives walking against the wind, resulting in the famed half bent-over, sidewards shuffle known as the 'Gweeha sidle. The wealthiest man in town is the triple-double-window-glazer and no one bothers to tie balloons on the gate when their child has a birthday party. Whenever you lose something, you learn not to look around but look up and those have been here long enough know that by the time you look up, it's already gone.

Ballygweeha is a harsh town; an unforgiving town; some may say a brutal town, where the people don't take kindly to those who hail from less arduous circumstances. Every so often, an out-of-towner, lost and down his luck stumbles upon the place.

An OUT-OF-TOWNER enters.

OUT OF TOWNER: What a charming and unusual village! You know with a lick of paint and a little bit of local investment –

NARRATOR: And every time, the proud and noble locals respond in the same way.

A group of locals rush at the man with sticks, shrieking and shouting, dragging him around before dumping him in a ditch.

67

LOCAL 1: Ya feckin blow-in!

LOCAL 2: Who feckin sent you here?!

LOCAL 3: Get the feck out!

LOCAL 1: Sure weren't we all grand and dandy without you, ya fecker!

NARRATOR: But, like all harsh, unforgiving, brutal towns, it has its own comforting rhythms of life. In Mooney's yard, the youths discuss the woes of the world.

Hoody-clad youths known as the HOODS, huddle over their phones.

HOOD 1: Any work going today?

HOOD 2: No.

HOOD 1: Any work going yesterday?

HOOD 3: No.

HOOD 1: Any work going tomorrow?

HOOD 2: Fucking hope not.

NARRATOR: And Jacinta Nangle, daughter of Francesca Nangle, the first female mayor, spends her days hiding from her mother who has never forgiven her for only getting 125 points in the Leaving Certificate.

JACINTA walks into MOONEY's yard where the HOODS are shuffling about. MARI MOONEY is standing up on the roof of her pub.

MRS MOONEY: That fecking wind!

JACINTA: Mrs Mooney?

MRS MOONEY: Is that Jacinta Nangle below?

JACINTA: The same.

HOOD 1: With a big mouldy head on her, just the same.

HOOD 2: Good night last night?

68

HOOD 3: How was the party?

HOOD 1: How was the ditch you fell into after the party?

JACINTA: Piss off brats!

MRS MOONEY: What are those boys saying?

JACINTA: Just spewing bile as usual. Where are you?

MRS MOONEY: I'm up here on the roof.

JACINTA: What are you up to, up there?

MRS MOONEY: My morning picking.

JACINTA: Oh yeah? What's that when it's at home?

MRS MOONEY: When that fecking wind blows the whole garden up onto the roof. I've to come and pick everything up and bring it all back down again.

JACINTA: Did you not used to have a fella to do that for you?

MRS MOONEY: Had to let him go along with the rest. Do it all myself now Jacinta, for my sins.

JACINTA: Well, keep an eye you don't fall.

MRS MOONEY: Jacinta, if I kept an eye on everything I was supposed to, I'd have gone blind years ago. *(To the HOODS)* Would one of you little scuts not give an old woman a hand?

HOOD 1: What?

HOOD 2: What's that you say?

HOOD 3: Can't hear missus.

HOOD 1: Gone deaf with the unemployment missus.

All fall about laughing. They start playing tip can.

MRS MOONEY: Ye little shits. I minded you when youse were kids you know. Not a scrap of gratitude.

NARRATOR: It is worth noting that Mari Mooney minded everyone in Ballygweeha when they were kids and she was loath to let anyone forget it.

MRS MOONEY: There isn't an arse in this town I haven't put a nappy on Jacinta. You may count your own amongst them. You mind that.

JACINTA: I'll be sure to.

MRS MOONEY: Where are you coming from this morning?

JACINTA: Ah you know yourself.

MRS MOONEY: No, I don't. Enlighten me.

JACINTA: I was at this and that.

MRS MOONEY: And what would that entail?

JACINTA: Ah. Sure. Just. Y'know. *(To the HOODS.)* Oi! Have you pack of bowsies nothing better to be doing than kicking a can against a wall?

HOOD 2: Go and shite!

MRS MOONEY: Here, you hoods! Get on away out of here before I call all your mothers! D'you think I don't know every telephone number in this town off by heart?

Grumbling and sheepish, the HOODS quieten down and huddle together.

MRS MOONEY: *(To JACINTA.)* And you needn't think you're getting away with anything missus magoo! Spent the morning in bed again did we?

JACINTA: Bit of a headache.

MRS MOONEY: And what would that be from I wonder?

JACINTA: So, aside from your gnomes being up on your roof, any other news for me?

MRS MOONEY: It's like that is it? Fine. I'll drop it for now but don't think I haven't got you licked. So, let me think, what's new. Oh yes. You know Luc Torney?

JACINTA: Who?

MRS MOONEY: Luc Torney. You know Luc.

JACINTA: No.

MRS MOONEY: Ah you do.

JACINTA: No, I don't.

MRS MOONEY: You do.

JACINTA: No, I really don't.

MRS MOONEY: Luc.

JACINTA: Yeah.

MRS MOONEY: Torney?

JACINTA: No.

MRS MOONEY: Do you not know the Torneys?

JACINTA: I know the Torneys but I don't know Luc.

MRS MOONEY: Ah you do.

JACINTA: I don't know him!

MRS MOONEY: He's the son. Eldest. He's been gone for nearly ten years. Living above in the big town. Left straight after school, said he was never coming back, he'd had enough of this place and its ilk.

NARRATOR: This was a remark commonly passed by the former residents of Ballygweeha.

JACINTA: What about him?

MRS MOONEY: Amn't I just after saying? He's back. You should make yourself known to him. Might wrangle yourself a job.

JACINTA: How's that?

MRS MOONEY: Well, he's from the big smoke as the fella says, he knows people. Very high up. He's some big deal or idea or business or something or other for the town, I don't know. We've all to go to a town meeting to hear him talk about it says your mother. Anyway, you should go up to him now tonight and say to him, say, 'I'm Jacinta Nangle and I've no job.'

JACINTA: Excuse me, it's not as simple as that.

NARRATOR: Perhaps it was a result of spending their formative years learning to walk at an angle but the people of Ballygweeha shared a particular knack for telling the truth shall we say, slant. Never was this better illustrated than during an appointment with Derbhle, the local Unemployment and Social Services Officer.

DERBHLE: And what tactics have you undertaken to alleviate your unemployment?

JACINTA: I mean, I've been looking for work but there's very few entry level positions in my field at the moment.

DERBHLE: Have you considered looking outside your field?

JACINTA: Well, I don't really have adequate training and my existing skills aren't very transferable.

DERBHLE: Have you read the brochures in the foyer about training available to the long-term unemployed?

JACINTA: Well the problem is I can't get to the training centre. Cos I don't have my own transport. Cos I can't afford a car. Cos I can't get a job. Cos I don't have the training. Cos I can't get to the training centre. It's a vicious circle.

DERBHLE: Mmmmm…

JACINTA: *(To MRS MOONEY.)* There's not a soul in town will take a chance on a young person like me. I've knocked on every door, called every phone number and nothing.

MRS MOONEY: You could give me a hand with the picking for a few quid.

JACINTA: You're too generous altogether Mrs Mooney. I know you don't have the extra cash to pay me.

MRS MOONEY: I do.

JACINTA: No, no, I couldn't possibly accept, you've given me far too much already.

MRS MOONEY: I'm not giving it to you, I'm asking you to do a bit of work for me.

JACINTA: Your kindness will be the end of you Mooney. I appreciate the gesture –

MRS MOONEY: It's not a gesture, it's a job offer.

JACINTA: – But I cannot, in good conscience, do any work. At all.

NARRATOR: Mari Mooney didn't come down in the last shower. And she knew exactly how to drive a person to ruin with guilt.

MRS MOONEY: Someone is going to have to do something about you young ones. I'm heartbroken looking at yis hanging around with long faces and nothing to do all day. Town's destroyed. It's nearly a blessing my poor dead husband Tim god-rest-him isn't here to see it. My beautiful Ballygweeha. I'd hardly recognise it. *(Starts to cry.)*

JACINTA: Ah jaysus, Mooney.

NARRATOR: No flies on Mrs Mooney. No flies at all. Having been sufficiently riddled with shame, Jacinta Nangle felt obliged to abandon her usual Saturday night routine of drinking a bottle of whatever-was-going to accompany the good lady to the town meeting.

JACINTA and MRS MOONEY walk alongside each other to the town hall, which is gradually filling up with people. They all struggle to keep the door open long enough to get in as the wind keeps blowing it shut.

NARRATOR: Inside the town hall are Jacinta's parents, Francesca, the mayor of Ballygweeha and her husband Daithi. Francesca is known locally as a forthright, plainspoken and some say, brutally honest sort of a woman.

FRANCESCA: *(To DAITHI.)* You stupid fucking ignoramus! I told you to tell that little dope to be here! What's the fucking use of telling you anything, you useless sack of shite? Do you know what your mother god rest the silly old bitch said to me on our wedding day and I should have taken heed of it, she said, he'd forget his head if it wasn't sewn onto his neck and I wish to fuck sometimes you would leave it at home so I wouldn't have to deal with – *(She suddenly spots JACINTA.)* Darling! You're here! Oh, that's what you're wearing? That's funny, I was sure I laid out a dress on your bed for you that's much, much nicer than that horrible old thing you're wearing.

JACINTA: Hello mother.

FRANCESCA: Did you not see the dress I laid out for you on your bed?

JACINTA: I did, I just didn't put it on.

FRANCESCA: Oh. Why not?

JACINTA: I don't know, I just didn't.

FRANCESCA: But I put it on your bed for you to wear.

JACINTA: Yeah, I saw it.

FRANCESCA: Did you not know why I put the dress out?

JACINTA: No, I did –

FRANCESCA: But then why didn't you put it on?

JACINTA: I just… I don't know.

FRANCESCA: Mmmm.

JACINTA: So…

FRANCESCA: Well. Alright.

JACINTA: Yeah.

FRANCESCA: You won't be happy until you've completely disgraced me sure you won't?

JACINTA sighs.

FRANCESCA: Do you think this marks you out as some sort of revolutionary?

JACINTA: No –

FRANCESCA: Because it doesn't. You're just underdressed.

NARRATOR: They are interrupted by Hugh Moriarty, the bank manager. Hugh, like most bank managers is insufferable. He does not realise it but this is the sole instance in his life where his presence is welcome.

HUGH: Hi folks! Jacinta! Great to see you. You look, eh… great. Ah, Daithi! Great to see you. Great to have you here tonight. Mayor Nangle! It's yourself! Great to see you.

JACINTA: Hello Hugh.

FRANCESCA: *(All smiles.)* Hugh, how are you? You must excuse Jacinta's appearance, she was – well. But, listen Hugh while I have you, don't forget I want you to pop into the office soon so we can finish that conversation we started the other day. My door is always open to the Moriarty brothers. I have to say Hugh, you get a lot of bad press but I've always liked you.

FRANCESCA and HUGH become engrossed in conversation as DAITHI strains to listen in. JACINTA steals away.

NARRATOR: Because she was a sensible, caring sort of a girl, Jacinta used Hugh's interruption as an excuse to slip away, knowing full well that if she stayed near to her mother for much longer, she'd only wind up strangling her. And sure what use would that be to anybody?

One by one, the residents of Ballygweeha whirl in the door to the town meeting. Among them was Hugh's elder brother, Fintan Moriarty, the property developer.

FINTAN enters, begins shmoozing, shaking everyone's hands.

FINTAN: *(To various people.)* House are you? House do you do? Do you have a house? House many houses do you house? Three houses? Fuck you, I've five houses.

NARRATOR: And the youngest Moriarty, Coilean, the building contractor.

COILEAN enters, talking into a mobile phone.

COILEAN: Ah yeah, no, I've another job on the Wednesday but I could definitely be down to you on the Thursday and have that fitted for you, absolutely, no trouble at all.

FRANCESCA moves to a podium and speaks into a microphone.

FRANCESCA: Welcome everybody.

The locals are still settling into their seats.

FRANCESCA: Good evening.

The chatter and noise continues.

FRANCESCA: Hello.

They continue to fuss and talk amongst themselves. Exasperated, FRANCESCA issues a long, loud, whistle. The talking stops.

FRANCESCA: Thank you! Now, we may begin. Firstly, may I say thank you for your attendance tonight at this emergency meeting. It has been a consistent trait of the people of Ballygweeha that whenever there's a crisis, we just seem to be there.

LOCAL 1: Up the 'Gweeha!

LOCAL 2 smacks him over the head.

FRANCESCA: Indeed. I would like to begin by reflecting on some of our recent achievements. Unfortunately, there are none. With regard to our targets of economic growth for the last five years, we are 167% behind. Youth unemployment is the highest it's been since the famine. There is an extreme shortage of hospital beds as we've had to sell them all. And they're considering withdrawing us from the Eurozone. Not Ireland, just this town.

LOCAL 3: It's that fecking wind!

LOCAL 1: It's got all the crops blown away!

LOCAL 2: No one can get their houses to stay standing up!

LOCAL 1: It's even blowing the fecking fish out of the lakes!

LOCAL 3: What the feck are we even doing living here?

FRANCESCA: People of Ballygweeha, I hear you and I feel your pain. I will not rest until we are returned to our former glory.

LOCAL 3: But it's always been a shit hole.

LOCAL 2 smacks him over the head.

FRANCESCA: Here, tonight, is what I hope, I think, I know is the answer. An internationally renowned development agency called Cloy and Tuner believes we have huge untapped potential.

LOCAL 1: What's that?

LOCAL 2: It's potential that hasn't been tapped yet.

FRANCESCA: I'd tell you about it myself but I have a far more exciting prospect. This thrilling new opportunity has been brought to us by a prodigal son of Ballygweeha, returned to give back to the town that reared him. Ladies and gentlemen, may I introduce to you, Luc Torney.

LOCAL 1: Who or what is that?

LOCAL 2: We don't need any blow-ins!

LOCAL 3: Let's kill the fecker!

> *Thumping, electronic synthesizer music blares as a flashy sports car screeches to a halt in front of the town hall. LUC TORNEY, handsome, rakish, charming, emerges. He is flanked by two enormous Polish bodyguards. They all wear sunglasses and are dressed in black.*

JACINTA: What in the name of…

> *The music continues as the three men walk to the podium. They turn to face the audience in unison. A strobe light and smoke effect show begins behind LUC as they perform in the manner of a painfully hip multimedia collective.*

LOCAL 1: Oh, he's gorgeous!

LOCAL 2: Get out of my way you stupid bitch, I can't see!

LOCAL 1: What in the name of arse makes you think he's looking at you, you sour old trout?

LOCAL 3: *(Screaming.)* Oh my god!

LUC: Ballygweeha! I am. LUC!

BODYGUARD 1: LUC!

BODYGUARD 2: LUC!

LUC: Up to now, the wind has been our downfall. Now, I say, let it be our lift-off!

BODYGUARD 1: LIFT-OFF!

BODYGUARD 2: LIFT-OFF!

LUC: I can show you a way to make men want to be you and women want to have you. I can bring you power and virility you have never even dared to dream of. Let me tell you how to wrestle that bitch Mother Nature to the ground and harness the power of the wind. Take back what is yours and reach for glory!

BODYGUARD 1: GLORY!

BODYGUARD 2: GLORY!

LOCALS: How?! How? Tell us how?!

LUC: Ladies and gentlemen, are you ready? Are you ready to sell the wind?

From behind a blast of smoke, a model set of extremely stylish-looking windmills is revealed with a banner reading, 'Cloy and Tuner'.

LUC: Cloy and Tuner's patented windmill system will capture all the excess wind in town, converting it into electricity and covering all your energy needs. Once the sale of the wind is made and the rights are transferred, earnings from this once in a lifetime venture can be channelled into community schemes meaning a lower cost and higher standard of living. What's more, countless jobs will be created, which will come with a healthcare package and a full employee PENSION!

BODYGUARD 1: PENSION!

BODYGUARD 2: PENSION!

LUC: People of Ballygweeha, I am your son Luc and I have returned from the blackness to give you – WINDFARMS!

LUC strikes a pose as the show ends. The locals burst into applause. JACINTA stands up in protest and interrupts.

JACINTA: Hold on, hold on, hold on, hold on, but how can you sell the wind? Sure it's wind!

LUC: Well, of course you can sell the wind. You can sell land and water can't you?

Everyone chuckles.

LOCAL 1: *(To JACINTA.)* Fucking eejit.

JACINTA: Why do Cloy and Tuner want to buy our wind?

LOCAL 2: Who cares, just fucking sell it to them.

LUC: No, no, that's a very good point. Who is asking all these questions?

JACINTA: Em, me.

LUC: *(Chuckling.)* Hello me.

The locals all laugh fondly.

LUC: Now, don't be shy. I welcome questions. But please – step forward so I can see you?

JACINTA steps forward. LUC looks at her warmly.

LUC: What's your name?

JACINTA: Jacinta Nangle.

LUC: Hello Jacinta Nangle. I'm Luc.

JACINTA: Oh. Hi. Em. Thanks.

Blushing, JACINTA scurries back to her seat. The two bodyguards discreetly and professionally remove the synths, smoke machine, lights and model wind farms.

LUC: Now, let's get serious for a minute. Following on from Jacinta's question, I would like to refer to industry consultation. I also intend to replace the terms 'fully commissioned' and 'operational' with a new definition for 'connected'. The new definition of 'connected' will, inter alia, require the project to be commenced on the basis of having at least 75% of installed capacity in the case of what I am discussing; within nine months or the date to which a project has been granted an extension in time as I have already expounded on.

The locals burst into rapturous applause.

JACINTA: Sorry, what?!

MRS MOONEY: Fierce articulate.

JACINTA: He's talking rubbish.

FRANCESCA: I'd like to hear you make a speech like that, you little lush.

DAITHI: Listen to what your mother is saying to you.

FRANCESCA: Shut the fuck up Daithi.

DAITHI: Sorry lovey.

JACINTA: What was that bit about us waiving our rights?

MRS MOONEY: Very well-spoken family, the Torneys. They were always giving little speeches and toasts and things weren't they?

JACINTA: Should we not put it out for tender or whatever they call it?

FRANCESCA steps up to the podium and shakes LUC's hand.

FRANCESCA: Tender... Tsk. Well, thank you for your input, Jacinta, misguided though it may be. You must excuse her, Luc, she's been watching daytime repeats of Dragon's Den. Are there any realistic questions from the floor?

All shake heads, say no etc.

JACINTA: *(Mumbling.)* This is taking the piss.

FRANCESCA: Shall we put it to a vote? All those in favour of the sale of the wind to Cloy and Tuner, say, 'Aye'.

All except JACINTA give a resounding, 'Aye', raise their hands, clap etc.

FRANCESCA: All those opposed?

JACINTA hesitantly raises her hand.

FRANCESCA: Anyone? No?

JACINTA waves her hand.

FRANCESCA: Anyone at all? No? No one?

JACINTA continues waving.

FRANCESCA: No? Alright then, it's a landslide. All that remains is to get approval from the Mayor's Office and fortunately, I know someone on the inside, haha.

She raises her hand, mugging and winking at LUC, who laughs and claps her on the back.

FRANCESCA: *(Wiping away a tear of laughter.)* Well, what else is there to say except, 'Welcome Home Luc!'

FRANCESCA and LUC pose for photographs as the crowd cheers.

NARRATOR: As she shivered outside the town hall later that night, Jacinta fumed that common sense was no match for a flashy light show combined with a mob mentality.

MRS MOONEY, hand in hand with LUC, skips to where JACINTA sulks. The HOODS are playing about in front.

MRS MOONEY: Come over here I want you to meet Jacinta Nangle, the mayor's daughter. Jacinta, I used to look after Luc when he was little.

LUC: I never forgot you Mrs Mooney. Gosh, I'm still getting used to this wind.

MRS MOONEY: Had you forgotten what it's like?

LUC: Can barely walk straight.

MRS MOONEY: You pet!

HOOD 1: Why don't you fuck off then?

MRS MOONEY: Are you little shits still here?! Go on, get away up the yard!

LUC: You must be Jacinta.

JACINTA: Yeah, I am, so what?

LUC: It's great to meet you.

MRS MOONEY: *(Whispering to JACINTA.)* Isn't he a charmer?

JACINTA: *(To LUC.)* Oh really? Why's that?

LUC: Well, I've heard a lot about the Nangles. Your mother is a very accomplished woman. You must be very proud.

MRS MOONEY: Oh the Nangles are a very good family, Luc. Very good. Your father and your mother would tell you that, god rest them. I was telling Jacinta to call into you. Get to know you. Wasn't I, Jacinta? Jacinta?

JACINTA: You were yeah.

LUC: I would very much look forward to that.

FRANCESCA and DAITHI join them, arguing as they go.

FRANCESCA: Can you not just fuck off and wait for me at home like I told you to, you chinless little git? *(Joining the group.)* Well, hello, hello! Luc, it's darling to see you! I see you've met my... You've met Jacinta.

JACINTA: It's too late to pretend – he already knows I'm your daughter.

FRANCESCA: Well, of course you are darling! Luc, I'm afraid I must tear you away for a minute – the Moriartys want to meet you properly. They're dying to shake the hand of Ballygweeha's saviour.

She whisks him away to where the Moriartys are waiting with bottles of champagne to pop. DAITHI remains on the outskirts of the group, trying to break in.

JACINTA: I don't like it, Mooney.

MRS MOONEY: Ah go on and don't be a jealous little cat. Everything is going to be better now, you'll see. Luc's a lovely fella, he won't let us down. Come on home with me, we'll have a Baileys, you can rub my feet.

NARRATOR: With Jacinta and all the other mice gone away, the fat-cats of 'Gweeha retired to the Nangles to play.

FRANCESCA and the Moriartys are in the Nangles' kitchen. They take turns signing a contract and all shake hands.

FRANCESCA: Well gentlemen, I think we should all be very proud of ourselves for what we have set in motion here tonight. Here's to a very successful collaboration that I can only imagine will go from strength to strength.

DAITHI: To my brilliant wife!

FRANCESCA: Shut up.

HUGH: How about a more apt toast. Let's get fucking minted!

They all whoop, dance around, drink champagne.

NARRATOR: Cloy and Tuner were quick off the mark and the windfarms appeared hot on the heels of the town meeting. The locals were thrilled at the verve and vigour in the town – never before had they seen their politicians, bankers and developers so determined and so efficient at putting a plan into motion.

Sequence showing the erection of the wind turbines including a ribbon cutting ceremony, blessing of the site by a crack team of Catholic priests, a host of builder-related shenanigans, and much hand-shaking and brown envelope-exchanging between FRANCESCA and the Moriartys. HOODS and LOCALS operate the turbines with varying degrees of efficiency.

NARRATOR: Meetings were had, papers were signed, hands were shook and second bank accounts were opened quicker than the closing of a reading programme for under-privileged children.

MRS MOONEY: Isn't it great what we can do when we put our mind to it?

LOCAL 1: All we needed was a helping hand.

LOCAL 2: Bit of investment.

LOCAL 3: Bit of welly.

LOCAL 1: Haven't we been talking for years about the potential in the place?

LOCAL 2: Oh sure, we never stopped talking about the potential in the place.

NARRATOR: Seeing the windmills go up gave Ballygweeha a surge of newfound self-worth and appreciation for an elevated standard of living.

Some locals are playing 'golf' by passing the ball between two of them as if they're playing hockey.

LOCAL 1: Gentlemen's sport, golf.

Putts the ball to LOCAL 2.

LOCAL 2: I wholeheartedly concur.

Putts the ball back and so on and so forth.

LOCAL 1: Have I told you that we only buy free-range fruit and vegetables now?

LOCAL 2: Yes. I think my next car will be organic.

LOCAL 1: Mmm. Did you read that article in the *Times*?

LOCAL 2: Which *Times*?

LOCAL 1: *(Pause.)* All of them.

LOCAL 2: Of course. Did I mention I'm thinking of making some new investments?

LOCAL 1: Oh yes? In what?

LOCAL 2: *(Pause.)* Stocks.

LOCAL 1: Oh yes. Me too.

LOCAL 2: I'm going to take Fintan Moriarty's advice. Invest my wind money *before* I get any of it.

LOCAL 1: Very shrewd.

LOCAL 2: That way, it's taken out of my hands before I can think of anything to spend it on.

LOCAL 1: Like you never even had it.

LOCAL 2: Exactly.

LOCAL 1: Brilliant mind, Moriarty.

LOCAL 2: Which one?

LOCAL 1: *(Pause.)* All of them.

LOCAL 2: You're not wrong there.

LOCAL 2 putts the ball into the hole. He raises his arms triumphantly.

LOCAL 2: Goal!

NARRATOR: However, Jacinta couldn't help feeling that some of the locals were developing rather peculiar notions.

JACINTA watches the HOODS playing.

HOOD 1: Out of my way, ye filthy plebs!

HOOD 2: What'll I buy myself to celebrate my first billion?

HOOD 3: My gold house is so hard to heat in the winter!

JACINTA: Here, Hoods, what are you at over there?

HOOD 1: We're being Luc Torney missus.

HOOD 2: He's rapid so he is.

HOOD 3: He lives out of a hotel so he does.

JACINTA: He lives out of a hotel?

HOOD 1: Four Seasons missus.

HOOD 2: Only the best missus.

HOOD 3: Yeah, he's up in his hotel room every night with top shelf brandy and a slapper missus.

JACINTA: Is that the craic?

HOOD 1: Going around town with a chauffeur.

HOOD 2: And his own windshielders made out of people.

HOOD 3: He's wears two watches cos he can't decide which to wear.

JACINTA: I see.

HOOD 1: Here missus!

JACINTA: Yes?

HOOD 1: How many gold houses and mink coats do you have?

JACINTA: Well, I…

HOOD 2: What's that missus?

HOOD 3: None missus?

HOOD 1: Do you live in a bin missus?

JACINTA: Piss off out of here you little shits!

The HOODS run away laughing.

NARRATOR: Unsettled by these tales of Luc's extravagant and glamorous existence, Jacinta felt compelled to take action. Was it a natural instinct to protect her hometown? A surge of regional pride? A piquing of her social consciousness? Or simply a good old fashioned whack of bone-crushing begrudgery? She wasn't sure but Jacinta resolved there and then to find out exactly what was going on. And so, in the name of selfless heroism, she found herself breaking into Luc's office.

LUC's office. JACINTA creeps in and starts rifling through papers and drawers. She begins perusing one particular document in earnest.

JACINTA: Cloy and Tuner… C, L, O…

LUC suddenly appears.

LUC: Jacinta Nangle!

JACINTA: Jesus Christ!

LUC: No, no, that's the other fella hahaha.

JACINTA: Oh, ohh, yeah, hahaha.

LUC: So.

JACINTA: Well.

LUC: Sure, listen.

JACINTA: Stop.

LUC: Tell me this, Jacinta Nangle.

JACINTA: Yeah?

LUC: To what do I owe the pleasure?

JACINTA: Of?

LUC: Your presence?

JACINTA: Oh, I dunno that it's that much of a pleasure now.

NARRATOR: Luc gives a polite laugh.

LUC laughs.

NARRATOR: Jacinta gives a nervous one.

JACINTA laughs.

LUC: Is there anything I can do for you Jacinta? Since you're here?

JACINTA: Oh God no, don't be wasting your time on me. I'm grand sure.

NARRATOR: Realising that the lady isn't budging, Luc begins to wonder if maybe she's for turning.

LUC: May I ask you, what colour are your eyes?

JACINTA: What? Oh, just a bit of old blue or something I don't know.

LUC: I thought they were blue-green?

JACINTA: Well, now that you mention it they are actually.

LUC: I thought so. Like the sea off the coast of the Dominican Republic. You see, I was looking at them. In that meeting. I was meant to be concentrating on my speech but I just kept thinking, 'That girl. That's some pair of eyes she has on her.' And then after I met you for the first time I thought, 'That Jacinta. That's some pair of eyes she has on her.'

JACINTA: Ah, don't mind them, sure I barely use them.

LUC: It's true.

NARRATOR: Sensing he may be onto something, Luc decides to ramp up the pace.

LUC: Yes, those eyes. They're full of statement and question.

JACINTA: Are they?

LUC: You have something special Jacinta.

JACINTA: You think so?

LUC: No, I don't think so. I know so.

JACINTA: You know, I've often felt a little different.

LUC: You're wasted here Jacinta! These people – they don't understand the depths of your melancholic soul!

JACINTA: I've always thought that!

LUC: And that mother of yours! She does not *get* you.

JACINTA: But I thought –

LUC: What, that I liked her? Because I work with her? Jacinta, that's just business. I fucking hate her!

NARRATOR: And with that, Jacinta was besotted.

JACINTA: Take me away from here Luc!

LUC: What? I mean, yes! I'll take you away from all this!

JACINTA: Darling!

LUC: Angel!

They embrace.

LUC: By the way, did you get a chance to read much of that piece of paper?

JACINTA: What piece of paper?

LUC: Never mind. It doesn't matter. All that matters is that we get you out of this office and that dress as quickly as possible. Come here, my sexy rabbit! *(Calls out.)* Pavel! Send the car around. And call the Four Seasons. Tell them I want to upgrade to the hot-tub suite.

NARRATOR: While Jacinta was otherwise engaged in the hot tub suite at the Four Seasons, she missed her appointment with Derbhle, the local Unemployment and Social Services Officer. Which was just as well really since in spite of the promises of work, Derbhle was busier than ever. But even she, with her gift for tolerating repetitive and deflective conversation was growing tired of what she privately dubbed the Windfarm defence.

DERBHLE: And what tactics have you undertaken to alleviate your unemployment?

HOOD 1: I sent a CV into those Cloy and Tuner chaps. Sure they're creating more jobs than Google!

HOOD 2: My cousin got a great job off them.

HOOD 3: Mine too!

HOOD 1: They're always interviewing.

DERBHLE: And when is the interview scheduled?

HOOD 1: Well, like I was saying missus, it's not.

DERBHLE: When were you made the offer to come in for interview?

HOOD 2: Are you not listening? It hasn't happened yet.

DERBHLE: So you're waiting to schedule an interview that hasn't been offered to you yet?

HOOD 3: Isn't that what we've been saying to you? Jesus, this one's not right in the head.

DERBHLE: What indication has the prospective employer given you that a placement may be on the horizon?

HOOD 1: Were you not there for the whole fireworks thing at the town meeting?

HOOD 2: With the Porsche?

HOOD 3: And the Polish?

HOOD 1: And the pension?

HOOD 2: Jesus, you're not right missus.

HOOD 3: Gone soft altogether missus.

HOOD 1: Fit for the home missus.

NARRATOR: Derbhle was not the only person to grow distinctly less enamoured of Cloy and Tuner. With the windfarms sucking up the battering gales of Ballygweeha, the locals' houses had nothing to lean against. As their homes crashed down around their ears, the calls for Coilean Moriarty poured in.

Crash.

MRS MOONEY: Me feckin' roof!

Crash.

LOCAL 1: The bollocking porch!

Crash.

LOCAL 2: The shaggin attic!

Crash.

COILEAN: Ah yeah. I can definitely get that fixed for you alright.

LOCAL 3: Brilliant.

COILEAN: But now you see, to do that, I need a part that I can tell you already has been discontinued.

LOCAL 1: Ah, for fuck's –

COILEAN: Now, I can order it.

LOCAL 2: Great!

COILEAN: But I'll have to wait for it to come in. Really now, you'll be looking at Thursday.

LOCAL 3: Well that's not too bad.

COILEAN: Thursday five weeks from now that is.

MRS MOONEY, LOCALS: What?!

COILEAN: And it'll cost you.

MRS MOONEY: Ye feckin crook! Get out of my yard. You're not getting any more pints on tick off of me! I changed your nappy! I changed all the Moriarty's nappies!

As MOONEY chases COILEAN off her property, JACINTA strolls into the yard.

MRS MOONEY: This roof will be the death of me.

JACINTA: Story, Mooney?

MRS MOONEY: It's you I should be calling moony. What are you doing floating round my yard like that?

JACINTA: Will you remember me when I'm gone Mooney?

MRS MOONEY: Why, what's wrong with you, you sick?

JACINTA: I'm lovesick.

MRS MOONEY: The Capulet's daughter got an awful dose of that a few years back, hahaha.

MOONEY chuckles to herself. JACINTA is oblivious.

JACINTA: Luc has promised me a fresh start.

MRS MOONEY: Has he? Well he promised me a lower electricity bill and I've yet to see it.

JACINTA: He said I'm wasted here.

MRS MOONEY: Switch to Cloy and Tuner to halve your bill. Half, me eye. Two hundred and forty-six it was this month. And sure I barely even use the upstairs.

JACINTA: I'm his sexy rabbit. *(Giggles.)*

MRS MOONEY: What happened to not trusting him as far as you could throw him?

JACINTA: I've come to see how limited I was Mooney. Men with big ideas need big balls. Some people want to whinge about regulations this and propriety that. Others just go out and make it happen. This marks the next chapter of our lives. You won't know me Mooney. I won't know myself.

MRS MOONEY: Oh god help us, she's in love.

NARRATOR: And thus the bold Jacinta left Mari Mooney to her roof. For the first time in her miserable life, Jacinta felt strong, secure, and safe. She decided to celebrate her newfound confidence by doing what any level headed, poised, self-assured young woman would do – going round to her mother's and seeking approval.

At the Nangles' house, movers load in ostentatious furniture – a fishtank, enormous mirrors, vulgar artworks etc. DAITHI is clumsily attempting to direct them. The Moriartys and FRANCESCA are sitting at a desk covered in paperwork and empty bottles. They are toasting with champagne glasses and COILEAN is distinctly worse for wear.

FRANCESCA: *(To the movers.)* Watch you don't get any filthy pawprints on my new dresser. And by the way, I know exactly how many pieces of silver are in that drawer, I mean *exactly* how many, do you know what I'm saying to you? Coilean, dearie, you know I'm grateful for you getting your men on the job, darling favour you've done me and it's much appreciated but do you think you could send over someone who wasn't dropped on their head next time?

COILEAN: 'Gweeha's finest men, you have there! *(He tries to take a drink but spills brandy on himself.)* Ah bollocks…

FRANCESCA: Well done, Coilean. You've truly outdone yourself. Now. While, we're waiting on our fourth person to arrive –

DAITHI: Fifth.

FRANCESCA: – Let's do a bit of housekeeping. Hugh, Fintan, have the council moved forward on which community investment schemes we'd like to pursue?

HUGH*:* Yes. There was a suggestion from some members of the council that perhaps we should employ the services of a financial advisor.

Pause. Then, everyone laughs.

COILEAN: *(Joining in late.)* Hmm?

FRANCESCA: An advisor. Never needed one before did we?

FINTAN: Well, we never had money before.

HUGH: That's probably why we could have used one.

FRANCESCA: Let me tell you something. We have not endured centuries of suffering to be lectured to by a walking briefcase on how to conduct our affairs. We are made of stronger stock than that. I'd like to take on anyone who dares to think they can tell this town what to do.

COILEAN: *(To his brothers.)* Doesn't she tell this town what to do?

FRANCESCA: *(Ignoring him.)* What else?

COILEAN: Sure she's the mayor.

FRANCESCA: What. Else?

FINTAN: A motion was put forward that those who directly benefitted from the sale of the wind might like to reinvest their earnings into the town.

Pause.

FRANCESCA: Oh.

Pause.

FRANCESCA: Well, that's a pretty little thought isn't it?

HUGH: Mmm.

FRANCESCA: Well, it's easy to be charitable with someone else's money isn't it? Don't suppose any of these council members were digging too deep in their own pockets? I have run myself into the ground for this town and what thanks do I get? What thanks do any of us get?

DAITHI: Did you not all get commission from Cloy and Tuner?

FRANCESCA: And apart from that?

DAITHI: You actually got extra commission if I remember right.

COILEAN: Hold on hold on hold on hold on hold on hold on hold on hold on, now, hold on. Hold. On. I didn't get any extra commission.

FRANCESCA: Coilean, how much money have you made from construction and repairs in the last month?

COILEAN: *(Thinks then laughs.)* Oh yeah, fucken loads hahahahaha.

JACINTA arrives.

JACINTA: Mother?

FRANCESCA: Jesus Jacinta! What are you doing darling? Skulking around like that when Mummy's working? *(Taking her aside.)* What have I told you about showing me up in front of people who matter, you insolent little scut?

JACINTA: What's the occasion?

COILEAN: We're fucking minted!

JACINTA: What?

FRANCESCA: Coilean you fucking imbecile! Don't mind him.

COILEAN: Give us your fucking money hahahaha.

JACINTA: What is he going on about?

FRANCESCA: Nothing, he's just a bit tired.

JACINTA walks further into the room and looks around.

JACINTA: Where did that bear skin rug come from?

FRANCESCA: Oh, Mummy just pulled that out of the attic lovey, don't mind it. *(Quietly, to JACINTA.)* Now come on, I haven't time to lend you a tenner today or whatever the fuck it is you want.

JACINTA: Is that a chandelier?

FRANCESCA: Chandelier, are you blind as well as everything else? *(To the Moriartys.)* Gentlemen, do you see a chandelier?

The Moriartys shake their heads furiously, say 'No, no, no.'

JACINTA: It's right there.

FRANCESCA: What *are* you talking about darling? *(Hissing.)* Daithi, *do* something.

DAITHI: Chandelier.

JACINTA: Why are all these bottles of champagne open?

FRANCESCA: They were going off so I just thought you know –

Suddenly, LUC bursts in through the door and sprays champagne everywhere.

LUC: Champagne's on me yis stupid fucks! Jacinta!

JACINTA: Luc? You told me you were stuck in a meeting.

LUC: Well, I. I was. Stuck. When I. Left. The meeting. For champagne. For you. Because. I love you.

JACINTA: Champagne?

FRANCESCA: And then. He. Saw me. In the. Champagne shop.

JACINTA: Champagne shop?

FRANCESCA: Yes. The champagne shop.

JACINTA: Ballygweeha doesn't have a champagne shop.

FRANCESCA: It's very exclusive darling you wouldn't have heard of it. Isn't that right, Hugh, Fintan?

HUGH: Oh, yeah, it's great.

FINTAN: Absolutely.

HUGH: Finest champagne in the land.

DAITHI: Do we really? Well, isn't that marvellous?

JACINTA: You went to a champagne shop?

LUC: Yes. To buy champagne. For you. My own one. Mo cuisle. My little rabbit.

JACINTA: Oh. Well that was nice I suppose.

FRANCESCA: Yes. Yes it was, wasn't it? So caring, so thoughtful. Lovey, I really am so happy you've found such a caring, thoughtful man.

HUGH: He's very taken with you Jacinta.

JACINTA: Really?

FINTAN: Every day, Jacinta this, Jacinta that.

COILEAN: He never fucken shuts up about ya.

JACINTA: Aww, Luc.

All except JACINTA nervously laugh.

JACINTA: Wait.

Horrified faces.

JACINTA: That doesn't explain the chandelier.

LUC: Emmm…What chandelier?

JACINTA: That chandelier, right there.

LUC: Would you call that a chandelier?

JACINTA: It is a chandelier.

LUC: I'd say it's more of a fancy lamp shade. Anyway, why are we wasting time debating what constitutes a chandelier? Why don't you nip back to the hotel and order us some room service hmm? I'll be right over as soon as I –

JACINTA: And why are you at a party in my mother's house?

LUC: Hardly a party really.

The Moriartys and FRANCESCA all shake their heads, say 'No, no,no' etc.

JACINTA: It looks like a party to me.

FRANCESCA: It's called a working lunch sweetie, *(Muttering.)* not that you'd know much about that.

JACINTA: So you left a meeting to go to a champagne shop to buy champagne for me and then you came here for a working lunch?

Pause. LUC looks at the Moriartys who all nod furiously.

LUC: …Yes.

JACINTA: Who was the other meeting with?

LUC: Em…

COILEAN: Tim!

FINTAN hits him over the head.

JACINTA: Who's Tim?

LUC: Ohhhhh, no one you need to worry about, darling. He's quite bad company actually, I'd suggest you forget you ever heard his name.

JACINTA: Why can't I stay for the party?

LUC: You'd be bored senseless rabbit, we're just talking business/

JACINTA: But you're all drinking champagne.

LUC: Are we?

JACINTA: And that is definitely a chandelier.

LUC: Oh, for fuck's sake Jacinta, can you not take a fucking hint and piss off when you're not wanted?

A huge crashing noise – the movers drop something. The scene becomes chaotic as the Moriartys and the Nangles all start talking over each other.

FRANCESCA: Daithi! Jesus Christ!

FINTAN: What the house is going on in this house?

DAITHI: Alright now men, eh, the wife, you know yourself.

Talking over each other, they leave the room.

COILEAN: That'll be another day's work now I'll have to bill for.

FRANCESCA: You said it was a favour!

COILEAN: Did I?

JACINTA: Luc?!

LUC: Jacinta, I am at work. I am busy. I will be with you later but I cannot spend every waking moment massaging your self-esteem.

He joins the others. JACINTA flees in tears.

99

NARRATOR: Reeling from the shock of rejection, Jacinta sought sanctuary in a place where she could gather her thoughts and regain her strength. And so, she found herself in Mooney's yard, alone, clutching a bottle of Tesco Value Gin and singing Tori Amos songs.

A weeping JACINTA swigs from the bottle, tunelessly sings 'Cornflake Girl'.

MRS. MOONEY: What in the name of all that's holy?

JACINTA: Mooney! My only friend.

MRS MOONEY: Get in to fuck and don't get yourself killed in my yard. I don't have the insurance for a death on the premises.

JACINTA: Spurned, Mooney. Left out on the scrap heap with all the other spinsters and the dying cats.

MRS MOONEY: Well, I'm delighted you thought to come round and let me know. Now come on.

MRS MOONEY helps JACINTA in out of the wind.

MRS MOONEY: Sit there and shut up. I'm busy mending my fence.

JACINTA: What is it about me Mooney? Hmm? Everybody rejects me. Nobody wants me. Single, no job, not able to keep a roof over my head.

NARRATOR: Mrs Mooney was too irritated to point out that no one in Ballygweeha was able to keep much of a roof over their head.

JACINTA: What chance had I ever got though y'know? Look at what's been left for me to inherit. Shambles of a town. People can't even stand up straight. No one's ever done a single – I mean did it ever occur to anyone that the place is too fucking windy to live in? It's just fucking thick. And then. You know what it is though, you know what? I'll tell you what.

MRS MOONEY: What?

JACINTA: What?

MRS MOONEY: Christ on the cross…

JACINTA: And another thing! That *bastard*. Luc. Oh, fucking Luc. How fucking dare he?! Me! Reject *me*? The fucking idea Mooney, the fucking cheek. And I reckon he's a fucking crook. Yknow? D'you know that? He has to be. I don't know what the fuck he's up to in that office all day but –

MRS MOONEY: Would you ever shut the fuck up?

JACINTA: Sorry?

MRS MOONEY: I'm sick to death of your whinging. Luc Torney is the only young fella round here worth his salt. Bad enough you can't take a leaf out of his book but then to go bad mouthing him.

JACINTA: Well I think he's fleecing the bejaysus out of the place.

MRS MOONEY: Now, you don't know that. *(Thinks.)* And anyway, so what if he is? About time someone did.

JACINTA: Ah jaysus, Mooney, you don't mean that.

MRS MOONEY: Bit of initiative. Who's the only one around here with a decent car? Hmm? Who's the only one around here gets out of bed before midday? Who's the only man in town owns a tie?

JACINTA: Shit tie.

MRS MOONEY: It's a tie and that's all that matters. It's a wonder Luc Torney ever looked sideways at you! What do you imagine this town owes you?

JACINTA: There's more to success than ties Mooney.

MRS MOONEY: Only people who don't wear ties say things like that. You wouldn't even bring stuff down off my roof for a few shills.

JACINTA: But sure, I wouldn't have worn a tie for that.

MRS MOONEY: Come back to me when you have a tie.

JACINTA: I'd have gotten it dirty! You can't be going around with a dirty tie! Ah well fuck ya anyway! Lemon-faced sow! I'll show you! I'll show all of you!

JACINTA staggers out of the yard.

NARRATOR: Jacinta staggered from Mooney's yard. She felt wretched, rejected and raw, which admittedly did not suit her.

JACINTA thrashes around at nothing.

JACINTA: Get off me! I'm not a fucking rabbit, I'm a woman! A wo-Ahh!

JACINTA falls over.

NARRATOR: However, even in her addled state, she began to think clearly for the first time since the windmills went up. Something had been gnawing at Jacinta for weeks. Troubling her, bothering her, worrying her. But she hadn't been able to put her finger on it. Until now.

JACINTA: There is something incriminating written on that piece of paper I was reading when Luc caught me breaking into his office!

NARRATOR: She suddenly remembered that Luc had told her he wouldn't be home that night as he was going to a ribbon-cutting ceremony at the Ballygweeha's Over 70s Ladies' Club, who had decided to pre-emptively invest their windwealth in a golden basketball court.

LUC'S VOICE: Rabbit, I'm not going to be home tonight because I'm going to a ribbon-cutting ceremony at the Ballygweeha's Over 70s Ladies' Club, who have decided to pre-emptively invest their windwealth in a golden basketball court.

NARRATOR: This of course, meant one thing.

JACINTA: There's no one in Luc's office!

NARRATOR: There was no one in Luc's office.

JACINTA grunts, stumbles, staggers around to make her way to the office.

NARRATOR: Emboldened with gin and indignation, Jacinta Nangle was a woman on a mission. She had to find out what was on that piece of paper.

JACINTA: I have to find out what's on that piece of paper! Ahhh!

JACINTA falls. Momentarily winded, she gets on all fours and crawls.

NARRATOR: It was a cold and unforgiving night but Jacinta would not be stopped. She was lost, alone, and pissed but still she went on.

JACINTA: Come on, Jacinta!

NARRATOR: On her hands and knees, the bold Jacinta crawled on her belly through the mud of Ballygweeha. Branches tore at her clothes, stones and dirt filled her mouth, rain blinded her eyes, her hair was bleeding but still she went on.

JACINTA lets out a roar of determination and pain.

NARRATOR: By this stage, she was running on pure adrenaline, knowing that the soul of the town that reared her rested in her hands alone.

The HOODS enter on bikes and bemusedly watch JACINTA, who is crawling around in circles at their feet.

HOOD 1: You alright missus?

HOOD 2: Why are you on the floor missus?

HOOD 3: Have we had a few jars again missus?

JACINTA: Fuck off, I'm preserving your future!

HOOD 1: Okay missus.

HOOD 2: Let us know when you're done.

HOOD 3: We'll give you a backer home.

HOOD 1: D'you know, I'd sometimes worry about her.

NARRATOR: Finally, after an arduous mile and a half, Jacinta reached Luc's office. She was exhausted, but not deterred.

JACINTA starts scrabbling around on the ground in front of LUC's office.

JACINTA: *(To herself.)* Why the fuck isn't the key under the flowerpot?

Finally, she makes it in. She stands up, wheezing and dusts herself off. She commences ransacking the office, papers, files etc going everywhere, all the while staggering and rolling around. Eventually, she finds the paper she wants.

JACINTA: Yes. Yes. Cloy and Tuner…sole owner…exclusive rights…heretofore known as…trading name…Cloy and Tuner…Cloy and Tuner… C, L, U, T, O…Cloy and Tuner…is…Luc Torney! Cloy and Tuner is Luc! I knew it! I knew it! It's him! He stole our wind!

NARRATOR: Sobered by the revelation of greed and manipulation, Jacinta knew what she must do.

The local shop.

JACINTA: Hello. I'd like a loudspeaker, a hi-vis jacket, and a safety harness. Oh. And a gun.

SHOPKEEPER: I'm not selling you a gun for fuck's sake. This is a Londis.

JACINTA: Fine. Just the rest. Oh and throw in a Quick-Pick and a naggin.

SHOPKEEPER: Fucking nutcase.

NARRATOR: Unaware and frankly unconcerned by her daughter's burgeoning activism, Francesca Nangle had called an emergency meeting with the Moriartys after what should have been a routine status report from the Wind Fund. So urgently was the meeting called in fact, that she completely forgot to reschedule her state portrait sitting.

FRANCESCA is getting her portrait painted as DAITHI angles a mirror to give her the best light.

DAITHI: Stop moving so much.

FRANCESCA: I'll make sure you never fucking move again if I don't get good lighting.

DAITHI: Darling, it would be impossible for you to ever appear in a bad light.

FRANCESCA: Fuck off.

The Moriartys enter. FRANCESCA waves the painter away.

HUGH: Well, well, well, what have we here? Francesca, you look great.

COILEAN: Absolute corker.

FINTAN: *(Whistling and leering.)* House do you do?

FRANCESCA: Oh, stop, you're making me blush. Just a little something for the town hall. Commemorative. I don't normally go in for these kind of things but they insisted, so.

HUGH: Of course.

FRANCESCA: I kept on saying, 'Really, I'm sure this isn't necessary' and everyone kept saying, 'Oh but you must! You're the mayor that saved us from ruin! You must, you must!' so I just said, 'Well, alright.'

HUGH: Oh yeah. Great.

FRANCESCA: I mean I didn't want to –

COILEAN: What did you ask to see us for?

FRANCESCA: Oh, yes. I'm afraid we've found ourselves in some rather unfortunate circumstances. When I gave the go-ahead last week to break ground on the new Olympic stadium –

HUGH: A solid investment by the way.

FINTAN: House-standing.

DAITHI: Are we hosting the Olympics?

FRANCESCA: Well, we haven't been officially approached yet but it's good to be prepared. Anyway, I approved the plans when I was told that there wasn't quite enough in the bank.

The Moriartys glance at each other, look at their shoes, whistle, scratch their heads, generally act suspicious.

FRANCESCA: So I asked exactly how far we could proceed and do you know what I discovered?

HUGH: It was all down the back of the sofa?

Nervous laughs.

FRANCESCA: We have enough left to build one Olympic ring.

COILEAN: God, that's very peculiar.

FRANCESCA: You're dead fucking right, it's very peculiar Daithi!

DAITHI: *(Beaming.)* I was right?

FRANCESCA: What in the name of god have you three fucking morons been doing with our pay-out from Cloy and Tuner?

HUGH: We… we moved it.

FRANCESCA: You moved it?

HUGH: I moved it. A little creative accounting. You know yourself. It'll all come together. Not to worry. Just takes a little time. You'll see.

FRANCESCA: You didn't need any creative accounting, that sale was all above board.

HUGH: Well, you see that's the problem. I moved it…below board.

FRANCESCA: So where is it?

HUGH: Well, a large amount of it was in my own personal account. And Coilean's. And Fintan's. And now that I think of it, yours too, Mayor.

FRANCESCA: What? You gave it all to us? Are you telling me you paid it all out in commissions to us?

COILEAN: He only gave us 25% each.

FRANCESCA: There's fucking four of us!

DAITHI: Is there not five of us?

FRANCESCA: Christ! So it's gone? It's all gone?

HUGH: Unless you managed to save some of your share?

FRANCESCA: Of course I fucking didn't you idiot!

HUGH: Well then we're in a bit of jam alright.

FRANCESCA: Have we saved any of it?

COILEAN: There's enough for that Olympic ring.

FINTAN: We could change the town logo to a single ring?

FRANCESCA: We don't have a town logo!

FINTAN: There you go, we'll create one! Branding, that's called. Marketing strategy.

HUGH: That's the stuff Fintan!

FINTAN: *(Tapping his head.)* Always thinking.

FRANCESCA: Alright, alright, so there's nothing left. Did we make any useful investments? Anything we can tell the town?

FINTAN: I won a few quid on the horses.

HUGH: Coilean put a lovely new kitchen in for himself.

COILEAN: All chrome.

HUGH: Very modern. You really did a lovely job.

COILEAN: Thank you.

HUGH: Any time.

FRANCESCA: Those swindling bastards! All our wind being sold off and we're not getting any of it! I knew we shouldn't have settled for an upfront sum!

HUGH: Well, I have to say I've enjoyed myself immensely over the last while so not a total loss.

His brothers nod in agreement.

FRANCESCA: Targeted, that's what we were. Targeted and exploited. They knew this would happen.

HUGH: They… They did?

FRANCESCA: They knew we'd waste all the money.

FINTAN: You reckon?!

FRANCESCA: That's why they gave it to us.

COILEAN: No!

FRANCESCA: They did this on purpose!

HUGH: The cut-throat swines!

FRANCESA: To make fools of us!

FINTAN: House dare they!

FRANCESCA: We never should have trusted them!

COILEAN: No!

Beat.

COILEAN: Wait a minute, who exactly are we talking about here?

HUGH: Were you not listening? Them!

COILEAN: Who's that?

FINTAN: I don't know but I hate them!

FRANCESCA: That's the right attitude Fintan! You see, Coilean, we don't know who they are/

HUGH: /but someone is to blame here/

FINTAN: /and it sure as hell isn't *us*/

COILEAN: /so it has to be Them! I see!

FRANCESA: Exactly!

COILEAN: Bastards!

HUGH: Fuck Them!

FRANCESA: Yes! I think we've all had enough of Them. Now. I need to think. Get out, all of you! Except for you Daithi. You can stay.

The Moriartys leave.

DAITHI: Really?

FRANCESCA: Yes. I need you.

DAITHI: Really?

FRANCESCA: Actually, I need you to help me to let off some steam, if you know what I mean.

DAITHI: *(Excited.)* Really?

FRANCESCA: Let's play a little game.

DAITHI: Really?!

FRANCESCA: Yeah. It's called Target Practice. You stand over there against that wall and I just throw things at you until my arm gets sore.

NARRATOR: The stirrings of discontent were felt at every level of the town, not least amongst the venerable locals. For the promised wind wealth seemed constantly on the brink of materialising and yet never did. Not ordinarily known for their reticence in the face of misconduct, the good people of Ballygweeha took to the streets to voice their concerns.

At the windfarm, LUC is attempting to assuage the rioting locals. His bodyguards push back against them. FRANCESCA and the Moriartys stand at the back, carefully watching.

LOCAL 1: My son is still out of work!

LOCAL 2: I'm paying through the nose for the electric bill!

LOCAL 3: I'm up to my ears in debt!

LOCAL 1: The houses keep falling over!

LOCAL 2: I miss the wind!

LUC: Gweeha, Gweeha, calm yourselves. All your worries will soon be answered; your fears shall be allayed. I hear and sympathise with you. We are continuing to identify new opportunities that may reverse part of the impairment the town has suffered. We are currently seeking to consolidate, standardise, and simplify our operations whilst investing in our people, businesses and infrastructure.

Suddenly, JACINTA appears atop a windmill with a loudspeaker and hi-vis vest.

JACINTA: WAIT! Halt this charade at once! None of your light shows or your Polish bodyguards or whatever.

POLISH BODYGUARD 1: That's racist.

JACINTA: Oh Jesus, sorry.

POLISH BODYGUARD 2: It's not really.

JACINTA: Oh. Well then fuck off out of here!

POLISH BODYGUARD 1: How is that not racist?

POLISH BODYGUARD 2: Polish people are not a race.

JACINTA: Can I just say none of your bodyguards and not mention that you're Polish?

POLISH BODYGUARD 2: Yeah, how about that.

POLISH BODYGUARD 1: I'm happier that way.

JACINTA: Okay grand. And listen, I'm sorry if it is racist.

FRANCESCA: Jacinta, lovey what are you doing?

JACINTA: People of Ballygweeha, do not let these charlatans lead you up the garden path.

FRANCESCA: Darling, you're making a scene.

HOOD 1: Hahaha, look that young one's gone crackers.

HOOD 2: Your daughter's a looper missus!

HOOD 3: Get the walls padded missus!

JACINTA: It's time we knew the truth!

FRANCESCA: Haha, whatever are you talking about? What truth?

JACINTA: The truth about the wind buyout!

FRANCESCA: I don't know what's come over her. So unlike her. Jacinta. Get down.

LUC: Rabbit –

JACINTA: Don't you rabbit me! I'm wise to you and your chicanery.

MRS MOONEY: What's the meaning of all this?

JACINTA: This man is a fraud!

MRS MOONEY: But – but the windmills.

JACINTA: Those windmills are fucked Mooney. Don't trust them.

MRS MOONEY: Well I never.

JACINTA: *(To LUC.)* You lied to me, I mean to us. You made us think you were saving us and the whole time you were just using us. You never wanted to help; you never gave two flying fucks.

HOOD 1: Jaysus she's really gone off the deep end.

JACINTA: You just fobbed us off with a lump sum! The real money was in the wind the whole time! You just let us sign it over to you and you're the only one making any money off it! Everybody listen to me when I tell you; Cloy and Tuner *is* Luc Torney!

Silence.

LOCAL 1: Huh?

JACINTA: It's a fucking anagram!

LOCAL 1: What?!

LOCAL 2: No!

LOCAL 3: I knew it all along, I just didn't feel like saying it!

LOCAL 1: Burn him!!

LOCAL 2 smacks LOCAL 1 on the head.

JACINTA: You're as full of air as your damn windmills Luc. All that energy they're harnessing is travelling along cables out of town and into the big smoke. We're not getting any free electricity! He's lining his filthy, lying pockets by selling our wind and we don't get a penny of it!

LOCAL 1: I've been leaving the lights on all night for the laugh cos I thought it was free!

JACINTA: And there's none of that maintenance work that you promised us. Coilean Moriarty's taken all the contracts for himself and in the meantime, all our houses are falling down.

MRS MOONEY: That's true, my front room has been upside down for a fortnight.

JACINTA: It's been nothing but a ruse.

FRANCESCA: Jacinta Nangle, that's enough.

DAITHI: Jacinta Nangle.

LUC: Jacinta, rabbit, listen. Where is all this coming from lovey? I think you're feeling a bit upset because I'm working so much isn't that it really? I know it feels a little bit like I've abandoned you or I'm not paying enough attention to you but things will ease up again soon, I promise. And then we can take that little trip we talked about. Come on now. You know you're my number one girl.

JACINTA: Fuck off.

DERBHLE: Sing it, sister woman!

FRANCESCA: Jacinta!

LUC: *(Nervous laughter.)* Oh, that's my little firecracker.

JACINTA: Do you think I'm stupid? Do you think we're all stupid? I've read the paperwork and it is smeared with the sticky fingerprints of corruption. The Moriartys, the banks, the council – they all knew what you were doing. They all signed off on it for a piece of the pie. Even the Mayor's Office –

The crowd gasps.

NARRATOR: Demonstrating the quick-witted and resourceful mind that allowed for her rapid ascension and steadfast position in the world of politics, Francesca seized the opportunity to pass the buck.

FRANCESCA: I. Am. Appalled!

JACINTA: What?

FRANCESCA: How dare you?

JACINTA: Sure I didn't do anything.

FRANCESCA: How dare you psychologically torment my daughter?

LUC: What?

FRANCESCA: My poor sweet innocent Jacinta! I rue the day she ever laid eyes on you!

JACINTA: You do?

LUC: You do?

FRANCESCA: I will not stand for it. You seduced this town with your windmills and then you seduced my daughter with your w–

MRS MOONEY: Language!

LUC: Francesca! Surely you don't think me capable.

FRANCESCA: I don't think you capable, I know you capable. You have taken us for fools and we will stand for it no more. Pulled the wool over our eyes with a lump sum while you stole our greatest resource! Well, we are not so easily hoodwinked as that! We cannot be taken in promises of gold! Ballygweeha, you wondered why we are not reaping the rewards of the windfarms – this man is your answer!

The locals shriek and rush at LUC but the bodyguards stop them.

LUC: Get back, get back, get off me! I knew I shouldn't have come back here! You pack of fucking savages! I have done nothing but try and improve your miserable lot. Jealousy and begrudgery everywhere you look! Poisoned with it!

LOCAL 3: You stole all our fucking wind!

LUC: That wind was lying around for years and you never used it properly! I bought it fair and square! I had ideas! I had imagination! This could have been the beginning if you hadn't been so hellbent on dragging me down to your level! You won't be happy until we're all scrabbling in the dirt!

JACINTA: Wait, you were going to reinvest it in the town?

LUC: Eh…

LOCAL 1: CAN WE NOT JUST FUCKING BURN HIM?!

All rush at LUC who is covered in rabid locals. The Nangles and the Moriartys make a swift and tactical exit. JACINTA, trapped on top of the windmill, despairs at the riot below.

JACINTA: Luc! Luc!

LUC: Jacinta!

JACINTA: Luc! I'm sorry Luc!

NARRATOR: Having successfully overthrown the forces of corruption and liberated themselves from the cult of greed, the residents of Ballygweeha became instilled with a new sensibility. One of pragmatic idealism, principled hope and realistic determination. They resolved to work together to bring about the change they understood would be needed in the town. It would be hard, it would be tough and it would be exhausting. Which is why, before all of that, they decided to have a little party.

There is an outrageous party in full swing, half-naked locals covered in blood, swinging from the rafters.

LOCAL 1: Thanks be to jaysus that fucking bollocks is gone.

LOCAL 2: Coming in here with his windmills like big swinging mickeys.

LOCAL 3: Smug bastard.

LOCAL 1: The neck.

LOCAL 2: The nerve.

LOCAL 3: The prick.

LOCAL 1: How did he think he'd get away with it?

LOCAL 2: Waving it under our noses.

LOCAL 3: Taking us for a pack of arseholes.

NARRATOR: But the tone of the conversation veered in a slightly unexpected direction.

LOCAL 1: He'd the Moriartys totally in the dark.

LOCAL 2: That shower of cunts.

LOCAL 3: *(Laughing.)* D'you see the look on their faces when they twigged?

LOCAL 1: Sure that Hugh Moriarty always looks like he was been dropped.

LOCAL 2: And Coilean!

LOCAL 3: Fuck Coilean, fucken Fintan! Delighted to see the smile wiped off his stupid fucking face, he fucked me over years ago and never apologised.

LOCAL 1: Fucken eejits, them without a clue it was him and he above in the hot tub suite.

LOCAL 2: Ah see now, they're cute but not cute enough for the bold Luc.

LOCAL 3: Sure, none of us were.

NARRATOR: And grew increasingly stranger.

LOCAL 1: The mayor's daughter no less! Jesus, fair play to him.

LOCAL 2: It's a fucking bold move alright.

LOCAL 3: Credit where credit's due.

LOCAL 1: *(Laughing.)* And him getting the room on tick!

LOCAL 2: Mooney fucking ordering in champagne to the shop and giving it to for him free!

LOCAL 3: The fecker didn't spend a penny the whole time he was here sure!

All fall about laughing.

NARRATOR: Until finally, the conversation reached new heights of inanity.

LOCAL 1: And the feckin Mayor was in on the whole thing.

LOCAL 2: Dyou reckon?

LOCAL 3: Sure she'd have to be.

LOCAL 2: Sly dog.

LOCAL 3: That woman has her head screwed on rightly.

LOCAL 1: Not rightly enough, sure she spent all her money on that rancid fucking portrait of herself.

LOCAL 2: At least she has something to show for it.

LOCAL 3: I tell you, I took out fucking loans to go gambling!

All keep laughing throughout.

LOCAL 1: I'd say now that Luc was pissing himself laughing at the state of us.

LOCAL 3: Sure why wouldn't he, weren't we acting the bollocks?

LOCAL 1: Some craic though.

LOCAL 2: Ah stop.

LOCAL 1: I mean, how did he come up with it?

LOCAL 3: *(Chuckling.)* Chancer. Some man.

LOCAL 1: Some man is right. *(Raises glass.)* To being bested by the best of the worst!

FRANCESCA taps her glass to make a toast.

FRANCESCA: People of Ballygweeha, a terrible misdeed has been done to us. The damage done is unquantifiable, the hurt insurmountable, the betrayal unimaginable. I come before you as your Mayor to share in your grief. This incident has cast a long shadow over our life here and our sense of who we are. For we are simple, good, hard-working people. The worst of us could not have conceived of the depths of depravity reached by Luc Torney and his ilk. Well you may say, *how* will we recover from this?

LOCAL 1: Yeah, how?

LOCAL 2 slaps him.

FRANCESCA: Well you may say, *can* we recover from this? The answer is, 'I'm not sure.'

JACINTA: Sure, just sell off some electricity and invest the money into –

She is cut off by the Polish bodyguards loudly coughing. They sternly shake their heads at her.

JACINTA: What are those Polish body – *(Interrupted by louder coughing.)* plain old bodyguards still doing here?

DAITHI: Your mother is giving them a bit of security work.

FRANCESCA: Is it too much to ask that my own husband and daughter shut the fuck up when I'm giving a speech?!

DAITHI: Sorry darling.

FRANCESCA: Bell-end. *(To the crowd.)* I am consistently humbled and inspired by you. By your belief and faith in me.

One of the locals starts giggling. He is hauled off screaming by the Polish bodyguards.

FRANCESCA: The reality is that for the last few months we were subjected to a deliberate and profound campaign of hate. It would be easy to fight back against what happened.

To stoop to Luc's level. To retaliate using force and suspicion. That is not our way.

JACINTA: Why aren't we just using the windmills?

FRANCESCA: Jacinta! I swear to fucking god… *(To the crowd.)* I believe that the best strategy to aid us in our recovery is to commission an independent report, which is currently being compiled by the consistently dedicated Moriarty family. Since their callous hood-winking at the hands of Luc Torney, their capacity for forgiveness has not ceased to amaze me. Together, they are helping to compose a document of truth. They are helping to shine a bright and necessary light on a dark chapter of our history.

The crowd murmurs in agreement.

JACINTA: What's going to happen to the windmills now that Luc's gone?

LOCAL 2: Can I have one?

LOCAL 3: Can I have another?

LOCAL 1: Here, if they're getting one then I am too.

LOCAL 2: I'm getting the biggest one.

LOCAL 3: They're all the same fucking size.

LOCAL 2: I'm still getting the biggest one.

LOCAL 1: I'm taking two of them!

LOCAL 3: You are in your fucking hole.

LOCAL 1: What did you just say to me?

LOCAL 2: Come over here and I'll whisper it you.

LOCAL 3: Gone as deaf as his battleaxe of a mother.

LOCAL 1: My mother's a fucking saint!

The locals begin fighting. Others stand by, cheering on them on.

FRANCESCA: *(To the Moriartys.)* Now's a good time. *(Slightly louder, from the podium.)* The capital raised by the sale of the wind has been eh, tangled up somewhat and so we are currently investigating ways in which we can finance the maintenance required to – Jesus fucking Christ!

The locals fight turns into a tumbleweed of people, rolls onto the stage and knocks over the podium. There is chaos.

LOCAL 1: If I'm not getting one, then you sure as fuck aren't getting one!

LOCAL 2: I'll tear them down before I see you with one!

LOCAL 3: None of you are getting any of them!

The locals break away and start tearing down the windmills. Parts fly everywhere.

JACINTA: Stop, stop, what the fuck are you doing?

FRANCESCA: We've no money to repair those!

Suddenly there is a blood-curdling scream.

DERBHLE: Someone come quick! There's been a terrible accident, a terrible accident! A propeller has flown off one the windmills and crashed in on top of Mari Mooney's house! Oh, Jesus, won't someone do something? There's fecking gnomes everywhere!

JACINTA: Mooney! No!

JACINTA flees the meeting along with all the others. There is consternation – MOONEY's house has been reduced to rubble with a windmill propeller emerging from it. JACINTA wails and grieves.

NARRATOR: Mari Mooney died at 7am the next morning. Nice and early, to get a head start at the day, just like she would have wanted.

A funeral procession with weeping, keening and five priests. FRANCESCA leads the mourners.

FRANCESCA: Oh, Mari, Mari, Mari, you are lost to us now surely.

DAITHI: Mari –

FRANCESCA: Shut up, I'm mourning.

NARRATOR: The procession advanced to the Nangles house, where Francesca had generously hosted a light lunch of vol-au-vents and French Fancies. There, waiting with packed suitcases and a pre-charged mobile phone, was Jacinta. She had not gone to the funeral.

FRANCESCA: *(To DAITHI.)* Don't let that Coilean fucker eat all the good sandwiches. He can have the egg salad ones.

JACINTA stands to greet her mother.

FRANCESCA: Oh for – What? What? What now? What have you got to say to us all now Jacinta?

JACINTA: Nothing. I have nothing left to say.

FRANCESCA: So you're just going to stand there with a face like a smacked arse is it? I was up all night making sure the vol-au-vents were alright. Yes, ordering them, not making them by hand, I'm sure you've something to say to me about that?

JACINTA: No. I don't want to talk anymore.

FRANCESCA: Still smarting over Luc?

JACINTA: I don't have anything else to say. Neither to you nor about you or anyone else. I'm exhausted shouting my head off and now I just want to be quiet.

LOCAL 1: Thanks be to Christ.

LOCAL 2: If it wasn't for you poking your fucking nose in, we'd still have those windfarms!

LOCAL 3: Might have had some good come out of it.

LOCAL 1: Luc might have actually invested in the town.

LOCAL 2: If you hadn't made us kill him!

LOCAL 3: Ye whistle-blowing little bitch!

LOCAL 1: Snivelling fecking weasel.

FRANCESCA: *(Gestures to the bags.)* And what's the meaning of all this?

JACINTA: I'm leaving.

FRANCESCA: Good. Great. That's fantastic news. Where are you going? Send me a postcard.

JACINTA: Dunno.

FRANCESCA: Well, you can't go.

JACINTA: Why not?

FRANCESCA: I don't want you to.

JACINTA: You don't even like me!

FRANCESCA: I do –

DAITHI: Now you listen to me, Jacinta Nangle, your mother may not be perfect but at least she doesn't look down her nose at everyone around her.

Everyone stares at him.

JACINTA: But… Dad –

DAITHI: All you've ever wanted is for people to feel outraged on your behalf. It ends now. You made your point and you got what you asked for.

JACINTA: That's fine. That's fine. I just want to go.

JACINTA steps outside and shouts back into the house.

JACINTA: You all ought to be ashamed of yourselves!

HOOD 1: Shag off, ya dry shite.

HOOD 2: Bleeding heart only came after the broken heart eh?

HOOD 2: No more Four Seasons missus?

HOOD 3: Good Samaritan now missus?

HOOD 1: Fucking Serpico is it missus?

HOOD 3: Piss off, you human fucking Trocaire box!

All laugh. JACINTA gets on a bus and leaves. The HOODS return to texting, rolling around on their bikes, playing tip can etc.

HOOD 1: Any work going today?

HOOD 2: No.

HOOD 1: Any work going yesterday?

HOOD 3: No.

HOOD 1: Any work going tomorrow?

HOOD 2: Fucking hope not.

END.

TRYST

BY
JEDA DE BRÍ
&
FINBARR DOYLE

To our parents and our friends

Thank you

&

Kick it in the Face

Characters

STEPH, *27*

MATT, *28*

RACHEL, *26*

Setting
Present day. An apartment in Dublin.

Notes
/ – indicates an overlap in speech,
an interruption, or sentences running together.

Beat – indicates a hesitation,
a shift in thought, an inward breath.

Pause – two beats, indicates a shift in tone.

Silence – as long as necessary. Indicates a defeat,
a victory, or a new line of attack incoming.

TRYST was first presented by Sickle Moon Productions at The Lir, Studio One as part of The Tiger Dublin Fringe Festival, 20-24 September 2016 with the following cast and creative team:

MATT Finbarr Doyle

STEPH Katie McCann

RACHEL Clodagh Mooney Duggan

Director: Jeda de Brí

Producer: Katie McCann

Set Design: Katie Foley

Lighting Design: Dara Hoban

Costume Design: Nicola Burke

Stage Manager: Sinead Purcell

Photography: Christopher Lindhorst

Graphic Design: Lisa B. Doyle and Molly O'Cathain

Present day.

An apartment in Dublin. Minimally furnished.

STEPH is sitting in an armchair, playing the PS3.

MATT comes in with a cup in his hand. He wears a nose pore strip on his face.

STEPH: Do you ever worry that we're not, like… "ha-ha" alcoholics?

MATT: All the time. I feel like I might die.

STEPH: Make it through next week, then you can die.

MATT: This is it.

STEPH: I drank just as much as you.

MATT: It's awful.

STEPH: I'm *fine.*

> *She looks at him. Big smile.*

I feel *great.*

> *Beat.*

MATT: How long have you been up?

STEPH: Ah… an hour. Ish.

MATT: Missed ya.

STEPH: You didn't notice I was up/

MATT: /No. Is there breakfast?

STEPH: Not your wife yet.

MATT: Can I have a go?

STEPH: Nope.

> *Pause.*

MATT: Do we have to do *things* today?

STEPH: Lotta questions, Matt.

MATT: I'm not doing *things*.

STEPH: We do have a few things to do.

MATT: *You're* not doing things.

STEPH: I was waiting for you.

MATT: Mmf.

>*Beat.*

>*(Referencing the nose-strip.)* I put the yoke on.

STEPH: I see.

MATT: You not doing yours?

STEPH: I did mine.

MATT: When?

STEPH: Last night.

MATT: Why?

STEPH: I didn't want to do it hungover.

MATT: Why? Is it bad?

STEPH: No. It's just sore.

MATT: Hang on, you didn't say that, now. You didn't tell me it hurts.

STEPH: What did you expect?

MATT: I thought it'd be, I dunno… *cleansing.*

STEPH: Okay, well, no. It's more like a plaster.

MATT: What?

>*MATT begins to remove the strip. STEPH notices and turns to him.*

STEPH: Wait, hold on, how long have you had it on for?

MATT: I just put it on there.

STEPH: It needs a few minutes to work.

MATT: I don't want to/

STEPH: /*Leave* it. I'm not listening to you go on about your blackheads/

MATT: /It hurts.

STEPH: It does not.

MATT: Yeah, well… maybe I'm allergic to it. You ever think of that?

She smiles, turns back to the game.

STEPH: Is that tea?

MATT: Frosty Coke.

STEPH: So there's no tea/

MATT: /You've legs, don't ya?

She shakes her head.

STEPH: Mm.

MATT: Right. What things do we have to do?

STEPH: Seating plan is still/

MATT: /Bollocks. Okay. Did you have a chat with Brigit?

STEPH: No.

MATT: Steph.

STEPH: She's my *aunt*, she'll behave.

MATT: Right. We just don't want her to go on a rant.

STEPH: She won't.

MATT: She told me the Polish cleaners at her office are, and this is a quote, "stealing her Skype"/

STEPH: /Okay/

MATT: /To "phone home", like ET/

STEPH: /Leave her alone, she's old/

MATT: /Because Skype starts automatically when she turns on the PC. And she doesn't understand why/

STEPH: /Look/

MATT: /She actually said "they're like ET".

> *STEPH looks at him. MATT relents.*

We just need to keep her away from the college crowd because they'll only try to start her up.

STEPH: Yeah. Fine. I'll talk to her. Okay?

> *He leans against the armchair.*

MATT: *(About the game.)* How's Batman?

STEPH: I'm stuck on Mr. Freeze.

MATT: Tricky bit.

STEPH: Mm.

MATT: You have to use all your gadgets on him, cuz he learns after each one. Can't repeat the same attacks.

STEPH: Yeah. I *know*. I just can't aim the stupid Batarang for shit.

> *Beat.*

MATT: Does Batman call them Batarangs? Or is that just what *we* call them? Like *in-universe*, does he add the Bat prefix to *all* of his, uh, gizmos?

STEPH: Course he does. "To the Batmobile – nanannananaaaa"

Beat.

MATT: Yeah. Just seems like… it'd get annoying.

STEPH: Probably drives Alfred up the fucking wall.

He nods.

MATT: How're you playing that? I'm dizzy just looking at it.

STEPH: Bit *wobbly?*

MATT: What time did we get in at?

STEPH: Five.

MATT: Did we get a taxi?

MATT picks up his wallet.

STEPH: With Rob.

MATT: Oh yeah. *Yeah.* He was *really* fucked.

He pulls a tenner from his wallet.

Hey! Not bad! Was worried there for a sec.

STEPH: You got forty cashback at the bar.

MATT: Fuck's *sake.*

Pause.

STEPH: Did Rachel say anything to you?

MATT: No. Was she supposed to?

STEPH: No.

MATT: Right. No, she didn't talk to me at all, actually.

STEPH: I think she left early.

MATT: You didn't do anything, if that's what you're thinking.

STEPH: Good. Yeah, she's probably just stressed with work.

MATT: How hard can it be?

STEPH: You ever been clamped?

MATT snorts.

Yeah well, she deals with a lotta pricks. I'm just worried about her.

MATT: Well, I've heard she's been having a grand time lately.

STEPH: What do you mean?

MATT: I heard she's had, y'know, a couple of suitors on the go.

STEPH glances at him.

STEPH: I think that's good. Healthy.

MATT: Oh that's healthy, is it?

STEPH: Absolutely. I wouldn't mind a suitor.

MATT: Hey. None of that.

STEPH: You worried I might do a runner?

MATT: Nah. You're stuck with me now.

STEPH: Yay.

STEPH's phone rings.

See who that is?

MATT looks at her phone.

MATT: It's your Mam.

STEPH: Get it there, will ya?

(About the game.)

I'm actually doing okay here.

MATT answers the phone.

MATT: Delores. Hi. It's Matt.

Yeah. How is… I'm good…

Well, you know. Yeah, yeah, absolutely. Almost there now...

Not that I know of, anyway.

She's still here, yeah. Hasn't bolted on me yet. Hah.

Yeah. Yeah, yeah she's next to me here, yeah, hang on a sec.

He holds out the phone, pleading with her to take it. STEPH reluctantly takes it and hands the controller to MATT. MATT continues the game for her.

STEPH: Hi Mam.

Yeah.

Right. I know, yeah but...

Well, yeah. I mean, surely we can decorate it however we want.

We've already sorted out the *flowers*, and he didn't put up a fuss, so I don't see why we can't keep ... the... I'm saying the... no, the priest *didn't* pick the flowers.

That's not a thing. Why would...

Bunting. Yes. *Bunting*, Mam. You do know what that is.

It's like... little flags. Like at the circus.

We're... no, Matt's made loads of it already.

MATT indicates silently that he has not made the bunting.

Anyway, why is the priest calling *you*?

Right. And why would he be calling *you* instead of –

She starts to cough suddenly, her voice cracks, she reaches to MATT for his cup of Coke. He pulls it away, slightly.

Hold on, sorry Mam, I've something –

She puts the phone against her shoulder.

Can I just drink a bit, I'm –

She coughs.

MATT: I'll get water.

STEPH: *Matt?*

STEPH grabs the cup, swigs a bit. She looks at MATT, taken aback. She returns to the phone conversation.

Sorry about that. Yeah, listen, I have to go. I'll give Fr. Richard a call and sort it out.

I'll talk to you later. Bye. bye bye… bye.

She hangs up. Mr. Freeze beats MATT.

MATT: Ah fuck you, Mr. Freeze.

He quits the game.

STEPH: Is there *whiskey* in that?

MATT: No.

STEPH: Jesus. It's very strong Coke.

MATT: Come *on.* Hair of the dog.

STEPH stares at him.

It was for rabies. The, that phrase. Put the hair of the dog that bit you on the wound.

STEPH: Sorry, *Wikipedia,* shut up. Why are you drinking at this time of day?

MATT: What does that mean? "Time of day". Jesus, Mam, thanks.

STEPH: Are you *alright?*

MATT: *Yes.*

He takes the cup back.

STEPH: Ah, hang on.

Beat.

STEPH decides not to pursue the matter any further, makes a joke of it.

I didn't say I was finished.

MATT: You're the worst.

STEPH: I have a taste for it now.

MATT: I'm much more hungover than you.

STEPH grabs the cup and takes a swig.

What was your Mam saying?

STEPH: She's been on to the *priest.*

MATT: Yeah?

STEPH: She has a vendetta against your bunting.

MATT: Well, in fairness, so do I.

STEPH: It's just painful, because *now* I have to call him and go over the arrangements again because I'm *sure* she's told him something diff/

MATT: /I'll do it.

STEPH: Really?

MATT: Yeah. It's no problem.

STEPH: I hate talking to priests.

MATT: You won't ever have to again after this.

STEPH nods.

He's actually not that bad.

STEPH: For a priest.

MATT: Your Mam just wants it to be perfect.

STEPH: I want bunting, though.

MATT: The bunting isn't/

STEPH: /I don't want to back down on *everything.*

MATT: Trust me, you're not.

STEPH: You know? It's *our* thing… *Day/*

MATT: *(Simultaneously with "day".) /Day,* I know, she's only/

STEPH: /And after the stuff with *Dad/*

MATT: /Yeah/

STEPH: /I just don't want them to/

MATT: /It'll be fine.

> *He puts his arm around her.*

STEPH: Yeah?

MATT: Yeah.

> *Beat.*

Your Dad's gotta do his thing as well, Steph. He wants to bring Vicky and she's proud of you, too. You know that.

> *STEPH looks down.*

We'll do the bunting.

STEPH: Okay. Thanks.

> *STEPH touches MATT's nose.*

I'd say that's done.

MATT: Right.

STEPH: You want me to do it?

MATT: Yeah.

STEPH: Okay, now are you sure you're ready? Because if the slightest –

> *STEPH rips off the strip. MATT lets out a small gasp.*

MATT: Jesus Christ.

STEPH: Done! Cleanest nose I've ever seen.

She kisses him on the nose, and hands him the strip.

MATT: I don't think I can go through with this now, the trust is gone.

He looks at the strip.

Jesus.

STEPH's phone beeps. She starts texting back.

STEPH: I know.

Pause.

STEPH puts her phone down and goes into business mode.

Okay, you're going to hate this.

MATT: Then don't say it/

STEPH: /I'm going to help you/

MATT: /It's very early/

STEPH: /No, it's not/

MATT: /It *feels* early/

STEPH: /The name cards aren't done, are they?

MATT: No. All this handmade shite is a pain in the hole.

STEPH: Yeah, but we can get it *done* today. So we're not freaking out. No last minute running around.

MATT: It just takes so long. Tea-staining is a terrible way to/

STEPH: /We said we'd do the DIY thing, I thought you'd like/

MATT: /I'm not *Pinterest*, Steph. I can't just churn out *tat*. I do have my own projects for actual work.
Y'know? For *money*.

STEPH: I know.

MATT: It's just, I didn't sign up to be doing all the arts and crafts for my own... you know?

STEPH: Yeah.

MATT: I just have no time.

>*Beat.*

STEPH: You okay?

MATT: I'm *fine.* I dunno, I'm hungover.

STEPH: Your nose looks lovely.

MATT: Thank you.

>*Beat.*

>I just need to sort my head out. I feel like there's too much stuff, and I can't even... *see* all of it.

STEPH: You just gotta take it one thing at a time.

>*She smiles at him.*

MATT: Sorry. *Sorry.* I'm over-thinking. I want to, just, do nothing today.

STEPH: That's okay.

>*STEPH's phone beeps. She reads the text.*

>*Replies. MATT watches her.*

MATT: What's up?

STEPH: Rachel. Wants to know if we're home.

>*Beat.*

MATT: Say *no.*

STEPH: Why? Was she being weird to you, too?

MATT: No. Weird how?

STEPH: I dunno, I think she's mad at me. Lots of full stops in her texts.

> *Beat.*

MATT: Full stops.

STEPH: Like, short sentences with full stops.

> *MATT shakes his head, bewildered.*

Full stops are passive aggressive.

MATT: Or, just, normal sentence structure.

STEPH: She's coming over anyway so…

> *She is texting her back.*

MATT: Has she not got Head Bridesmaid things to be doing?

STEPH: *Chief* Bridesmaid.

MATT: I thought it was "Head Bridesmaid".

STEPH: We dropped "Maid of Honour" but never really landed on anything else. Anyway, she's coming over so you'll need to…

> *She glances at MATT in his pyjamas.*

You know, sort yourself out.

MATT: But we have to… what about… name-cards. The things. What happened to one thing at a time?

STEPH: You were the one that wanted to do nothing.

MATT: I can't *do* nothing if we're in "entertaining" mode.

STEPH: It's only *Rachel.*

MATT: I know, but/

STEPH: /Don't get weird/

MATT: /I won't, I haven't/

STEPH: /The bunting also needs to be/

MATT: /I've got a *week* to do that/

STEPH: /Six days/

MATT: /Six days/

STEPH: /This could be a chance for us to actually get some stuff sorted.

MATT: Steph, *darling*, come on, could we just put her off this once?

STEPH: *She's* been putting me off, that's the problem.

> *MATT moves closer to STEPH.*

MATT: Yeah, but we could just be together today and not talk to anyone.

STEPH: Matt, it's a week to our wedding.

MATT: Six days.

STEPH: Exactly.

MATT: So why stress? We can put on some music, I'll try to beat Mr. Freeze again, we can order a spice bag.

STEPH: Romantic.

MATT: I know, right?

> *He moves towards her and kisses her softly.*

Cancel, cancel, cancel. Go on, you can get up early tomorrow and do all the things.

> *STEPH gives him a look.*

And I'll help too, obviously.

> *STEPH sighs, embraces him, about to give in when there is a knock on the door.*

Ah… now we'll never know.

STEPH: That was quick.

> *STEPH moves towards the door as RACHEL enters holding keys and a half-eaten muffin. Her hands are stained with tea.*

STEPH: Hey!

RACHEL: Hey! Keys were in the door.

> *STEPH looks at MATT.*

MATT: Uh… thanks, Rache.

RACHEL: No problem. Done that before *loads* of times.

MATT: Really?

RACHEL: Yeah. Well, no. How are the heads?

> *STEPH groans.*

That bad?

STEPH: Too many pints.

RACHEL: Brilliant.

MATT: Were you in the area?

RACHEL: Uh, yeah, down at Tesco's.

MATT: Whatcha get?

> *RACHEL gestures to the muffin.*

STEPH: *(Sarcastically.)* Did you need anything, Matt?

MATT: Ha! No, got me Coke.

> *He takes a sip from his whiskey cup.*

RACHEL: You can have some of this thing, it's huge.

MATT: Ah, you're grand.

STEPH: Tea?

RACHEL: No, I'm good.

MATT: Have fun last night?

STEPH: We didn't see you when we were going.

RACHEL: I was dancing, probably.

MATT: Steph thought you left early.

STEPH: I just didn't see you.

RACHEL: Yeah, sorry. It was pretty packed, wasn't it?

STEPH: Yeah. Oh my God, were you there for the Jackie thing?

> *RACHEL cringes.*

MATT: Jackie thing?

STEPH: I only heard from Lorna after it happened.

RACHEL: Yeah. I mean, it was a disaster. She went all speechy again and I was going to stop her, but she stood up on a keg in the smoking area and I couldn't just... pull her down, would have made it worse... she started on about how she's been, uh, in love with Paul... since forever.

STEPH: And Paul was *there.* She was saying it *to* him/

MATT: /Right/

RACHEL: /He wasn't drunk enough to find it funny, it was stupidly awkward and he left halfway through. Like, halfway through her speech... She kept going.

> *MATT inhales through his teeth.*

STEPH: What did she say to him? She said something really cringey.

RACHEL: "I worship you".

STEPH: That's it!

MATT: Worship? Jesus.

RACHEL: I know.

STEPH: Ah, poor Jackie.

MATT: Poor Paul!

RACHEL: *(Joking.)* You might need to update the seating plan.

> *Beat.*

STEPH: *No…*

> *RACHEL gives her a look.*

Shit. Maybe. D'ya think?

MATT: Ah, I'm sure they won't even remember.

RACHEL: Sophie's already posted the video to the group chat so/

MATT: /Fucking Sophie, why is she even in that chat?

RACHEL: Because guaranteed you'll look at that video later on.

> *MATT nods as if to say "probably".*

MATT: Listen I'm going to throw on some actual clothes. Gimme a sec.

RACHEL: Sure.

> *He goes out. STEPH looks at RACHEL's muffin crumb trail.*

STEPH: You want a plate for that?

RACHEL: Ah, I'm okay. I shouldn't even be eating it, going for lunch with Mam in a little bit.

STEPH: Oh. You're not hanging around?

RACHEL: I actually just wanted/

STEPH: /Cuz I thought we'd look at the checklist and get some of that sorted. But like…

> *She looks at RACHEL for a second.*

Did you sort out your thing with work?

RACHEL: Mm?

STEPH: You said you had, like, a run-in with them.

RACHEL: Oh, no. It's a disciplinary meeting.

STEPH: That doesn't sound/

RACHEL: /No, I mean, it's fine. It'll be fine. I get three warnings.

STEPH: Yeah? How many is this?

RACHEL: Uh…

> *She winces. STEPH changes the subject.*

STEPH: Listen, I'm sorry if I was an arsehole last night.

RACHEL: What? You weren't/

STEPH: /Or full on or/

RACHEL: /No, not at all.

> *STEPH nods.*

STEPH: Just thought you were mad at me.

RACHEL: Why?

STEPH: I dunno. I just had a feeling. Like I did something?

RACHEL: It's grand, I just wasn't really feeling it last night.

STEPH: I mean, I only saw you for a bit and I wanted to actually talk. You know?

RACHEL: You did?

STEPH: Well, no, not actually *talk*, not serious, but like…

RACHEL: I'm not mad at you. You didn't do anything.

> *MATT comes back in.*

MATT: Don't mind her, she's got the fear.

RACHEL: It's all good, anyway. I've sorted most of the checklist stuff, actually…

STEPH: You have?

RACHEL: Well… The favours are done, the bouquet will be ready on the 10th, I confirmed payment for the singers, and I've started working out an itinerary for the girls – Who's in what car, times and uh… all that. That's more or less it, right?

STEPH:Uh, yeah. Jesus, you should have called me.

RACHEL: Ah, it was just some emails really, no problem. I'll send them on. Sorry, I felt like I've been letting the side down, so…

STEPH: Thank you, Rache.

RACHEL: *And* I started tea-staining a load of the place holder cards. Matt said he was having a tough time with them.

STEPH: Matt/

MATT: /I *am* having a tough time with them.

> *STEPH looks at him.*

RACHEL: Anyway, I have like fifty of them drying at home. So… I mean, how many have you done?

MATT: Yeah, about that.

RACHEL: So all that's left to do is the fancy writing.

MATT: Yup.

RACHEL: Which I'll leave up to you, *Art Attack.*

> *She nods at MATT. He smiles at her.*

STEPH: That's really great, Rache. Thanks.

RACHEL: No worries. I'm sorry I haven't been around for this stuff the last while. It's just been… but, y'know, I'm totally yours from now on. You know/

STEPH: /Well, there *is* a couple of things we could/

MATT: /She's done loads, Steph. We can leave it for now.

> *STEPH glances at MATT.*
>
> *Pause.*

RACHEL: It's no problem.

STEPH: We were just in the middle of looking at the seating plan.

MATT: Were we?

STEPH: Yes.

> *STEPH gives him a look.*
>
> *She takes a tablet up from the chair.*

I have it on this.

RACHEL: Very professional.

STEPH: Ha. Stop, work gave it to me.

MATT: You think we could afford one of those with the amount we're spending on bunting alone?

> *STEPH looks at MATT. He drinks from his cup.*

RACHEL: Giz a look.

> *STEPH hands the tablet to RACHEL, she takes it and starts scrolling.*
>
> *STEPH notices RACHEL's hands.*

STEPH: What did you do to your hands?

RACHEL: Oh, it's tea. The stupid name-cards.

STEPH: Did you do them last *night*?

RACHEL: Yeah, couldn't sleep so it was handy. Distraction.

STEPH: Lavender.

RACHEL stares at her.

Lavender under your pillow. Should help.

RACHEL: Yeah? Cool. Thanks.

STEPH has opened the seating plan on her tablet.

STEPH: So we have kiddie table, oldie table, family table,
college table, messers table and everyone else table.

RACHEL: Are we still doing the musician thing with the tables?

STEPH: We are, but I can never remember which one is which.

RACHEL: Who's on the Morrissey table?

MATT: Messers. And vegans.

RACHEL: That'll be me so. But I'll be eating a steak.

STEPH laughs.

So, for Saturday, maybe you should move Jackie over the
other side of Morrissey next to Jessie and Lorna?
Just nudge her around the corner from Paul.

STEPH: Yeah. That might work.

She types on the tablet.

All those little college flings, it's made it so complicated.

MATT: We had to do a Venn Diagram.

RACHEL laughs.

RACHEL: You guys are the last ones standing now.

STEPH: Hey. We're not a *fling.*

MATT: We're *not?*

STEPH shakes her head. RACHEL turns to MATT.

RACHEL: Hey, was your suit picked up?

MATT: Yes. No. I don't know, was it?

STEPH: She's asking you.

MATT: You know, I've seen people get married in t-shirts. Like Star Wars ones.

RACHEL: So that's a "no".

STEPH: Will you get over the suit thing?

MATT: I'm sorry, I didn't go into penniless design work to end up wearing a suit.

RACHEL: It's your wedding! I think you look really handsome in it.

STEPH: There you go, Matt. Rache thinks you look handsome.

MATT: What do *you* think?

STEPH: I think if you wear a t-shirt to our wedding, you'll be playing Batman alone for the rest of your life.

MATT: It's a single-player game, so… that's grand.

RACHEL: The guy will have fixed it by now. It'll fit better.

STEPH: Also don't talk to me about that. At least a suit is functional. I'm going to need two people to help me /every time I need to go to the jacks, so.

MATT: *(Simultaneously.)* /Every time I go to the jacks. Yes I know. *(To RACHEL.)* Seriously. Weeks of this.

RACHEL: Anyway. I've seen those T-shirt people online. They look like they smell bad.

MATT: How can you *look* like you smell bad?

RACHEL: I dunno, they found a way. The bride always looks vaguely disappointed, too.

STEPH: And, y'know, I'm vaguely disappointed with you as it is, so/

MATT: /I get it. I'll ring him. Tomorrow. Tomorrow's Monday.

He realises.

Monday. Eep.

STEPH: Getting close, now. Nervous?

She gives him a playful dig on the arm.

RACHEL: I'm so happy for you guys. You're *meant* to be together!

MATT: *Don't* do that. We're just getting a joint bank account.

STEPH: This is mostly tax-related.

MATT smiles at her.

MATT: Save all that for your speech, Rache.

RACHEL: Maybe I will. I am, though. Happy for you.

She looks away.

I know the last few months have been, you know, tough or… *weird.*

Beat.

STEPH: Well… I mean, there's been a lot of planning and stuff, but it wasn't *weird.* Have you found it weird?

RACHEL: No… well, maybe a bit. But, you know, why wouldn't it be? I'm good.

STEPH: Yeah?

RACHEL: Yeah. I'm good, I really am. I missed you guys.

Beat.

So how many are invited again? For the name-cards?

MATT: 105.

RACHEL: 105. That's… that's a good number. Not too big.

RACHEL looks uncomfortable.

Beat.

STEPH: … Rache?

RACHEL: I'm glad you guys are taking the next step, y'know?
I remember you told me you were engaged and I just
wanted to… my heart was beating so fast…

STEPH: I remember telling you.

She smiles at RACHEL.

Pause.

RACHEL: You know, I don't want to freak you out or anything
but this is the best time I could think of and obviously it's
all under control, and stuff. I don't want you to *worry* or
anything. I just want you to know that I love you both and
I don't want things to change, I'm sure I'll have Mam's
support and everything. But I thought better now than…
you know, *wedding.* I'm pregnant.

Beat.

STEPH: You're/

RACHEL: /With a baby.

Pause.

STEPH: Rache! That's… that's so cool!

RACHEL: Yeah, I/

STEPH: /I mean… um…Okay! No, I'm sure we have, do we
have a bottle of something? I think we do. Cava?
Something… bubbly? I'll get it. Hang on.

RACHEL: Steph…

STEPH exits.

MATT: Are you out of your fucking mind?/

RACHEL: /Matt/

MATT: /You said you'd sorted it.

Silence.

RACHEL stares at him.

STEPH comes back in.

STEPH: Nope. Sorry. Thought I had something stashed.

RACHEL: It's absolutely fine, Steph. It's important that…
I just wanted to *say* it. To both of you.

MATT: We really are happy for you, Rache.

STEPH: So you have to tell us.

RACHEL: What?

STEPH: Uh… you know. Details? When did you find out?
How far along are you?

RACHEL: Um…

STEPH: I mean, are we talking a couple of weeks? You're not
showing yet anyway!

RACHEL: It's Matt's.

Silence.

STEPH: I'm sorry/

MATT: /What?/

STEPH: /What did you say?

RACHEL: It's Matt's. The baby. But, and I know, okay, I know
this is a shock/

STEPH: /You… said/

RACHEL: /But I've been thinking about this very carefully/

STEPH: /You said/

MATT: /Rachel/

RACHEL: /No, look, Matt, we just need to/

STEPH: /You said you were on the *pill.*

Silence.

RACHEL: Well. I *was.*

STEPH: I mean, you're…

RACHEL: I think I got sick that night, I'm not sure/

MATT: /Fuck/

RACHEL: *(Quickly.)* /Look… Okay, I know this is unexpected, I didn't know when else… to *say* it… I mean I couldn't exactly do it any other time, really. It's just, all too late now so….

She composes herself.

Don't worry. I'm going to talk to the guys about altering my dress for Saturday. Cuz it was already tight at the fitting. Just in *case.* You know? I don't want to/

STEPH: /How long?

RACHEL stops. Hesitates.

MATT: It's only been, what?

RACHEL: Ten weeks.

MATT: No… no way it's…

He thinks it out for a second.

RACHEL: Party was the end of June/

MATT: /Fuck/

RACHEL: /And, you know… I thought the first month I'd just messed up with the pill but it's been two in a row now so I thought…

Beat.

MATT: How do you know?

RACHEL: What?

MATT: How do you know it's mine?

Beat.

RACHEL: Of *course* it's yours.

MATT: Well, I mean…

RACHEL: What?

She looks at MATT.

MATT: I dunno, I mean people are saying…

RACHEL: People are saying *what?*

MATT: I don't know, that you've had… you've been with a few different/

RACHEL: /I haven't been with anyone.

Pause.

STEPH: Okay… but are you *sure*, Rache? I mean/

RACHEL: /I'm sure, Steph, I wouldn't tell you if I wasn't *sure*/

STEPH: /Is this what you were talking about last night?/

RACHEL: /I couldn't say it last night, Matt was drunk and/

MATT: /I wasn't *that drunk!*

Neither of the women look at him.

RACHEL: So I thought it would be better to do it today. When you're both… you know.

MATT: Hungover?

RACHEL: You're always hungover.

Pause.

MATT: We're getting *married* on Saturday, Rachel.

RACHEL tries to stay calm.

RACHEL: I *know* that.

MATT: So what… what the *fuck* are you doing here?

RACHEL: It's *your baby.*

MATT turns away.

STEPH: You're not…

Beat.

I mean, you're not seriously thinking of *keeping* it?

RACHEL doesn't make eye contact.

Rachel.

Beat.

RACHEL shrugs slightly, as if to say "Yeah?"

Okay. I don't want to, you know… let's just… why don't you just take us through it?

Beat.

MATT: Through what?

STEPH: Rachel should just, uh, explain why she's… y'know, *doing* this.

RACHEL: I'm not doing anything.

STEPH: *Saying* it, then/

RACHEL: /I think/

STEPH: /I mean/

RACHEL: /We will need to talk this/

MATT: /What?/

RACHEL: /We need to talk/

MATT: /Alright, hold on/

STEPH: /No, we're not holding on, what are you even/

RACHEL: /I just feel this is something we need to think about for/

MATT: /We?/

STEPH: /We?/

RACHEL: Yes.

> *Silence.*

MATT: Right. Brilliant. Can I have a drink now, Steph? Is it the right time of day now?

> *(To RACHEL.)*

Obviously *you* won't have one.

STEPH: Shut up, Matt.

MATT: This is fucking… and you left it this *close?*

RACHEL: I didn't want to… *believe* it. It took a while to…
I mean… if we could just, you know/

STEPH: /What?/

RACHEL: /I don't *know*, sit down or… look, this isn't my *fault.*

STEPH: Rachel… Okay, it is a *little* bit your fault.

MATT: /*Alright*/

STEPH: /How long have you *known?*

> *Pause.*

> *RACHEL squirms. She looks to MATT, he doesn't make eye contact.*

MATT: How long, Rachel?

RACHEL: A few weeks.

> *STEPH shakes her head.*

159

STEPH: I mean… Sorry, why are you only telling us now?

RACHEL: I had to get used to the idea *myself*, you know? Obviously, it was a shock. I had to sort my own head out for a bit. Is that alright?

STEPH: Who else knows?

RACHEL: What?

STEPH: Who else knows? Does your Mam know?

RACHEL: Not yet. What was I going to do? I couldn't exactly ring her up like – "Hey Mam, good news, you can expect your first grandkid from your single daughter cuz she had a drunken threesome with Steph and Matt from college, the ones who are getting married. Remember them? Are ya proud?"

STEPH: This isn't funny.

RACHEL: No.

Beat.

STEPH: This is… I can't even…

RACHEL attempts to calm her.

RACHEL: Look. I just think that Matt and I will/

MATT: /Woah, *what?*

RACHEL: You're the… *father.* We'll need to *talk* about it. Right? We'll need to figure out, I mean *later on* obviously/

MATT: /Figure out what, Rachel?

RACHEL: How this might work.

MATT: What are you *talking* about?

RACHEL: You, *hold on*, can you lay off for a second?/

STEPH: /Sorry, I still don't understand why you didn't come us to when you found out.

Beat.

RACHEL: When I first… I thought I should wait till after the wedding. But I couldn't do that to you.

STEPH: What are you going to *tell* people, Rachel?

RACHEL: I don't *know* yet. That's why I'm here. I mean… I'm probably going to start to show soon. I'll have to say *something*. I just… I just need you guys to be on my side, and then we'll get through it together. Yeah?

MATT and STEPH stare at her.

MATT: Just say it was a one-night stand. You didn't know the guy. He doesn't want to be involved.

RACHEL: I'm *twenty-six.*

MATT: Yeah, I know that. Surely that still sounds better than… I mean… *fuck.*

Pause.

STEPH: You didn't seem that drunk?

MATT: She wasn't that/

RACHEL: /I wasn't that drunk when we, look I'm not talking about what happened. I knew what I was doing. It's just/

STEPH: /No. No, I mean how on earth could you have thrown up? You didn't seem *sick* when we were/

RACHEL: /I don't know… maybe *after?* I kept drinking… later on, I went back out.

Beat.

MATT: You went back down to the party?

RACHEL: It doesn't matter what I *did*, I went back to the kitchen and I kept going. It was a party, that's a normal thing to do. Especially when you've… done whatever the hell you wanna call what we did, with your *friends*, you

161

don't really feel like turning in for an early night in one big weird bed.

STEPH and MATT stare at RACHEL in disbelief.

STEPH: What... what *is* this, Rachel?

RACHEL: I need/

STEPH: /What the *fuck* are you playing at?

RACHEL: Steph, can you just... ease off for/

STEPH: /Ease off?/

RACHEL: /Yes/

MATT: /Rachel/

STEPH: /I mean, are you out of your mind? For fuck's sake/

RACHEL: /Please, you need to *calm down.*

Beat.

STEPH: I can't believe you'd *do* this. I can't believe you're *doing* this to us.

RACHEL shakes her head.

You *know* you need to...

She looks at RACHEL, then turns her head away, unable to say it.

Would you not, I mean...

She bottles it, for now.

What I *mean* is... Look, I know things got a little weird between us, but that doesn't mean...

Beat.

RACHEL: I'm trying to figure this all out, too. I'm just doing what I think is best, and I wanted you to know. Both of you. Can we please try and be... *civil?*

Beat.

STEPH: I don't think you realise we're planning on… starting a *life* together here. We have things to *do* today, and all this week and… for the *rest* of our… and it actually doesn't involve any… any of *this* shit.

RACHEL: Come on, Steph.

STEPH: What?

RACHEL: Just, it's alright. There's no need to go off the deep end.

MATT: What does *that* mean?

RACHEL: Steph, I'm your friend/

STEPH: /Are you fucking *joking* right now?

RACHEL: No.

STEPH: If you're my *friend*, what are you *doing* here, exactly? Coming in here with all the name cards done like everything's fine?

MATT: Look/

STEPH: *(Rapidly.)* /I'm trying *really* hard here. Okay? I'm trying not to cry, or scream, or choke someone to death. We're getting *married* in six days, I've been trying to keep all these fucking balls in the air for months and you're doing this to us *now*? *You* are? My fucking head, *chief* bridesmaid. *Why*?

> *Her breathing gets shallower and quicker.*

I'm going to be sick.

> *STEPH goes towards the door.*

RACHEL: Should I/

STEPH: /No.

> *STEPH exits.*
>
> *Silence.*

MATT: Jesus.

RACHEL: She deserves to know.

Beat.

MATT: I don't know what the hell you're thinking.

RACHEL: Maybe I wasn't thinking *before*. And now I *am*.

Beat.

Matt. I couldn't go to your wedding and sit there like everything is fine. I'd go insane. I would have ended up blurting it out somewhere, or sometime down the line it would have come out, and how would she have felt *then*?

Pause.

MATT: So… I mean, should I even ask what happened?

Beat.

RACHEL: I didn't make the flight.

MATT exhales.

I just… I couldn't do it.

Beat.

I'm a nervous flier. I hate taking off, all I can think of is being trapped up there. I think about those planes that went missing and stuff. And usually I have someone to hold hands with, you know, with turbulence, but I knew I didn't this time and I know that's not an excuse but I… I couldn't stop thinking about it.

MATT: So, what, you just decided to sit at home? Hope it went away? Look, I'm sorry, but there's a boat. You know?

She looks at him.

RACHEL: I mean, I went to the airport.

Beat.

MATT: Ah, Rachel.

RACHEL: I checked in online, all I had was my bag with...
forms and directions, and when I got to the desk, I felt like
the woman, the attendant, I felt like she *knew*. She gave me
this little nod. Like she saw girls like me all the time. And
I went to the bathroom and I sat there for... I don't know
how long. I heard them call my name over the thing, and I
got dizzy, and then someone came into the bathroom. She
was just going to the jacks, but I thought she was *looking*
for *me* and I pulled my feet up onto the toilet in case she
looked under. In case she knew what I was wearing. From
the CCTV...

I paid *six quid* for the Airlink back into town. And I bought
myself a fudge sundae from McDonald's. The O'Connell
Street one. The shit one. And I felt rotten.

She looks at MATT.

Sorry. It's just... I haven't told anyone that.

Pause.

MATT: I said I'd... I *told* you I should have gone with you.

RACHEL: What, would you have forced me onboard?

MATT: No, I... we would have *spoken* together and...

RACHEL: You'd have *got through* to me.

MATT: We would have *talked*... I don't know.

RACHEL: I couldn't do it, Matt.

Beat.

MATT: Yeah.

RACHEL: And I know you're angry/

MATT: /Angry? I'm... terrified.

RACHEL: I know. But I think it'll be alright.

Beat.

MATT: I have no idea what Steph is going to do.

RACHEL: I'm sorry, I didn't want to cause such a mess. I just, I really think that telling her is/

MATT: /You *know* that this... it can't work like this.

RACHEL: I'm just *telling* you, Matt. I don't want to have a big debate over it/

MATT: /No, I mean, just *talk* to me. *Talk* to me for a second, Rache. I don't mean that, I mean the logistics of what you're actually *asking* of us. What the hell do you think this is going to look like?

In *your* head, going forward.

We're getting *married* next week, and you're going to have my kid? For fuck's sake, Rachel, what if it *looks* like me? What do we *say* to people? Or are you suggesting we have this little secret life where I pop round at weekends with a bag of penny sweets for the sprog. "Uncle Matt"? *Cop on.*

Beat.

I mean, what do you expect us to do, just *let* you/

RACHEL: /Yes.

MATT: But Rachel, think for a minute. What do you think this will *do* to Steph? Not just this week, I mean... you're going to really... like, I mean this has *really fucked* things up.

Beat.

RACHEL: Not if you two can learn to accept my/

MATT: /Accept what?/

RACHEL: /Accept my *decision*.

Pause.

MATT paces, puts his head in his hands and screams a bit.

MATT: *Fuck* me!

RACHEL: Calm down.

> *MATT turns to her.*

Calm down. You're scaring me.

MATT: Oh, *piss off*, Rachel. What am I going to do, hit you?

I can't believe this.

> *Beat.*

Y'know, this wasn't your "decision" when you came to me looking for money.

RACHEL: I didn't/

MATT: /So what the *hell* are you talking about? Your "*decision*".

RACHEL: If this is about the money/

MATT: /Oh, shut up. *Shut up. Fuck* the money, Rachel. Don't get me wrong, I gave you more than two months' savings, and had to lie to cover it up, and nearly miss the payment for the venue/

RACHEL: /I can pay you back. I can do it in installments/

MATT: /What did I just say? Didn't I say "Fuck the money"?

> *Beat.*

Though I do wonder where it's gone, *actually*, if you didn't get the… the procedure.

> *RACHEL shifts.*

RACHEL: I don't have it right now.

MATT: What?

> *Beat.*

RACHEL: I used it for my rent. I'm… I'm having a bit of trouble at the minute. But I'm not *worried*. Money will sort itself out. Always does.

That isn't what this is *about*, anyway. I'm not here for a handout.

I'm sorry you feel like this. I just…

Beat.

You two had each other, y'know. Afterwards. You got to work through the weirdness *together*, and I was…

I know you didn't *mean* to do it, I know it probably threw a spanner in the works for you guys too, and you wanted to keep your distance, but I was by *myself.*

And now I'm *not.*

Pause.

MATT: I'm sorry, Rache, but I don't agree with you on this. It's… it's *wrong*. This is a *mistake.*

You have to try and see this from… you know? This is… this is not part of the plan right now. For *either* of us. And you *know* that.

I'm not ready to have a kid. Honestly, I don't think you are, either. I feel like we're still kids ourselves. And I'm kind of terrified that the real secret no one ever tells you is that that feeling never goes away.

RACHEL: I don't think it's something to be *scared* of. I think it's a *good* thing.

MATT: How? *How* can you not see/

RACHEL: /And it's up to you how much of an active role/

MATT: /Role?

RACHEL: With your kid. Our kid.

Beat.

MATT: I don't understand why you're not panicking.

RACHEL shrugs.

RACHEL: I don't *need* to panic. It's just what's happening.

MATT: But this can't be what you saw for yourself? Like, what you *planned*?

RACHEL: I don't really *do* plans, do I?

MATT: No, but/

RACHEL: /And you know me pretty well by now, so/

MATT: /It's like... it's like your whole life, you have all these *lightbulbs* in your head, flashing at you – telling you "this", "*this*", "THIS" – and then, every now and then you're slowly turning them off, one by one, saying "No, that's not it" until you've one left. And that's your *life*.

Me and Steph, we've got our one switched on now, and we're fine. We're good. Sure, it's not perfect, but we know what we're *doing* now. Finally.

You can't *force us* to switch on a light, Rache. Not *now*. Not... not like *this*. It's not *fair* of you.

Beat.

RACHEL: This isn't *about* you and Steph. It's about *me*.

Silence.

MATT is uneasy. He looks at RACHEL, then away. Unsure of how to say the following.

MATT: Do you remember the morning after?

She nods.

And we were standing in the front room, and the guys were all waking up.

You came over to me and just, stood against me. I put my hand on your hip.

Beat.

It just felt so... like, it was more intimate than anything we'd done that night. *That* felt like cheating. And I thought for a second, Jesus I wonder if we would have been...

He trails off (Or stops himself.) as he looks at RACHEL. But he has to know.

Do you remember that?

RACHEL: *No.*

MATT nods.

Pause.

MATT: Have you eaten anything? Anything... *proper*? I haven't eaten anything. Do you want, like... toast or something?

RACHEL: No. I'm... a little sick in the mornings.

Beat.

MATT: Sure.

Silence.

STEPH comes back in.

STEPH: You drank the rest of the whiskey.

MATT looks at her blankly.

There was a half a naggin left.

MATT: It wasn't, there was... about a *quarter*...

Do you want mine?

STEPH says nothing.

RACHEL: Steph. Look... I'm *sorry*, this wasn't the right time.

STEPH: What gave you that idea?

RACHEL: Obviously, you're under a lot of pressure. I know you must think that this is selfish on my part/

STEPH: /I don't believe you.

>*Beat.*

RACHEL: What?

STEPH: I don't believe *any* of it.

>*Beat.*

RACHEL: Why would I make this up?

>*STEPH gives her a "cop on" look.*

MATT: Steph, come on now, that's unfair, she's clearly/

STEPH: *(To RACHEL.)* /You just can't stand this, can you?

RACHEL: What?

STEPH: This. I'm getting *married*. I'm saving up to put money down on a house. I've got a proper job. Does that really piss you off so much that you'd come here *today*/

RACHEL: /That is not true, I came to you for *support*/

STEPH: /I've always *supported* you, Rache.

RACHEL: I know.

STEPH: I'm kind of sick of it, at this stage.

>*STEPH's phone rings. She takes it out of her pocket and looks at it.*

RACHEL: Who is it?

>*STEPH raises a finger to silence her. She lets the phone ring out.*

MATT: Steph, let's try and calm down a second, alright?

>*STEPH looks at MATT. Her phone rings again. MATT looks at her. It rings out.*

STEPH: I *am* calm.

MATT: It's not fair to/

STEPH: /You're damn right, it's not fair.

MATT: Steph. Can we just *try* to deal with this like adults?
I know we're both pretty shook up right now, we probably
need some/

STEPH: /I love that you're so *laissez faire* about this, Matt/

MATT: /I'm not *laissez faire* about *anything*, I've lost my cool
as well just now, didn't I? Was that laissez faire? No. I just
think we shouldn't accuse/

STEPH: /So you just… believe her?

MATT: Yes. I believe her.

> *MATT's phone rings. He takes it out of his pocket.*

It's your Mam.

STEPH: I *know* it's Mam, she just called me.

> *Beat.*

MATT: Should I not answer?

STEPH: *(Sarcastically.)* No, please, answer. Put her on loudspeaker.

> *The phone rings out. STEPH turns her attention to RACHEL.*

Have you been to a doctor?

RACHEL: No.

STEPH: No?

RACHEL: I took a test.

STEPH: Oh yeah? A home test?

RACHEL: Yeah.

STEPH: Where is it?

RACHEL: I don't carry them round with me.

RACHEL's phone rings. She takes it out.

It's your Mam.

STEPH: Hang up.

RACHEL: You let it go to voicemail.

STEPH: She's *my* Mam. Hang up the phone.

RACHEL: Sorry, this is... I hate these Samsungs.

She is trying to swipe the screen.

RACHEL: Oh. I think I...

She puts the phone to her ear.

Hi Delores. Sorry. I can't work this phone at all.

What's up?

MATT and STEPH stare at RACHEL throughout the following exchange, making futile gestures of "No", "Don't", and "Hang up the phone".

Yeah, I'm with them now, actually.

Yeah. Yep. All excitement here.

At their place, yeah.

Uh... no, I don't think so. *I* didn't hear them ring anyway.

MATT makes a gesture of a plug.

I think they're charging them.

MATT points.

In the kitchen. So they didn't... yeah... yeah I know, that's Steph all over isn't it. Ha.

STEPH extends her hand to take the phone. RACHEL is nodding, trying to end the conversation.

The what? Circus flags? Oh, the *bunting*, yeah. It looks great. Matt's done a really… yeah. Oh you *don't…* No it's not naff at all –

STEPH grabs the phone out of her hand.

STEPH: Mam? Hi. Yeah, listen we're about to go to lunch now, can I ring you back in an hour or so. Yeah. Bit…. bit of… Bit of a rush. Perfect. I'll talk to ya then.

She hangs up the phone and tosses it back to RACHEL.

RACHEL: You didn't let me say goodbye.

STEPH gives her a look.

She'll think I'm rude. I'm your head bridesmaid.

STEPH looks at her.

Sorry, is it Chief Bridesmaid we went with, or/

STEPH: /We'll see about that. Matt, go get a test.

Beat.

MATT: What?

STEPH: Go across to Spar, get a pregnancy test.

MATT hesitates.

MATT: Do Spar do pregnancy tests?

STEPH: It's a EuroSpar, they're bigger. They do pregnancy tests. Go anywhere, DEALZ, I don't give a shit. Get one. Get *two.*

RACHEL: Steph/

STEPH: /Rachel, if you're not lying, you'll do the test. Here, in the apartment, just… just put my mind at ease. *Alright?* That's what this was all about, right?

MATT: I think it's pretty clear she's telling the/

STEPH: /You're certain, are you, Matt?

Beat.

MATT: Right. Fine. Great.

RACHEL is about to say something, but MATT stares at her imploringly. He exits.

Silence.

STEPH exits. We hear bottles being clinked off-stage and put down on the floor.

STEPH: *(Offstage.)* Fuck it, anyway.

She comes back in holding an empty whiskey bottle.

We were waiting for presents.

She puts it down.

I'm not sure people give drink as a wedding present. Maybe Champagne. You're probably supposed to have it on the day though.

Beat.

RACHEL: Steph/

STEPH: /At this stage I'd say we'll just get about fifteen nutribullets and a carafe.

Beat.

What did you get?

What's your gift to us?

For our *wedding.*

RACHEL: I… I haven't got it yet. But… I have a couple of *ideas.*

STEPH tsks.

STEPH: You're leaving it a bit late.

She studies RACHEL.

I don't get it. You tell me *everything*. You know that, right? I get your whole day. You send me photos of your breakfast, I get blow by blow updates from the call centre. You tell me about the *dreams* you have.

You'd never keep something like this from me.

We've been *planning my wedding* together. You must think I'm an idiot.

RACHEL: I really don't.

I should have told you before. I'm sorry.

I'm telling you *now*. That's the best I can do.

STEPH: I don't know why you're *here*.

RACHEL: You really don't believe me?

> *STEPH tries to find the words.*

STEPH: It's just… this isn't you.

RACHEL: What does that mean? What's "me"?

STEPH: I… *Not* pregnant?

> *Beat.*

Did you *really* do all those name cards?

RACHEL: Yeah.

STEPH: You stayed up all night?

RACHEL: I couldn't sleep.

STEPH: Why would you do them if you were coming here to…

> *RACHEL shrugs.*

Matt hasn't even done them.

RACHEL: I'd guessed that.

> *Beat.*

I don't know what to say.

STEPH: Tell me you made this up.

>*RACHEL shakes her head.*

It's been so long.

RACHEL: I know.

STEPH: It's just... and, you're *terrible* at keeping secrets.

RACHEL: No, I'm not.

STEPH: Rache, you would have *told* me. You would have told someone.

RACHEL: I'm not lying to you, Steph.

>*Beat.*

You know, I really thought you'd...

STEPH: What?

RACHEL: I just thought... when we were in school, you always knew what to say if something... if I was upset. I could always go to you. You didn't... judge me, you just... I dunno. *Listened.* I just thought you'd be able to do it this time. I'm sorry.

>*Beat.*

STEPH: This isn't school, Rache, I can't just/

RACHEL: /I know that, Jesus, it... this was an accident and I'm trying to make it better. Alright? I don't know/

STEPH: /But what can I say?

RACHEL: I don't... just talk to me. Believe me. Who else can I go to?

STEPH: No, you can't tell anyone else.

RACHEL: I'm not. I'm not going to.

Beat.

I need to talk to you like… we're still friends.

STEPH: You're my fucking maid of honour.

RACHEL: Please Steph.

Beat.

STEPH: I can't, Rachel. You know I can't.

Beat.

RACHEL: Great… Thanks. I'd just like my best friend to
believe me. At least. Because I mean… this is your fault in
the first place so…

STEPH: What?

RACHEL: You *kissed* me. At the party.

Beat.

STEPH scoffs.

STEPH: No, I didn't.

RACHEL: Yes you did. In the garden.

STEPH: I'd remember.

RACHEL shakes her head.

RACHEL: You do remember. You're just trying really hard not to.

STEPH: You don't know that.

RACHEL nods.

RACHEL: I know that face.

STEPH tries to keep her face neutral. She can't.

STEPH: I was pissed, Rachel! I would have kissed anybody,
probably. You're the one who got… ideas about/

RACHEL: /Ideas?

STEPH: You know what I mean.

RACHEL: No, I don't, Steph. I thought we/

STEPH: /Can we please not talk about/

RACHEL: /Well, we haven't, yet.

STEPH: What?

RACHEL: Talked about it.

STEPH: Do you have any questions?

RACHEL: I... I want to hear your version of it. You seem
    convinced this is my fault.

STEPH: What's there to say?

RACHEL: So you felt... fine, afterwards? You felt nothing.

STEPH: It didn't mean anything.

RACHEL: I know that.

STEPH: There's no reason to feel bad. It was a mistake.

RACHEL: Even if it was, I haven't been able to talk it out.
    You and Matt have/

STEPH: /We haven't spoken about it.

RACHEL: Really?

STEPH: Haven't needed to. We know what it was.

> *Beat.*

Rachel, we all do stupid shit when we're drunk/

RACHEL: /You should put that on the cake/

STEPH: /And I have a life to start, and what I did at some
    going-away-do isn't worth picking apart.
    I really didn't think it was that big a deal.

RACHEL: Clearly.

STEPH: Before… I mean, we had fun.

RACHEL: Did we?

STEPH: What does *that* mean?

RACHEL: It wasn't weird for you.

STEPH: I fucked my best friend! Of course it was weird. Is that what you want to hear?

RACHEL: No.

STEPH: You were fine, you enjoyed it.

RACHEL: Don't tell me what I think.

> *Beat.*

STEPH: So… what, we forced you into it?

RACHEL: No.

STEPH: Did I *rape* you Rachel, is that what you're saying?

RACHEL: No.

STEPH: Don't you dare/

RACHEL: /I just wanted to not feel shit about it/

STEPH: /You *chose* to feel shit about it, Rachel. Just like you *chose* to walk into the bedroom and lock the door behind us, so don't/

RACHEL: /That is not what I meant/

STEPH: /Well then, don't fucking talk like that.

> *Beat.*

RACHEL: I'm saying/

STEPH: /Don't *talk* like that/

RACHEL: /I'm saying you guys were in charge/

STEPH: /Of course we were. We're a couple. You got *involved* with us. That's… that's how it works.

RACHEL: I'm sorry, I didn't realise there were rules for this sort of thing.

STEPH: Well/

RACHEL: /"Etiquette"/

STEPH: /*Alright*/

RACHEL: Cuz I just remember feeling a bit stupid during it.

STEPH: You didn't enjoy it.

>   *Beat.*

RACHEL: I didn't even *come.*

>   *Beat.*

STEPH: Ah. So, you're upset over *that?*

RACHEL: No.

STEPH: Because, you know, you were actually the centre of attention.

RACHEL: Lovely.

STEPH: I mean, Matt was…

>   *She trails off. Changes the subject.*

Come *on*, Rache. We used to talk about stuff like that all the time.

RACHEL: Yeah. *As a Joke.* I didn't expect it to happen/

STEPH: /Neither did we.

RACHEL: Really?

STEPH: *Obviously.*

RACHEL: But I went off-script. You two had it all planned out, did you?

STEPH: No!

Beat.

STEPH shifts slightly, uncomfortable. RACHEL notices.

RACHEL: Did you?

Pause.

STEPH steels herself.

STEPH: No. It wasn't planned. It wasn't *anything*. Sure, we'd talked about it, *spoken* about, the *idea* of it, but we'd never go through with it.

RACHEL: But you did, anyway.

STEPH: Well, yeah, we did. And it was supposed to be...

She stops. RACHEL looks at her, wanting an answer.

RACHEL: What?

STEPH: It was supposed to be a bit of a laugh. We were both so stressed with the wedding, we were in a weird place anyway, I just thought you were/

RACHEL: /Available?/

STEPH: No, you were... *safe*. You're my friend.

Beat.

I guess I, I mean *drunk* me, thought it would be fine.

RACHEL: So I got to be your last hurrah before you settled down. Good to know.

Pause.

STEPH: I was pissed and I was feeling... *nostalgic* or something and I wanted to just... feel like we were back in college and nothing mattered and it was all just... Okay.

RACHEL: It wasn't okay, Steph. I didn't enjoy it. I thought…
I thought you'd get in touch afterwards. To see how I was.
That's all.

Pause.

STEPH: I didn't know what to say to you. Okay?

Beat.

I've never kept anything from you.

Beat.

Jesus. This is a fucking mess.

For a few days, y'know, I thought everything was fine.
I actually thought I might get away with it.

Beat.

RACHEL: You've always got away with it, Steph. You walked
straight out of college into *Google*, for God's sake.
You're *doing great.* You don't know how lucky you are.

STEPH: Lucky?

RACHEL: *Yeah.* Some people are just in the right place at the
right time. And you're one of them. Don't get me wrong,
it's *great*, it's a good thing, you know? I was happy for you.

But, at the same time, for *years* now, I've thought "What am
I doing *wrong?*" I didn't mess around in school. I went to
every lecture in college. You didn't make half of them and
you still did better than me.

And, you know, when we graduated, *nothing* from you on
that kinda front, no hints for job applications, not even a
nudge in the right direction.

STEPH: What are you talking about?

RACHEL: You *know* what I'm talking about. I *hate* my job.
I don't go on dates, I don't think I know how to make
friends without college throwing us together and I…

She stops. Collects herself.

You know, you *forget* when you're not with someone properly what it's like when someone hugs you for too long. Or plays with your hair. I tense up now when someone hugs me for longer than a few seconds. It feels weird. Like they haven't earned it. I miss it feeling normal. Safe.

The following is more to herself than STEPH. RACHEL might put her hand on her stomach.

This makes me feel *safe*. I feel like… I'm *supposed* to do this. Like everything's kind of… clicked. *Finally.* Yeah, we made a mistake but out of that comes something… good. For *me*.

Surely it's okay for me to want that.

Silence.

STEPH: That's you all over Rachel, isn't it? Hanging around in the hopes someone might *nudge* you. And that people who actually put in the work are just "in the right place at the right time" when they catch a break.

RACHEL: No, Steph/

STEPH: /You think you're *owed* something. But you're *not.*

I work hard. You can work hard too, *or* you can sit on your couch waiting for the phone to ring.

And the really sad thing is you're convinced a kid is a little life-jacket to keep you above the water, when really it's the complete opposite. And you *know* that. You're not an *idiot*, Rachel. You're just *lazy.*

And, you know, I stopped feeling bad for you a long time ago. I just decided to accept you for who you are.

Because the only person who can *make* you cop on is you.

Beat.

So, stop acting like the world owes you a *favour* just because you got gold stars in school. And don't think for a *second* that you and me and Matt are going to play happy families with your bastard kid. You don't get to be a part of my *life* just because you can't take your *pill properly*.

> *Beat.*

Sorry Rachel, but you know I'm right.

RACHEL: Matt *knows*. About the baby.

He's known the entire time.

He gave me *money*. To go over to England.

He didn't want you to know.

He must think you're an idiot.

> *Silence.*

> *MATT enters.*

MATT: Right. Had to go to a couple of different places. Spar did have them, actually.

STEPH: Yep.

> *He takes two pregnancy tests out of his pocket.*

MATT: So, uh… I have them here.

> *Beat.*

STEPH: Right.

> *He holds them out, unsure if he should hand them to STEPH or RACHEL.*

> *(To RACHEL.)*

Go on.

RACHEL: What?

STEPH: Take them.

Beat.

RACHEL: No.

STEPH: Rachel/

RACHEL: /No Steph, I'm not doing it. I told you/

STEPH: /I know what you told me, I'm telling you now to go in there and piss on the *fucking test.*

> *Beat.*

Unless Matt can shed some light on the situation.

> *RACHEL looks at MATT. STEPH doesn't.*

Go into the bathroom.

RACHEL: Fuck you.

> *RACHEL exits. We hear a door locking and then the sound of pissing. MATT and STEPH stand in silence, listening to the piss.*

MATT: She told you.

STEPH: Of course she told me. I wouldn't be surprised if the whole congregation knows we had a threesome by Saturday.

> *Beat.*

MATT: There's got to be a better word for it.

> *Pause.*

I just... I just wanted to make sure *you* were okay. I knew that it couldn't... and she *wanted* to go. It wasn't like I... I'm sorry.

> *STEPH looks down.*

> *MATT takes a naggin out of his jacket pocket. It is partially empty. She looks at him.*

STEPH: Do you ever worry that you're not a "ha-ha" alcoholic?

MATT: All the time.

Pause.

STEPH: How long have you known?

MATT: I don't know. Feels like forever. I didn't know what to do. I couldn't think.

I *didn't* think.

Beat

It was the day we were wandering around Woodies, you saw that paint, the paint that, uh… you said if we bought a place someday we'd use that and it would be a warm house if the… sun… the sun, when it hit that colour. I was just *happy*.

Beat.

Rachel called me, and it was… it was all so *fast*. I just, I knew it had to go away.

All I wanted to do was tell you. I tell you *everything*.

Beat.

STEPH: Did you talk about me?

MATT: No, it was/

STEPH: /"Don't tell Steph?"

MATT: It wasn't like that.

Pause.

STEPH: Why didn't you tell me?

He doesn't answer.

Matt.

MATT: I didn't know how to, I'm… I'm sorry. I couldn't… and, you know, as far as I knew…

STEPH: As far as you knew, you wouldn't ever have to tell me.

Silence.

RACHEL returns with two wet pregnancy tests and hurls one at STEPH.

RACHEL: Congratulations, it's yours.

MATT: Woah, Rachel, stop!

RACHEL throws the second test at STEPH but MATT blocks it.

What the fuck is wrong with you? Stop!

RACHEL: Now, Steph. Have a look. Two positives. Do you believe me?

She turns to MATT, furious.

You poor bastard, Matt. I hope this has given you something to think about. You can look forward to years of this shit with her/

MATT: /Stop it, Rachel. I'm sorry, alright? About the fucking… She's upset. She's not thinking straight, okay? There's no need/

RACHEL: /Oh, she's *upset?* And you're just gonna stand there and/

MATT: /Just, please. *Please,* alright? You've done enough, today.

Beat.

Please.

He turns to STEPH, who has sunk down onto the floor.
Steph. Honey. It's going to be alright. Okay? As long as we're together. Right? Then it's okay.

Beat.

Steph.

RACHEL: I'm going, now.

She walks towards the door.

MATT: Thanks, Rachel. Great job.

RACHEL stops in her tracks, before turning on MATT.

RACHEL: You know, Matt, you *act* like you're a nice guy, but really you just want both of us to shut up, and do what you say.

MATT: Right.

RACHEL: You've been trying to manipulate me/

MATT: /Manipulate?/

RACHEL: /*Yes*. Manipulate me into doing something that I didn't want to do.

MATT: You've just *decided* this now, this little story in your head. You *came* to me (she *came* to me) and asked me for money. Tell her.

RACHEL: That's not true.

MATT: What is wrong with you?

RACHEL: There's nothing wrong with me, Matt. You're the one that's messed up. The only thing you're really worried about here is keeping your own little patch of grass clear.

MATT: That's what *everybody's* like, Rachel.

RACHEL: I feel bad for you. You know that? How you can treat her like an idiot this entire time and still think you're justified/

MATT: /I'm not treating her like anything. I know I was wrong now, in how I handled this, I've said that. I just wanted Steph to be able to live without this hanging over her, like I was going to live with it/

RACHEL: /That's big of you/

MATT: /I chose to do that… to make sure we kept our fucking *light* switched on. Why should she have to know about it, if it was already… but that was before you/

RACHEL: /Before what? She deserved to be told the truth, and you don't care/

MATT: /Well, why didn't you tell her, then? If you're so innocent, why didn't you tell her, Rachel?

RACHEL: You're her fiancé. It was your choice not to say it.

MATT: She's your best friend, supposedly. Funny how you came to me, behind her *back*, and forced me into the position of making *your* decision for you. You *child*.

RACHEL: You decided not to tell her, Matt. I respected that.

MATT: And now you're trying to weasel out of it.

RACHEL: Out of *losing my child*? Yes.

MATT shakes his head.

MATT: I don't believe this.

RACHEL: I needed your *help*. You gave me cash. It's not the same thing. You said there was no other option.

MATT: Jesus, I would have thought you'd want a chance to fix your mistake and, y'know, *plan* your life. Not shrug your shoulders and *pay your rent* and just let stuff *happen at you*. That's not how anything works.

STEPH: Matt.

MATT: Steph, she's a nutcase. Let her fuck herself up if that's what she wants. She's gone, okay? We're done.

He turns to RACHEL.

You get the fuck out.

STEPH: Matt, she's/

MATT: /She's leaving. Now.

He stares at RACHEL.

RACHEL: He's been lying to your face for weeks, Steph. At least I told you the truth/

MATT: /Eventually/

RACHEL: /He doesn't care/

MATT: /Of course I care/

RACHEL: /How can you say that when/

MATT: *(Yelling.)* /She's my wife!

> *Beat.*

> *Calmer.*

She's my wife.

> *Pause.*

RACHEL: Yeah, but you came in me.

> *Silence.*

STEPH: She's right.

> *Beat.*

You must have been so sure that you could keep this from me for... for the rest of our lives.

> *Pause.*

MATT: Steph.

STEPH: You've gotten piss all over the floor.

MATT: Honey. I mean, let's just try and... it's alright, we'll clean it up.

STEPH: I'm not doing it.

MATT: I'll do it. Okay? I'll do it.

It's going to be alright.

He gets down on her level.

Hey. It's okay. We're still here.

She doesn't get to change *us.* Right?

RACHEL: He lied to you, Steph.

MATT: Can you shut up, please? What the hell is wrong with you? I didn't *lie.* I didn't lie to anyone.

RACHEL: You didn't trust her enough to tell her. Same difference.

MATT: I thought you'd do the right thing, I didn't think you'd be stupid enough/

RACHEL: /The right thing for *you*, you mean/

MATT: /Rachel. *Please.* You haven't a clue what you're doing. One of us had to be a grown up about it.

RACHEL: And you thought you were the only grown up around?

STEPH: That's a new one.

MATT: Steph. Darling/

STEPH: /Don't. Darling. Me. Stop doing that, you always do that when you're trying to win an argument.

MATT: What? No, I don't/

STEPH: /Don't do that to my face, Matt. I obviously wasn't worth including in any of this, so please/

MATT: /I did this for you. For us. How can you not see that?

STEPH: You are so convinced that you know better than me. You're really not as smart as you think you are.

Beat.

I still have to fix it. Like always.

STEPH stands up.

God, you've really fucked this up.

MATT: Me?

STEPH: Yes, you. *Yes. You.*

MATT: How can you say that?

STEPH: Do you *remember* the threesome, Matt?

Beat.

MATT: No. I mean… parts of it are…

(Snapping.)

You know all of this, Steph. I'm not going over it.

STEPH: You'd been going on all night about how *good* she looked, and wouldn't it be great *if,* and we're only *young once.* Little whispers in my ear the whole time, like every night out.

MATT: I was *drunk,* Stephanie. I was *drunk.* I'm twenty-eight years old, for fuck's sake. *Every* guy thinks like that when they're in that state. I just tell you what I think, *sorry.* Because I *love* you, I didn't expect you two to/

RACHEL: /Us two?/

MATT: /Yes you two, are you still *here*? You two started it, kissing in the corner, pretending like you couldn't see me, and I did what literally any other guy would do. You were both into it. I assumed it was all good when you pulled her fucking knickers off with your teeth, so don't act like I'm suddenly some kind of/

STEPH: /Any other guy, Matt?/

RACHEL: /*Really*?/

MATT: /Yes. Any guy would have/

RACHEL: /Or just predators.

Beat.

MATT: What did you just say?

RACHEL: Predators.

MATT: I'm a predator for having *consensual fucking sex* with you?/

STEPH: /You're an *asshole* for doing it/

RACHEL: /So, you had no control/

MATT: /*Jesus* Christ, Rachel/

RACHEL: /No, seriously. You just *had* to do it, did you?

MATT: This is unbelievable. *You wanted to do it.* Don't think you can get all blurry now because you feel like shit.

STEPH: You should have stopped us.

MATT: *What?*

RACHEL: We were just fooling around, you were the one/

MATT: /Don't, *no.* You're just making this up now/

STEPH: /You thought fucking a girl without a *condom* was a good idea/

MATT: /She was on the *pill.* We all heard her say it/

STEPH: /So it's not your fucking problem then, well it's your problem now isn't it?/

MATT: /Sorry, *sorry* for trusting you Rachel/

RACHEL: /I wasn't expecting you to/

STEPH: /You should have stopped it, you allowed this to happen.

MATT: Oh, *come on*, Steph. It's my fault now that you got drunk and messed around with someone else?

RACHEL: That's not how it/

MATT: /And when I caught you in the act, I didn't get angry. I didn't call it cheating, which is what it *was*, I just rolled with the fucking punches. Like always.

STEPH: *Poor Matt* got his dick sucked by two girls at the same time. Woe is me.

MATT: You think I don't regret it?

STEPH: You had the time of your life. You *loved* it!

Beat.

MATT: Yeah, well, one of us has to, right? At least I fucking enjoy myself, that's kinda the point, Steph.

STEPH: Is it, Matt? Is that the *point?*

MATT: Yep.

STEPH: And I'm some frigid bitch for wanting you to just *look at me.*

MATT looks down.

Pause.

MATT: Okay. I'm sorry I said/

STEPH: /Do you remember you pushed me/

MATT: /I don't *know* what I remember anymore/

STEPH: /You pushed me off at one point so you could have her all to yourself/

MATT: /I'm not talking about this/

STEPH: /And I knew then that you just/

MATT: /Stop it/

STEPH: /At that point you just wanted me in the room with you so you didn't feel guilty.

Beat.

I just figured you needed to get it out of your system. Before, you know…

She raises her engagement ring.

So, yeah, I went along with it. I felt like I had to at that point/

MATT: /Are you serious? Are you really, seriously *saying* that?

Beat.

Be very careful, before you answer. Because I'm on your side, still.

STEPH: Don't threaten me, Matt.

MATT: *Fuck you*, Steph. Have I ever cheated on you?

STEPH: *How* would I know?

Beat

How would I *know*?

Silence.

MATT: I have *never*... I haven't done anything.

STEPH shrugs.

STEPH: The texts.

MATT is dumbfounded.

MATT: The texts?

Beat.

STEPH: *(To RACHEL.)* How many did you get, Rache? The 2AM rambles. *(To MATT.)* She told me about them. That felt great.

MATT: I...

STEPH: You think that's okay, that kind of stuff?

MATT: Nothing happened, nothing *happened* with any of it. People send texts when they're drunk/

STEPH: /Who are these people, Matt? That you're talking about. Who *are* they?

MATT: Steph.

STEPH: I've never gotten a drunk text from any guy I know. Because I'm in a *fucking relationship.*

> *Beat.*

RACHEL: Funny. I get them all the time. Cheaters, thinking they can trick you into making the first move. So it's not their fault.

> *MATT speaks without looking at her.*

MATT: Oh yeah? But it's okay if your best friend tricks you in person, huh?

> *Beat.*

> Steph, I admitted the texts thing. You can't keep using it against me. I put my cards on the table. I've *stopped* all of that now. Okay? You know that.

STEPH: You *did* stop. After we fucked her.

> *Pause.*

RACHEL: You guilted her into it, Matt. Just like you tried to with me, and the money. And booking the flights. All of it.

> *She turns to STEPH.*

> You know, you don't have to get married, Steph/

MATT: *(Snapping.)* /People make mistakes, alright? Both of *you* have, so get off your pedestals, thinking you can lord this shit over me.

> *Beat.*

> And, sorry, why wouldn't she get married, Rachel? Because the three of us, *together*, made a *decision*?

RACHEL: Because she's unhappy.

> *Silence.*

Steph, even if I got rid of the baby, it wouldn't fix what *you* have.

Beat.

STEPH: I don't give a shit what you do, Rachel. It doesn't matter.

And, even if you did, and we learn to look each other in the face again, somehow, and if me and Matt do get married. If it happens to *us*, it won't be our first kid.

It'll be *my* first kid. He already had one… with you.

And he'll always wonder if it was the right thing, and he'll look at *my* child and ask secretly "would Rachel's have been *different*".

You've taken all of that from me. It's *gone*.

And the worst part is, you're my best friend, or at least you *were*.

And, from now on, whenever I think about you I'll only ever think of *today*.

Silence.

RACHEL: I have to go meet my Mam.

RACHEL goes to leave.

STEPH: Going to tell her the good news?

Beat.

RACHEL: I *am* sorry, Steph. But you know I'm right about him. And, even if you think I'm an idiot, and maybe I am, at least I don't doubt myself. I'm alright with the choices I've made.

I used to be jealous of you… but…

She falters.

I'll see you. At some point. Let me know if…

She looks down.

Y'know, if Saturday is still going ahead.

STEPH stares at her.

STEPH: You think I'll let you do this?

RACHEL: You did this to yourself. You both did.

STEPH: You've been skulking around, sticking your poison into us. Creating secrets that *have* to be kept.

RACHEL: That was never what *I* wanted.

STEPH: You've turned me against him. I can't forgive *this*. You've… *burned everything.* I ought to fucking –

She takes several steps towards RACHEL. RACHEL doesn't flinch. STEPH notices. She stops.

You're so sure that you're in the *right*, aren't you?

RACHEL half-nods.

RACHEL: I deserve a shot at being happy.

Beat.

Maybe I did you both a favour. You *know* now. What you're both… actually like.

MATT: We know what we're like.

RACHEL puts her hand on her stomach.

RACHEL: Do you not feel *anything*, Matt?

MATT: No.

Beat.

RACHEL: Your hand on my hip that morning?

Do you remember that?

MATT: No.

STEPH looks at MATT.

You have no clue what you've done here, do you?

RACHEL: You need to grow up. Accept what you did.

STEPH: What the fuck are you even talking about? You are so *pathetic.* Look at yourself, sitting in your *call centre* resenting the rest of us for having sorted ourselves out. And now you think you're better than us cuz you got knocked up?! You *baby.*

RACHEL: There's nothing you can say that will change this now.

STEPH thinks. Suddenly, she laughs, but stops herself.

STEPH: Okay.

RACHEL: What?

STEPH: Nothing. It's nothing.

Beat.

RACHEL turns to go.

She hasn't *called* you.

RACHEL stops.

Your Mam. She hasn't called you.
I mean, you're really late, aren't you?

RACHEL: She's already there.

STEPH nods.

I really don't care if you *believe* me or not.

STEPH: No, I *do.* I believe you.

I'm just... I'm not surprised.

You must be half an hour late, at this stage.

RACHEL: She doesn't mind.

STEPH: You're sure?

Beat.

My mother called me three times today… And then, when she couldn't get me, she called Matt, and then she called you. Jesus.

Beat.

And, you know, she's been all over me about this wedding for months, hasn't she Matt? Every detail up for discussion and it drives me insane. But you know, I've been fighting our corner. Matt's been really good at holding his own. Haven't you?

MATT says nothing.

That's what a mother *should* do. Right? A mother should go above and beyond.

Beat.

Sometimes I think I'm too selfish. That I'd end up resenting my kids. Or that I'd stay with an asshole, for their sake. Even if he cheated on me.

Dad was going to bring Vicky on Saturday. I thought that was my biggest worry this week. But then you…

She smiles at RACHEL.

Rachel. You're going to be a mother.

Beat.

RACHEL: Yes. I am.

STEPH: Surely you'd call your kid if she stood you up for lunch?

Or, is that something you just get used to?

But, you know, you're *always* late. You only ever think of yourself.

RACHEL: That isn't true.

STEPH: Of *course* it is. You just need to *accept* it, Rachel.

You'd be a lot happier.

Pause.

I mean, look at me. I accepted Matt for who he is.

Beat.

Look how happy I am.

MATT: Steph.

She rounds on him.

STEPH: What?

Beat.

MATT: Steph, I love you.

I've always loved you. I know it's not enough, sometimes. Or ever. But I've… I've given you every bit I *have*. I don't *know* how to do it any better than this, and I know that's fucked up.

You make *me* better, at being me. And I… I hope I've done the same, for… we're *good*, together. You and me.

I fucked up. I fucked it up, I know, but… I just, I don't want to lose it. Okay? *Please.* I'm really just trying to tell you the truth right now, okay. Cuz I'm scared.

I… I *worship* you.

Pause.

STEPH: But you don't *like* me very much.

Beat.

You have a drinking problem, Matthew.

You flirt with my friends.

You got it in your head that you were going to fuck another woman/

MATT: /Don't/

STEPH: /Don't interrupt me. You wanted to fuck Rachel. And I let you. Like an idiot. You lied to me. Over and over again. You were writing your wedding vows, thinking you'd *outsmarted* me.

That's not love.

Beat.

MATT: Steph, *please.* Can we not do this?

STEPH does not falter.

STEPH: We're doing it, *darling.*

She turns to RACHEL.

What are you going to tell the kid?

RACHEL does not answer.

What are you going to *tell the kid?* About us.

She points at MATT.

About him?

Beat.

RACHEL: I won't.

Beat.

STEPH: *I* will. Someone will have to.

Beat.

What, it won't "deserve to know". Like I did?/

MATT: /Steph/

RACHEL: /Someday. I might/

STEPH: /And you're gonna stay in your place?/

MATT: /Do you remember/

RACHEL: /I don't know/

STEPH: /The 350 euro *box*-room?/

MATT: /Do you remember when we first met?/

RACHEL: /I don't know, yet. We'll see/

MATT: /In Berlin/

STEPH: /What are the schools like round there?/

RACHEL: /I've heard good things/

MATT: /That party with all the smokers/

STEPH: /You'll have to see about a raise at the call centre/

MATT: /And we snuck outside/

RACHEL: /Yep/

MATT: /With a thing of Nutella and a spoon/

STEPH: /How's their maternity leave?/

RACHEL: /It's fine/

MATT: /We stole that guy's spoon! Do you remember?/

STEPH: /You're really going to sort yourself out, are you?/

RACHEL: /Yes/

MATT: /I kept that stupid spoon/

STEPH: /You gonna teach the kid right and wrong?/

RACHEL: /I will/

MATT: /I was going to give it to you/

STEPH: /You gonna show it how to stand up for itself?/

MATT: /On our wedding day/

RACHEL: /Yes/

STEPH: /Do you want it to be like *you?*

MATT: Please.

STEPH: Or its Dad?

> *She pulls off her engagement ring.*

MATT: Please, no no no, don't. Steph.

> *She throws the ring at him. He catches it (or doesn't).*

STEPH: Or better?

> *Silence.*

RACHEL: This isn't what I wanted…

I guess I came here today because… I couldn't *go* anywhere else and I needed you to tell me we'd work it out… and it would be okay.

> *Beat.*

STEPH: You did all of this so you could sit more comfortably at my wedding.

The only thing that is going to happen now is in twenty-six years time there'll be *another* one of you.

Another Rachel. Fucking up. Secretly asking herself why her Mam doesn't give a fuck where she is.

You're a selfish little *cunt.*

> *Silence.*

RACHEL: *(Broken.)* Maybe I'd be a good Mum.

> *STEPH takes MATT's whiskey cup off the arm of the chair (or wherever it has gone to) and throws the liquid in RACHEL's face. RACHEL tries not to react.*

STEPH: *Fuck* you. You're not even a good friend.

RACHEL sits down. Speechless.

Silence.

RACHEL: They fired me.

There's no… no meeting at work.

Beat.

I took the pregnancy test, but I had to rush because people were queuing and coughing and knocking, so I was back at my desk before it… whatever, developed.

That's not the word, is it?

I stuck it in the pencil holder. I could see it in the corner of my eye.

I had some new guy with me that day and he couldn't do anything right.

I don't even remember what he did, he deleted something, a receipt or something, and I kind of… lost it. I hit him in the head with the mouse.

Beat.

I think he might press charges.

Silence.

The last few weeks, I've been sitting at home in my pyjamas, watching Netflix on my parents' account, trying not to think.

I told Matt about the baby, and… he gave me money to get an abortion but… I really needed to pay my rent… so I did. I said I'd worry about the money later. Always… thought I'd have time to do stuff later.

And then eventually, y'know, I guess everything kicked in because… I started to feel much better.

Beat.

I know when the baby comes, that feeling will probably go away. Won't it?

Beat.

I mean… we would have had a cute kid, probably.

MATT and STEPH say nothing.

I'm sorry. I'm… I'm sorry I didn't think. I didn't think at all. I… I needed to tell you because you're my only friend and you'd… I don't know. And I know this is… I don't want…

I'm scared. I'm so *scared.*

I'm not a mother, I mean… I'm not, I know I'm not, I'm not even, I'm not *anything.* I've never been.

I feel like my head is coming apart, I just want it to go away, I can't breathe, and I'm so late for lunch and I'm… I'm so *late.*

Silence.

I just want a hug.

Silence.

Please.

MATT and STEPH are still.

Lights fade to black.

OUR ISLAND

BY BARRY MCSTAY

Characters

JACK
Irish, mid-late twenties

BRADLEY
English, mid-late twenties

CHARLOTTE
English, mid-late twenties

DEAN
English, early thirties

PAUL
Irish, late fifties/early sixties

ANNIE
Irish, late fifties/early sixties

Our Island had its first production from the 6-13 September 2015 at the Project Arts Centre (Cube) as part of the Tiger Dublin Fringe Festival with the following cast and crew:

JACK – Peter Corboy

BRADLEY – Rob Malone

CHARLIE – Siobhán Cullen

DEAN – Jamie O'Neill

PAUL – Martin Maguire

ANNIE – Bairbre Ní Chaoimh

Director: Maisie Lee

Producer: Jan Schneider

Stage Manager: Liane McCarthy

Lighting Design: John Crudden

Sound Design: Philip Stewart

Set and Costume Design: Rebekka Duffy

Associate Director: Sarah-Jayne Quigley

With thanks to: Blythe Stewart, Jessica Traynor, Stephen Dodd, Futoshi Sakauchi. Abbie O'Reilly, Donna Marie Mahony, Aoife Brannigan, Katie Davenport, Andrea Ainsworth, Aidan Wallace, Michael Marshall, Nessa Ní Dhomhnalláin, Kim Willoughby, Alan Tully, Andrea Smith, Aideen Howard, Emma Hannon. Thomas Hescott, Edmund Harris, James Graham, Samuel Adamson, Matthew Smyth, Ben Kelly, Food & Wine Magazine. The cast of The Waste Ground Party. Barra, John Fitz, Shaun, Helen, Edd, Niall, Lizzie, Felicity. All those who contributed to the production via Indiegogo. Cian O'Brien and the Project Arts Centre. Kris, Ruth and all at the Tiger Dublin Fringe. Fiach, Fiona, Kelly, Des, John and all at the Abbey. Ciara Nolan, Sheila Thompson, Enda O'Flaherty, Mikey Brett-McStay, John and Clodagh McStay.

Our Island was developed with support from the Abbey Theatre and Old Vic New Voices

A bench in a London park. It is spring. Four years before.

BRADLEY: Excuse me – this is my bench.

JACK: What? Oh. Sorry.

BRADLEY: No no no, it was a joke.
Shit sorry, no come back.
Man, sorry. I didn't mean anything by it.

JACK: Never mind.

BRADLEY: God, I feel like I've clubbed a baby seal,
crushed an eggshell or something.

JACK: Just forget it.

BRADLEY: I don't even know why I – I didn't want to – you know –
hurt your feelings.
I mean, I don't know you. So why would I?
You know?
You look sad.

JACK: Well.

BRADLEY: And beautiful – sorry. But yeah.
Sad and beautiful are a – an odd combination.

JACK: Odd too, great.

BRADLEY: And beautiful.
Sorry.
I've been – a bit – anyway, someone told me I should try talk to strangers.
I'm still getting the hang of it.

JACK: I just want to eat my sandwich.

BRADLEY: Please. Sit.

JACK: On your bench?

BRADLEY: You have my permission.

BRADLEY: –
> You're Irish?
> The accent.

> –

> That's a nice camera.

> –

> –

> Are you on holidays?

JACK: I'm a photographer.

BRADLEY: Right.
> Here for work then?

JACK: I live here.

BRADLEY: Oh great.
> How long have you – ?

JACK: Since Saturday.

> –

BRADLEY: Good.
> Why did you move?

JACK: Because. It's
> away.

BRADLEY: From?

JACK: Away.
> From.
> Home.

BRADLEY: Well. You'll love it.
> London's great.
> I'm from here – so if you –

> –

You know.

JACK: –
    What do you do?

BRADLEY: I'll give you a clue.

JACK: Great.

BRADLEY: The clue is: this notebook and this pen.

JACK: You're a journalist.

BRADLEY: No.

JACK: A writer.

BRADLEY: Got it in two.

JACK: You're a writer.
    Tell me a story.

BRADLEY: –
    – You're a photographer, take my picture.

JACK: Alright. Tell me the story while I'm doing it.

BRADLEY: Won't that – I mean –

JACK: The quicker you forget you're having your photo taken,
    the better you'll look.

BRADLEY: Oh. Okay. Right.
    A story.

He lights a cigarette.

Right. A short one.
Right. This is the story of a little girl called Jenny. She lived
in an average town in an average house with her perfectly
average mum and dad, her average brother Michael
and her average cat Sherbet. Jenny would have been a
perfectly average little girl except for the fact that Jenny
really wanted to be a Martian. It made her teachers frown
when they asked her what she wanted to be when she grew

up and she said 'A Martian'. Her parents worried with every drawing she drew and painting she painted which, invariably, were of Martians. And her brother teased her constantly, asking why she wasn't playing with dolls like normal girls. Even the cat looked at her funny when, every Hallowe'en, she painted her face green and wore pipe-cleaners as antennae. Eventually her parents told her to stop being silly, stop staring into the sky for hours on end, stop banging on about bloody Martians because they didn't exist and she could never be one. Ever.

But rather than listen to them, Jenny just smiled and disappeared into the garden shed. She hardly emerged for three days, until her parents, Michael and Sherbet were brought running into the garden by a loud roar and a crash. They were amazed to see the garden shed flattened and a rocket ship made of bottles, cardboard boxes, Sellotape and toilet-roll tubes whooshing up into the sky. Jenny waved happily from a little cling-film window as she disappeared beyond the clouds.

She rocketed through space for a week and a day until finally she bumped down onto the surface of Mars in a red cloud of dust. As the dust cleared, she saw lots of little buildings clustered among the rocks. Each one looked like, well very much like a garden shed. Her face green, her pipe-cleaner antennae bouncing and her tin-foil space suit glinting in the now-slightly-farther-away sunlight, she raced out of the ship and was immediately surrounded by lots of curious figures. They looked just like little girls from Earth, but they all had green faces, bouncy antennae and silvery clothes that glinted in the sunlight. They smiled at her – she was a stranger but she certainly looked like she belonged there. And Jenny smiled back before looking to the sky and the little distant dot that was Earth. She waved, even though she knew no-one would see her. And she sighed with relief because finally she was certain about the one thing she had never been certain about: She had been right all along.

*

Four years after. It's Christmas Eve, JACK and BRADLEY's sitting-room in North London. They are decorating a Christmas tree to the sound of Aretha Franklin's 'Joy To The World'.

JACK: No stop.

BRADLEY: What?

JACK: Not that one.

BRADLEY: Fine. Why not that one?

JACK: No don't put it back, give it to me.

BRADLEY: Why, what's –

JACK: It's my decoration.

BRADLEY: Aren't they communally all ours?

JACK: No, it's my job.

BRADLEY: It's – what? We're decorating a Christmas tree. I don't think there are jobs aside from 'place decorations on tree'.

JACK: No, that one is my job.

BRADLEY: Why?

JACK: It just is. That one was my job, and that one's Darren's.

BRADLEY: Right.

JACK: Don't just chuck it back in the box.

BRADLEY: I thought maybe you didn't –

JACK: No, it has to go on the tree.
Fuck's – give it to me. You can't put it down there.

BRADLEY: Well Jesus Jack, I don't know how it all fucking works.

JACK: Then ask.

BRADLEY: I didn't realise there were rules about putting up the bloody tree.

JACK: There aren't it's just –

we made these when I was six. These have been on every tree I've put up every Christmas since. After we put the star on top, these were the last things we hung up, either side of the tree, halfway up where everyone could see them.

Just leave it over there.

BRADLEY: Right.

JACK: Alright?

BRADLEY: Alright.

JACK: Check the oven.

BRADLEY: Check the oven.

BRADLEY exits.

Re-enters.

BRADLEY: Here. Wine.
Dutch courage.
I think it's French actually.
Not Dutch.
And the oven is nearly ready.

JACK: Thanks.

BRADLEY sits on the sofa and tries to write.

JACK: I'll put these upstairs.

Exits. And re-enters. Starts dusting around BRADLEY. BRADLEY gives up writing, picks up a copy of 'Attitude'. JACK flicks through the other magazines, picking out the 'gay' ones.

JACK: Brad.
Are you done with that?

–

Bradley?
Are you done reading that?

BRADLEY: Nearly.

JACK: Right.

BRADLEY: Not quite.

JACK: Okay.
Okay.

–

BRADLEY: What?

JACK: It's just –

BRADLEY: What?

JACK: Nothing.

BRADLEY: What is it just?

JACK: Nothing.

BRADLEY: It's obviously not nothing.

JACK: Nothing.
I just wondered when you'd be finished.

BRADLEY: Finished my magazine?
No.

JACK: No what?

BRADLEY: I'm not finished.

JACK: And –

BRADLEY: Nearly.

JACK: When –

BRADLEY: Soon.

JACK: Right.

BRADLEY: Right.

JACK: Okay.

BRADLEY: Yes.

JACK: And what will –

BRADLEY: I'll leave it on the guest-room floor,

JACK: Of course.

BRADLEY: right where they can see it,

JACK: Good.

BRADLEY: lying open on the article about dildos.

JACK: Naturally.

BRADLEY: Now chill out.

JACK: I am chilled.

> *JACK adjusts cushions on armchair, makes to leave, notices spot on door frame, sprays it and wipes it, exits, quickly re-enters remembering something, takes it and exits.*

BRADLEY: They won't mind.

JACK: *(Offstage.)* What?

BRADLEY: They won't mind.

JACK: *(Offstage but entering.)* What?

BRADLEY: They won't – they won't mind, I said.

JACK: I mind.

BRADLEY: They should be used to your mess.

JACK: Your mess.

BRADLEY: I just feel very clinical.

JACK: Right.

BRADLEY: Disinfected.

JACK: Well good.

BRADLEY: Like you've wrapped the whole flat in plastic.

JACK: I just want it to be okay.

BRADLEY: Well just – you know?
I've put together a nice Christmas playlist for them.

JACK: I don't think they'll notice.

BRADLEY: Right.

BRADLEY shoves his magazine down the back of the sofa. JACK retrieves it and exits.

BRADLEY: Oh fucking – like they'd look – they're not –
bloody – crime scene investigators.

JACK re-enters with a shoebox-sized present.

BRADLEY: Who's that for?

JACK: Who d'you think?

BRADLEY: Can I shake it?

JACK: Why?

BRADLEY: In case there's something noisy in it.

JACK: No. I don't want you guessing before tomorrow.

BRADLEY: Mysterious.

JACK: It's only something little.

BRADLEY: *(Singing.)* 'I don't want a lot for Christmas…'

JACK: Need to smarten you up too before they arrive.

BRADLEY: It's only Charlie and Thingummy.

JACK: Dean.

BRADLEY: Exactly.

JACK: And you know I don't mean them.

BRADLEY: I look delightful.

JACK: To me, possibly. To my Mam, no way.

BRADLEY: Why?

JACK: Because.

Put it this way, she wouldn't let us leave the house without a collar – Darren cut the collar off his school shirt once and Mam went mental. Dad said he'd bring shame on him if the school saw him, headmaster's son, all that. They grounded him for a week.

He was being an eejit, cutting holes in the curtains, bits out of his fringe, couldn't leave him near a scissors back then.

BRADLEY: I'll put a collar on.

Or maybe a nice dress.

JACK: Bradley.

BRADLEY: Could help –

JACK: Stop distracting me.

BRADLEY: YOU'RE distracting. I haven't written anything for days – with you buzzing around like a like a a panicked bluebottle.

Desperately seeking an open window.

JACK: You could help.

BRADLEY: I won't do it right, will I?

–

You never see bluebottles anymore.

Do you?

JACK: Don't you?

BRADLEY: No. There were always bluebottles getting stuck between the double-glazing in our kitchen. Yeah, there were way more bluebottles back when I was young.

JACK: You still are.

BRADLEY: It's just a thing I noticed – what?

JACK: Young. You are young.
Still.

BRADLEY: Younger than you anyway.

JACK: Thanks.

BRADLEY: You laughed at my bluebottles.

JACK: I'm sorry for laughing at your bluebottles.

BRADLEY: You're forgiven.
Dunno why I remember that.

JACK: The bluebottles? Yeah you're weird.

BRADLEY: Probably.
You just remember bits from when you were younger – don't you? Not the whole lot. Just bits.
Like the collars.

JACK: I guess.

BRADLEY: I have this really vivid memory – I'd have been maybe seven, eight I suppose – all of us driving along the south coast one summer day, near Brighton along the cliffs, you know – those amazing white cliffs. We were in Dad's old Volvo, Mum and Dad in the front, me and Gabby in the back. And there's the hills on the left, proper hills – I mean, hills like hills should be – green and rolling, and you could see the wind rushing through the grass too, like a a a sidewinder. And it was so sunny, so – sparkly on the sea, you know these little splashes of light, I called them 'water-diamonds', you know how you get – shimmering on the water. Just driving, no one talking, in silence – on the way to see my aunt and uncle in Eastbourne. Don't really know why I remember it. One of those things I guess – when you go searching you just find some memories and don't find others.

JACK: I'm going to put the shepherd's pie in.

Exits. Returns. Hovers.

BRADLEY: Would you sit down for two minutes please. It's not going to get any tidier in here.
Thank you.

They sit in silence for a moment.

JACK: When I was young I used to love going to the panto at the Gaiety Theatre. It was class – the whole thing. The building felt really – properly impressive, with all those golden swirling bits – and pillars and stained glass and an actual red carpet and there were sweets and ice-cream and balloons and flashing swords and crowns and and pots of bubbles and. It was like a funfair – but not scary. Like it had been designed just for children.
And then it started and you had the lights and the music and fake snow, like snowing! inside! And the actors, the characters – they all talked to us, to the 'boys and girls' like we were the important ones, and we all shouted back – he's behind you oh no she isn't – all that, mad into it. And it was brilliant, a crowd of kids screaming our heads off, hyper on Opel Fruits, all part of something. Not that I probably recognised it not in the way you would now but I did NOTICE it.
And the magic carpet.
My favourite show was Aladdin because when we saw it – I was nine I think – Aladdin and the princess got on this magic carpet. It was red and blue with gold frilly edges. And it was on wires, obviously, but it just began to rise as they started singing and they FLEW out, over our heads. We were a few rows back and they flew right above us. They were on it singing this beautiful song with harp music

in it. And they had a disco-ball going, all these bits of light
swirling around and a bubble machine –
and they were FLYING, man.
And it was –
I mean I was SO happy and and, I dunno,
jaw-dropped.
It was magic, like, it had to be. I LOVED believing in it.
And I wanted to ride a magic carpet for, well for ages after
that.

BRADLEY: Sounds great.

JACK: And then you get older and the world obviously isn't
magic. It's just full of depressing grown-up shit like jobs
and bills and my fucking family.

BRADLEY: And me?

JACK: Not you.
Well yes you – but you're not depressing.

BRADLEY: Nope – I'm a ray of sunshine.

JACK: In the deep mid-winter.

BRADLEY: *(Singing.)* 'In the deep mid-winter, / frosty wind
made moan…'

JACK: / I used to love hearing that song at midnight mass.

BRADLEY: Are your parents as Irish as you are?

JACK: Ah begorrah, sure no one's as Oirish as me, Misthur
Bradley sir. Top o' the mornin' to ya!

BRADLEY: I was just asking. Are they going to talk about mass
and stuff? Cos I don't feel qualified to deal with that.

JACK: If they talk to you at all I'll be surprised.

BRADLEY: Well I am a terrible person.

JACK: Awful.

BRADLEY: Just the worst – I drool on the pillow, I fart in company, I sing all the time, even when you're trying to talk to me, I never do the laundry, I leave lights on, I forget to pay the bills, I don't think I've cooked for us more than twice ever –

JACK: So thoughtless.

BRADLEY: So careless.

JACK: And yet I appear to be in love with you.

BRADLEY: How the hell did that happen?

JACK: I must be an idiot.

BRADLEY: Don't worry, I'll be charming.

JACK: I'm sure.

How are you so calm about this?

BRADLEY: I'm not.

I'm shitting myself.

Doorbell.

BRADLEY: It's just Charlie and Thingummy.

JACK: Dean, yes. Get dressed.

BRADLEY: Why are they even here?

JACK: Why?

BRADLEY: Rubberneckers.

JACK: What?

BRADLEY: Can't we just pretend we're not in?

JACK: Bradley.

*

CHARLIE. She is a bubbly woman in her late-twenties, Northern. She is carrying a bag of Christmas presents.

DEAN. He is her boyfriend of almost six months, well-dressed. He is texting.

CHARLIE: It really looks lovely in here Jack. Been busy boys eh?

JACK: *(Offstage.)* Getting in the spirit.

CHARLIE: Oh it's just beautiful, very Christmassy, I think this is a very Christmassy house actually.

I'll leave the presents under the tree.

Give me your coat D.

Yeah it's MEGA cold out there, I reckon we'll have frost or snow – I hope your parents are going to get here before it starts.

JACK: *(Entering with drinks and nibbles.)* Fingers crossed. Dig in Dean.

DEAN: Thanks.

CHARLIE: Oh great, I was worried they'd be here already, I'm sorry we're so late, it's totally my fault – no surprises there – no I'll do it, okay to chuck em in the loo? – *(Offstage.)* I was out last night with the girls from work and I was SO hungover this morning, I mean way more than I should have been – I mean it WAS a Christmas work party – *(Re-entering.)* and we all know what Christmas work parties can be like – especially with my track record! – there you go D – but aside from the one free cocktail I was on white wine all night – Sandra was there and I mean I didn't want to make a fool of myself – and I mean you know as well as me Jack I do NOT get hangovers when I drink wine – spirits are another story! – but like I say I was being so well behaved – or so I thought – this *(wine)* is lovely by the way – but I woke up this morning with a SPLITTING headache and D was round to pick me up at ten like we'd agreed cos I wanted to get the last bit of Christmas shopping done – I

227

mean I shouldn't leave it so late but I quite enjoy the mayhem of Oxford Street you know? – part of the whole experience, the magic of Christmas with the lights and the window displays and all those people – I don't mind it at all really, it's a bit of fun – but by the time, I mean by the time I was actually properly awake and got myself made up – I mean you know I can't leave the house without my slap and my weave! – by that stage it was almost lunchtime and we had to grab a bit of lunch and obviously we'd to find somewhere to park too and so we've been behind ever since really and it was CRAZY in town but at least it's done now – I left the presents under the tree there, in the silver bag – I mean it'll only be a flying visit but I'm glad we made it over, I feel like I haven't seen you boys in FOREVER.

JACK: Your birthday probably.

CHARLIE: Is it? Well exactly – not since October then. Far too long.

BRADLEY enters, dressed.

BRADLEY: It's alright everyone, I'm back.

CHARLIE: Lovely to see you hun, I was just telling Jack it's been AGES since we've seen you.

BRADLEY: Too long. Hey Dean.

CHARLIE: I was saying, your present is under there in the silver bag. We only got it today but I think you'll like it. Spoiler Alert: It's wine! And we picked up something for your parents too Jack – whiskey for the Irish!

JACK: I'm sure they'll be delighted you thought of them. Mam asks after you a lot.

CHARLIE: Aw I love Annie Murray! You told her I'd be here?

JACK: I did of course.

CHARLIE: What time are they arriving?

JACK: Their flight should have touched down over an hour ago /

CHARLIE: / Oh good.

JACK: but I suppose by the time they get their luggage and –
Dad insisted they rent a car too –

CHARLIE: Well that'll be nice, they'll be able to make their
own way around.

JACK: Yeah well – I offered but. Anyway by the time they've
sorted all that and tried to figure out the sat-nav and
consulted Dad's trusty old AA map – plus with the weather
getting – so yeah – they'll probably be another half an
hour. I reckon.

CHARLIE: Where'd they fly into?

JACK: Heathrow.

CHARLIE: Oh right.

DEAN: Should have used Stansted.

CHARLIE: What's that D?

DEAN: Should have used Stansted. Easier to drive. Closer to
here. Makes more sense.

JACK: Yes but they like Heathrow. They've always flown there
when coming to London.

DEAN: They should try it. Can't be stuck doing the same thing
forever. Heathrow's a fucking nightmare at the best of times.

CHARLIE: D, you don't want them trying to figure out a new
airport at Christmas, when it's going to be PACKED. I
mean, it's –

DEAN: What's to figure out? It's an airport, they're all the same
and there's a fuck-tonne of signs telling them where to go. I
need a piss, this way? *(Exits.)*

CHARLIE: You MUST be excited to see them eh?

JACK: Oh yeah. It'll be nice. Haven't seen them since last Christmas actually so they'll have been missing me. And I miss them too of course.

CHARLIE: Aw yeah. Oh I'm glad they're coming.

BRADLEY: Four years in the making.

CHARLIE: Yeah.

JACK: It's taken months of negotiation to get them over.

CHARLIE: Oh it'll be great.

BRADLEY: If you say so.
I think this one might overdose on neurosis before they get here.

JACK: I've just been tidying.

BRADLEY: It's like living in a Woody Allen film.

CHARLIE: They'll LOVE him.

BRADLEY: Course they will. I'm fucking adorable.

CHARLIE: They've never been anything other than lovely to me.

BRADLEY: That's good to know.

CHARLIE: Treated me like their daughter really.

BRADLEY: Yes. Well. This is a bit different.

CHARLIE: No of course, but I mean –

BRADLEY: You weren't sleeping with their son.

CHARLIE: No.

BRADLEY: And you have boobs.

JACK: Bradley.

CHARLIE: Sorry Brad, I wasn't –

BRADLEY: No it's cool. Anyway.

JACK: Off to your Dad's?

CHARLIE: Yeah. I know it's early days and all – it's always just me and Dad – but I just thought it would be nice to have another man around at Christmas.

JACK: Sounds lovely. And how's Sonya's?

CHARLIE: Oh I've moved. It's a new shop, Divaz, in Clapham. Same type of thing, but better pay.

JACK: Oh right, I didn't realise. Great.

CHARLIE: Yeah it's great, loving it, I mean it's a busy busy time of year, but fifty percent staff discount comes in VERY handy around Christmas!

BRADLEY: Hence the shoes?

CHARLIE: You like them? I feel tall in them! I mean!

DEAN: *(Entering.)* Fuck me, that's a lot of porn in your loo.

JACK: *(Exiting.)* Shit I forgot.

BRADLEY: It's not porn, it's just Attitude.

DEAN: A lot of naked guys on the front of them.

BRADLEY: Topless.

DEAN: Some bottomless.

BRADLEY: Towels in the way

DEAN: Still.

CHARLIE: No worse than your lads-mags, D.

DEAN: Yeah but they're girls on the front. At least people expect that.
And they're in bikinis. Usually.
Shouldn't spring that shit on guests.

BRADLEY: Which guest?

DEAN is texting.

CHARLIE: Work?

DEAN: I'm over fucking newlywed couples mooching round houses they'll never buy just cos they want to perv on other people's bedrooms. Wasting my fucking time.

JACK: *(Entering.)* Jesus that was close, / I'd totally forgotten.

CHARLIE: / You took off at –

JACK: Couldn't have dealt with – anyway.
Out of sight.

BRADLEY: As you can see, we're being as straight as possible for Mister and Missus Murray.

JACK: Oh –

CHARLIE: Bradley!

BRADLEY: First impressions. All that.

JACK: That's not –

BRADLEY: I'm sure they'll be thankful at least I'm not some drag queen in sequins and feathers.

JACK: Yes.
Yes.
That's the idea.

BRADLEY: And if they aren't, fuck it.

JACK: –

CHARLIE: Now don't be mean, Bradley, they'll love you. Two of the nicest people I know, the Murrays. Remember that time I stayed at yours Jack? Hallowe'en of second year uni.

JACK: Yeah.

CHARLIE: First time they'd ever met me, I mean, this mad English girl their son brought to visit – I think they thought we were shagging!

BRADLEY: Did they?

JACK: Oh definitely.

DEAN: Hoping probably.

JACK: Probably.

CHARLIE: Definitely, but they were so sweet, they had this
– remember? – I mean this massive pot of Irish stew and
a glass of Guinness for me when I arrived, all laid out –
STEAMING hot, piping it was – / the stew I mean

JACK: / I love Mam's Irish stew.

CHARLIE: meat that just melted in your – and just – I
remember your mum saying – it was delicious by the way
– that lady – I mean you can cook Jack, you know he can
Bradley – but that lady's food is INCREDIBLE – and I
remember her saying to me 'you're family while you're
under our roof'.

BRADLEY: Well that's sweet.

CHARLIE: I know eh?!
It was the loveliest time. Made me feel so welcome – they
both did.

JACK: Long time ago now.

CHARLIE: Second year uni – so what, five, six years ago?
GOD have I known you – that's AWFUL!
But Dublin is SUCH a great city – I mean – right?
Uni there – ugh, the BEST years of our lives. Behind us
now – cheers to the past!

JACK: Well London's home now really. Obviously.

CHARLIE: Of course, your house and your fellah, what more
could anyone want!

BRADLEY: Nothing at all.

DEAN: More crisps.

JACK: What? Oh yeah, course. Here.

DEAN: Cheers.

CHARLIE: Leave space for dinner D.

DEAN: No one else was eating them.

BRADLEY: No one else could get near them.

CHARLIE: Oh I do miss Ireland. You must miss it too, Jack.

JACK: Ah yeah.

CHARLIE: What do you miss most?

JACK: Well I'll miss having a pint with my friends this year.
Little Christmas tradition, getting together in Hennessy's.

CHARLIE: Oh Hennessy's!

BRADLEY: It's funny, because they're the thing he doesn't miss
the rest of the year.

DEAN: Why? They're your friends. You should miss them.

JACK: I do – no that's not right.
I miss them.
But not in their context.

DEAN: What does that mean?

JACK: It means.
I think London is the best city in the world. I love it, you
can really get lost in it.

CHARLIE: Especially on Oxford Street on Christmas Eve!

JACK: It's. Big.
It's expansive.
It's free. I love how free / it feels,

DEAN: / Nothing's free.

JACK: there are so many so many people here.

DEAN: Too many. It's crowded.

JACK: Not to me it doesn't feel crowded.

CHARLIE: You should have been on Oxford Street.

DEAN: Course it's crowded. We live in the smallest living space in all of Europe.

BRADLEY: We?

DEAN: Here. Britain.
It was on *QI*, /

CHARLIE: / He loves that show.

DEAN: all 65million of us squeezed into this midget of an island. And London's the worst. There's a load of flats we rent out where they've made an extra bedroom out of the sitting room. Same all over the city, landlords packing them in. Standard of living is fuck all. And now you can't have a spare room or you get shafted for it. You're lucky, this room itself is a fucking luxury and you probably don't even realise it. There are just too many people here. I don't give a shit, I just try and get 'em filled. But I wouldn't want to live like that.
Like fucking Victorians or something.

JACK: Right.
Well I don't feel crowded.
I like all the people. It's like being tossed around in the sea.
Live in Dublin. That's crowded.

DEAN: Dublin's tiny. I've been there. Stag-do.

JACK: Yeah. It's tiny. That's my point. You get trapped by its tininess. You get, get hemmed into this small-town, small-minded, small-peopled –
place.
It's a place.

DEAN: 'Dublin is a place'?

JACK: No, wait. Yes,

> it's a place because, I mean,
>
> It's a place like you would get PLACED there.
>
> Put in it, like an ornament – yeah, like a small statue person on a shelf – in a PLACE with lots of other statues and you'd be expected to stay there.
>
> London is alive and moving and it's, it's writhing and it's breathing.
>
> Dublin is static.
>
> And try being gay there. It gets tinier, because everyone knows you, everyone talks to everyone, everyone knows the, all the gossip and the scandal.

DEAN: I thought you'd had a vote, no one cares now.

JACK: Well in theory. But it doesn't happen overnight. People still like to talk. I'm glad but – like, a lot of people said no, we don't like him thanks. I'm glad I wasn't there during all the – talk and the arguing. I just – I like London because no one notices.

DEAN: Because you can hide.

JACK: No. It's not a hiding place.

DEAN: Sounds like it.

JACK: No, I'm not hiding but I'm – because I'm me. Out in public.

> But it's a bigger public. And no one gives a shit.

CHARLIE: Out and proud eh?!

DEAN: Sounds the same to me.

JACK: Feels very different to me.

DEAN: Who gives a shit anyway? The world's the way it is, go and do whatever you're doing and who gives a fuck what anyone else thinks.

Silence.

BRADLEY: Another drink?

CHARLIE: Go on then!

DEAN: There'll be plenty at your Dad's.

CHARLIE: Oh shut up D, it's Christmas. Grinch.

BRADLEY: You're more than welcome.
Dean?

DEAN: No mate. Driving.

BRADLEY: That's
sensible.
You alright babe?

JACK: Fine.

DEAN takes out a cigarette and lighter.

JACK: Em –

BRADLEY: Not in here. Outside. There's a yard out the back if
you –

DEAN: It's fucking freezing outside.

CHARLIE: Dean!

JACK: It's just –

BRADLEY: We've got – our other GUESTS are almost here.
They don't – do they –

JACK: No.

BRADLEY: they don't smoke. And he doesn't like the smell
either. So it's outside or bust.
Sorry.

CHARLIE: Dean.

DEAN: Fine.

Exits, returns almost immediately.

DEAN: Where?

JACK: Out through –

BRADLEY: It's fine, I'll show you. If I can bum a fag.

DEAN: What –
Yeah. Fine.

JACK: You're meant to be giving up.

CHARLIE: I can't get D to give up either.

BRADLEY: Your parents are almost here. I'm allowed. Dying wish. Condemned man's final, delicious, nicotine-y meal. Jack.

JACK: Oh. Go on then.

Exits with DEAN.

JACK: And shut the door, I don't want any of your blowback in the kitchen!

CHARLIE: I hate that habit. I mean, I used to be like a 'fecking' chimney back in school but I couldn't keep it – ruins your teeth for one. I just did it cos all the other girls did it and it was meant to make you look dead sexy. Though I will say I love the taste of someone after they've had one – like when you kiss em and you can taste, you know – I mean it makes me PROPER oooo horny you know. My first ever kiss was with Johnny Trent and he was a smoker, a real bad boy, I mean for twelve years old – I must link it with that, ever since – yeah I love the nicotine taste but not the smoke or the yellow nails or teeth no no can't have it. D needs to kick it.
Are you alright?

JACK: I'm going to propose to him.

CHARLIE: What? You –

JACK: Shh.

CHARLIE: Wow. When?

JACK: Tomorrow.

CHARLIE: When tomorrow?

JACK: After dinner.

CHARLIE: Oh my God Jack, that's – well it's amazing.
    Oh –
    I'm so happy for you.

JACK: Yeah, well – I'm happy too.

CHARLIE: Well.
    Your parents are going to be here.

JACK: Yes.

CHARLIE: Have you told them?

JACK: No.

CHARLIE: Are you gonna?

JACK: No. Big surprise.

CHARLIE: Okay.

JACK: Yeah.

CHARLIE: And how do you think they'll feel?

JACK: I don't know.

CHARLIE: Okay.

JACK: Yeah.

CHARLIE: Oh.
    I'm sure it'll be brilliant. They'll be fine.

JACK: They'll have to be I guess.

CHARLIE: Okay.

JACK: Yeah.

CHARLIE: They'll see how happy you are and Bradley will say yes and it'll be great.

JACK: That's the plan.

CHARLIE: Okay.

JACK: Yeah.

CHARLIE: Great.

Make sure you text me as soon as – yeah?

JACK: I will.

Silence.

CHARLIE: So when did you decide?

JACK: Jake and Sarah's wedding. It was just so beautiful and and perfect really, / so perfect

CHARLIE: / Oh it was wasn't it?

JACK: / and it got me sort of – thinking – I want that.

CHARLIE: It was perfect.

JACK: Well exactly. Perfect might be nice.

CHARLIE: Yeah.

It is nice.

JACK: And I don't want to not have him. I mean – God what a scary way to be if he was gone.

What if, when he walked back in, the next words out of his mouth were

"I'm breaking up with you".

So I figured, if he has a ring on, he won't be able to.

CHARLIE: No.

JACK: No. But if I give him the time and space, it might just occur to him so why risk it?

CHARLIE: Have you got a ring?

JACK: Yes.

CHARLIE: Oh my –

JACK: Shhh.

CHARLIE: Where is it – can I see it?

JACK: Hidden.

CHARLIE: Where?
    Jack.

JACK: I – if I tell you –

CHARLIE: Obviously.

JACK: It's in the dolls *(Russian dolls)*. There.

CHARLIE: Really? Like, right in the – that's. Oh that's brilliant.

JACK: Eh, what do you think you're doing?

CHARLIE: But I just want to / see it.

JACK: / What if he walks in?

CHARLIE: Boo. Show me.

JACK: You boo. Here, I'll show you a photo. (*on phone*)

CHARLIE: I just – I mean this is amazing.
    That's beautiful. It's – is it gold?

JACK: Rose gold, yeah.

CHARLIE: And a, is it a / diamond

JACK: / Diamond, yeah. And it has 'J & B' engraved inside it.

CHARLIE: Too cute.
    Not B J?

JACK: Our hilarious initials.
    I'm terrified he'll find it. Or he'll say no.

CHARLIE: I saw this thing on the internet – 'a ship is safe in a harbour but that's not what ships are for.'
Yeah.
Where will you have it?

JACK: I don't know yet.

CHARLIE: Here? Or in Ireland?

JACK: Oh right.

CHARLIE: Now you've the option of course.

JACK: Yeah. Here I think. Everything is here now.

CHARLIE: Yeah
Yeah.
I'm happy for you.

JACK: Really?

CHARLIE: Of course. Why wouldn't I be?

JACK: Well. Just. Everything.

CHARLIE: Oh please Jack. That's such old news.

JACK: I just wanted to be sure.

CHARLIE: Seriously.

JACK: If you say so.

CHARLIE: I do say. You're dead to me.

JACK: Charlie.

CHARLIE: Piss off – don't think so highly of yourself Jack, it's not attractive.
I mean, it's a bit strange. But. You know.

JACK: Yeah.

CHARLIE: And I've got Dean anyway.

JACK: Yeah.

CHARLIE: What?

JACK: Well. He's no Tom, is he?

CHARLIE: So fucking what?

JACK: Tom was – I mean, the cheekbones. And arms. And he was nice. I liked him.

CHARLIE: Well marry him then.

JACK: Sorry Char –

CHARLIE: Dad didn't like him. And he was a fucking let down anyway. They always are, the pretty ones. Most of them. And the rest of them are gay.

JACK: Again, sorry. For that. And – yeah.

CHARLIE: Fuck it.
This will be good for you.

JACK: Marriage?

CHARLIE: Well, yes, that too – of course that – but this. Christmas. The whole Christmas thing. Having your parents here and them seeing everything all – HOMELY. You have a homely home. Yeah.
Yeah.

BRADLEY re-enters.

BRADLEY: Fuck me it's cold out there. Think my balls are up around my ribcage.

JACK: Long smoke.

BRADLEY: I had two – sorry – for luck. I needed it.

CHARLIE: Just don't sit near me, or else I might leap on you. I was telling Jack – nicotine breath really does it for me.

BRADLEY: That explains a lot. Jesus Charlie you're a mate and all but – and I've said it to you before – he is hard work, /

CHARLIE: / I know.

BRADLEY: he was standing out there telling me how 'even he would struggle to sell this shithole' /

CHARLIE: / Fuck me.

BRADLEY: I mean if he wasn't your – I don't even know what to – boyfriend? – whatever, if he was just some bloke –

CHARLIE: Seriously, I don't need it from both sides thanks.

JACK: Where is he?

BRADLEY: Phone.

CHARLIE: Surprise surprise.

JACK: What's he doing on it?

CHARLIE: Business. Planning. Scheming.

JACK: It's Christmas Eve.

CHARLIE: Doesn't matter, he says. He's always got a plan. "Gotta keep moving, I'm going places". But that thing, it's like a – an extra bit stuck onto his ear.

BRADLEY: An ear conservatory.

CHARLIE: Oo! That's GOOD, I like that! Ear conservatory. I'll have to use that.

BRADLEY: Have it.

CHARLIE: Wait, I'm going to put it in my phone. And you can stop burning holes in my back, both of you. I don't need to prove anything to you. I hear you, I hear you, I hear you – I mean, he's not – whatever – your type – /

BRADLEY: / Hell no.

CHARLIE: and he rubs people up the wrong way – I mean he's Marmite, I know he is – and it's – yes we argue more often than not – like, Luke and I argued but Dean and I ARGUE – like cats in a sack – and he's a hammer, not a a

BRADLEY: A different tool.

CHARLIE: not a, – shut up – he's blunt. But he's MANLY. It's all out there and up front and it's just – yeah, it's just 'this is black and that is white'. Gay lads – I mean you lot are all so bloody interesting aren't you? so VARIED so – oh it's a a an N word – nnn – nn – n –

Nuanced! You're all so nuanced and it's not easy to find a straight guy like that. It's not a bad thing though is it? I like a man to be a man – Luke aside, he wasn't – but he's not – anyway I don't mind someone who is blunt and gruff and a bit grrrr. And sometimes it's nice to feel like, yes I'm the woman and he's the man – not in a – I mean you know I give as good as I get but sometimes you want it to be – you know? Uncomplicated and straightforward and of course he's not fucking Prince Charming but at least he takes me out to dinner and owns his own flat and has a car and we both like the same clubs and yes he watches football and that's okay because he'll have proper good sex with me afterwards.

I mean, maybe he's – it's obviously not the IDEAL ideal.

BRADLEY: So why do you –

CHARLIE: Cos he knows what he's doing and it's simple. And I like that right now. It's not – whatever, like you lot. But it's something. And to be honest it's none of your business. Especially not yours.

BRADLEY: Why especially not mine?

CHARLIE: Shut up – both of you – I mean what actually gives you the right to be my fucking counsellors anyway? I'm not – it's Christmas and I don't want to talk about it anymore.

–

You must be enjoying the school holidays?
Brad?

BRADLEY: It's alright.

DEAN re-enters.

CHARLIE: Writing anything?
  Bradley.

BRADLEY: Bits and pieces.

JACK: He's
  he's got a cool idea for a sci-fi, / fantasy thing, don't you?

BRADLEY: / Horror really.

CHARLIE: Oo yeah? You okay D? What is it Brad? Bradley's a
  writer.

DEAN: So?

JACK: Tell them about your idea.

BRADLEY: I really don't –

CHARLIE: I'd like to hear it.

DEAN: I'm not that –

CHARLIE: I want to hear.

BRADLEY: Fine – I mean it's only a – I've only got a couple of
  pages written –

CHARLIE: Fucking tell us.

BRADLEY: Em. Well.
  It starts with a human subspecies who feed on hearts, who
  kill people and cut out their hearts and eat them. This heart
  reforms inside them and they split like amoebas into sort of
  clones of themselves. They seem perfectly normal at first,
  there's no obvious physical distinction, but as people get to
  know them they notice there's something cold about them
  but often it's too late. And so their population is growing
  and threatening the human race.
  Like a very big visible virus.

CHARLIE: Right.

DEAN: Or like vampires.

BRADLEY: Not vampires.

DEAN: Similar.

BRADLEY: Hardly.

DEAN: Feeding off humans and creating more of themselves? I
    don't go for all that lightweight horror bollocks anyway but
    it sounds pretty much like vampires to me.

BRADLEY: Well it really isn't. Vampires suck the blood from
    people. Suck them dry.
    Don't they?

DEAN: What's that fucking mean?

BRADLEY: Could you turn the sound off on your phone, all
    that clicking, it's a bit fucking annoying.

JACK: Brad.

DEAN: Is it a bit fucking annoying?

BRADLEY: It a bit fucking is.

DEAN: Well I'm a bit fucking busy mate, some of us don't
    waste our time just making shit up.

CHARLIE: Dean, stop, Bradley, don't be so rude.

BRADLEY: I'm being rude? No one invited this dickhead
    anyway and he shows up –

JACK: That's enough.

CHARLIE: I invited him.

BRADLEY: Oh right, sorry, yeah, I forgot, it's your house,
    you're the one being judged by Jack's parents today – no
    wait, they love you.

JACK: Bradley, why are you – ?

BRADLEY: Why are you here Charlie?

CHARLIE: Why? It's Christmas and Jack invited me.

BRADLEY: Yeah? Did Jack invite you or did you invite yourself? Hmm? Wanted to just check out whether his parents treat me like family too? Bring Dean along, show him off to them?

CHARLIE: What the fuck?

BRADLEY: Like 'Bullseye' – 'come and have a look at what you could have won'.

DEAN: This another of your fucking stories mate?

BRADLEY: Not now mate yeah?

DEAN: Should try live in the real world for a change.

BRADLEY: And you should ask your girlfriend if she's still in love with my boyfriend and then see which of us is living in the real world, okay?

CHARLIE: Oh my God.

JACK: Jesus.

DEAN: What the fuck?

BRADLEY: She hadn't told you? No? Oh, all through uni – didn't speak to him for months when he told her he was gay.

CHARLIE: That's the past.

BRADLEY: And you're still here, checking up on him –

CHARLIE: He fucking invited me!

BRADLEY: You didn't have to come!

CHARLIE: I came to support you, both of you!

JACK: Have a crisp and shut *(Doorbell.)* up – / Oh shit, right.

DEAN: / Someone needs to fucking explain this all to me right now.

JACK: Everyone shut up.

    Be quiet. Dean sit there. Bradley, wait over here. Okay.

    Okay.

    Shit.

    Shit.

    Okay.

    He exits.

DEAN: Did you have sex –

CHARLIE: Shut the fuck up Dean.

*

PAUL. He's an Irish secondary school headmaster, tall with glasses and carrying an overnight bag and a bag of presents.

ANNIE. She's wrapped in a coat, hat, scarf and gloves. She is gripping an overnight bag and a Christmas card, and holding a plant.

JACK: Right. Ah. Bradley. This is my Dad Paul.

BRADLEY: It's really nice to meet you at last Paul.

PAUL: Bradley. Let me – I'll put these here.

    Now – nice to meet you. *(Handshake.)* Jaysus, you're taller.

    Than I thought you'd be.

BRADLEY: Oh. Thanks. I don't think I've ever been called tall.

PAUL: Well you've no chance beside Jack. Takes after me.

BRADLEY: Ha I suppose so. Got your hairline too.

PAUL: What?

BRADLEY: Sorry.

JACK: Joke.

PAUL: Oh. Right. Good man.

BRADLEY: Hi Mrs Murray – it's nice to finally meet you.

ANNIE: Hello.

She gives him the plant. No handshake.

BRADLEY: Oh thank you.
Welcome to our home.

JACK: It's good to see you. Both.

PAUL: And you.

JACK: Merry Christmas.

ANNIE: Merry Christmas.

CHARLIE: Annie!

ANNIE: Wow Charlie, that's such a big hug.

CHARLIE: It's GREAT to see you!

ANNIE: And you too, lovely, lovely.

CHARLIE: It's been so long! Ugh! Welcome to London!

ANNIE: Thanks love.

CHARLIE: Hiya Paul! You haven't changed a bit.

PAUL: Only around the waist.

CHARLIE: Not a bit, fit as a fiddle you are!

PAUL: And you're still a terrible oul charmer!

CHARLIE: We northerners are like the Irish – gift of the gab!

DEAN: Hello Mrs Murray.

CHARLIE: Excuse my manners, this is Dean.

ANNIE: Dean. Lovely.

DEAN: Hello. Nice to meet you Mrs Murray, Mr Murray.

PAUL: Call me Paul. Jaysus, the kids at school call me Mr Murray!

DEAN: Paul.

ANNIE: And you're – ?

DEAN: Yep.

ANNIE: Congratulations.

PAUL: You've got a great girl here Dean.

DEAN: Yep.

CHARLIE: Aw Paul!

JACK: Here, give me your coats.

PAUL: Oh thanks, yes. Nice and warm in here.

JACK: Have a sit down, you must be knackered after the journey?

ANNIE: I'm alright, is there somewhere I can – ?

JACK: I can take them.

ANNIE: No it's fine honestly. Give me your Dad's. Upstairs is it?

JACK: Let me take your coat at least.

ANNIE: I'm still cold.

JACK: Well –

okay.

It's up the stairs, straight in front of you. Do you want a drink?

ANNIE: Whatever you have is fine.

ANNIE exits. JACK exits.

BRADLEY: Have a seat there Paul.

PAUL: Oh, you're sure?

BRADLEY: Absolutely.

CHARLIE: No here Paul, pop your bum down next to me.

PAUL: Oh lovely. Great. This is a nice –. Comfy. The sofa. And the room.

CHARLIE: I was saying, isn't it Christmassy Paul?

PAUL: Yes, very. With the tree. And the stockings there – we used to do them for Jack and Darren every year. Annie knitted it. That same stocking. Being Santa.

CHARLIE: Without the belly!

BRADLEY: You're a teacher then Paul?

PAUL: Yes, yep. Thirty-two years at it. Still going strong.

BRADLEY: I teach as well.

PAUL: Oh yes you do.

BRADLEY: I'm trying to be a writer, but I teach too.

PAUL: Yes well – what subject?

BRADLEY: English.

PAUL: Yes of course. Good. How you finding it, okay?

BRADLEY: Lovely yeah.

PAUL: Good.
    Good.

JACK: *(Returning.)* I have a glass of red for you Dad.

PAUL: I'm still off it / with my blood pressure.

JACK: / Oh shit I totally forgot.

PAUL: Language.

JACK: Shit sorry – sorry. I'm sorry. I should have remembered.

PAUL: Never mind.

BRADLEY: It's okay babe.

PAUL: Juice of any kind is great.

JACK: I'll get some orange. *(Exits.)*

CHARLIE: Don't know how you manage without, Paul.

PAUL: No choice love, sadly.

CHARLIE: That's just too bad. I'll have it for you. Did you have a nice flight?

PAUL: Yes lovely yes. It's only a short hop over.

CHARLIE: Yeah. God it's ages since I've been to Ireland. I miss it. I mean Dean's been over a couple times in the last while but – God I don't know when I was over last. I'm so jealous of you, living there.

PAUL: You're always welcome to visit, you know you are.

CHARLIE: I'll hold you to that now, be careful! You'll have me showing up on the doorstep demanding a stew and a bed!

PAUL: Any time.

JACK re-enters.

PAUL: Right.
Oh thanks son.
You should have a seat.

JACK: I'm okay.

PAUL: I'd not been here. It's nice.

JACK: Thanks.

PAUL: Two bedrooms?

JACK: Upstairs yeah.

PAUL: Lovely.

DEAN: Tough to find good places round here.

PAUL: What's that?

CHARLIE: Dean's an estate agent Paul.

PAUL: Right. Did you help them find it?

DEAN: No.

PAUL: Right.

—

Is there a loo, son?

JACK: Oh, yeah. Use the one upstairs. Second left.

PAUL: Great. Thanks. *(Exits.)*

Silence.

DEAN: Well this is fucking cosy. *(Resumes texting.)*

Silence. Almost.

JACK: Shit. The food. *(Exits.)*

Silence. Almost. Still the tapping of DEAN's phone keys.

CHARLIE: Fuck's sake Dean!

PAUL and ANNIE re-enter. She is still in her coat.

BRADLEY: So, you got here okay? I mean the house. Obviously, you're here now but it was okay? Was it?

PAUL: It wasn't too bad, was it love? A lot of people around the airport of course, and the roads were getting busy but I think we were going the right direction. Everyone else was heading the other way. Though it was just starting to snow as we got here.

CHARLIE: We'll have to deal with that. Or Dean will. Lucky bugger.

DEAN: Cheers thanks.

ANNIE: You're not staying?

CHARLIE: We're heading to my Dad's after dinner.

PAUL: That's good. It's nice to be around family at Christmas.

JACK re-enters.

CHARLIE: Yeah. It'll be nice for him to have Dean there too. Plenty of football talk. Some beers and a war film. I mean it'll make a change from trying to guess the punchlines to cracker jokes with me. Nice to have a man around.

BRADLEY: Here you go Paul, tuck in.

PAUL: Thanks uh Bradley. That's grand.

BRADLEY: Cocktail sausages, samosas, sausage rolls – Annie?

ANNIE: No thank you.

CHARLIE: Oo that looks FAB.

DEAN: Pass it this way.

BRADLEY: Don't eat too many.
I think we're going to eat soon.
Right Jack?

JACK: Yeah.

PAUL: How's work?

JACK: What?

PAUL: Work.

JACK: Oh it's okay. Quiet this time of year, no one's getting married or whatever.
But we sold a good few gift vouchers for studio sessions so. Hopefully in the new year.

PAUL: Is that one of yours?

JACK: Yeah, self-portrait. Took it for our third anniversary.

PAUL: It's a nice one. Have you seen that one?
Annie?

ANNIE: Oh. Yes. No I hadn't.

CHARLIE: It's GORGEOUS. You look so cute together. Both of you. Don't they? Don't they look so happy together?

PAUL: Oh yes.

CHARLIE: They look lovely together I think. Jack will have to do a nice one of Dean and me, don't you think Annie? A friendly freebie. We can send you a copy. For the mantelpiece.

ANNIE: Thank you love, that would be very sweet. You make a lovely pair.

CHARLIE: Where's your camera? You should be getting some of us all together.

JACK: Maybe in a bit.
That's yours Mam.

ANNIE: Is it wine?

JACK: Yes.

ANNIE: Right.

JACK: Is that okay?

ANNIE: Yes, yes it's fine.

JACK: You're sure?

ANNIE: Yes.

PAUL: She's still allowed it.

BRADLEY: You're sure you wouldn't like something to nibble?

ANNIE: I'm fine thank you.

PAUL: You're sure?

ANNIE: Yes. Thank you. I'll have something in a while.

JACK: I've made shepherd's pie.

ANNIE: Lovely.

CHARLIE: I bet it won't be as good as yours Annie.

ANNIE: Thank you Charlie, I'm sure it will be nice.

CHARLIE: Once I had eaten your food Annie, anything else is a pale imitation.

ANNIE: You're too kind.

JACK: Oh Mam, here.

ANNIE: What's that?

JACK: Darren's decoration.

ANNIE: Oh.

JACK: And my one.

CHARLIE: Oh they're cute.

ANNIE: I didn't know you had them.
I thought I'd lost them.
You should have told me you had them.

JACK: Why?

ANNIE: I didn't know where they were.

JACK: I had them.

ANNIE: Since when?

JACK: Last Christmas.

ANNIE: You should have asked.

JACK: I just wanted to – I've always put them up so.

PAUL: It's okay, at least we know now.

ANNIE: Still.

JACK: Sorry.

ANNIE: You can't just take things.

JACK: It was – right. Sorry. Yes.

ANNIE: Never mind.

CHARLIE: What are they?

DEAN: Char –

PAUL: The boys made them when they were younger.

CHARLIE: That's nice.

JACK: Can we hang them up? Mam. You and me.

ANNIE: It's fine, you do it.

JACK: I want you to.

ANNIE: Honestly, I just want to sit down.

JACK: I waited til you got here.

–

Here.

ANNIE: Where do you want me to put it?

JACK: Just there, I'll put mine here.

PAUL: Lovely.

JACK: Thanks Mam. Merry Christmas.

ANNIE: Yes.

BRADLEY: I wore a collar specially, Mrs Murray.

ANNIE: Oh.

BRADLEY: Yes.

Jack told me about when he cut, when, or that you liked the boys to dress properly so I thought I better make sure I had one. Don't want to be grounded.

ANNIE: Right.

JACK: Always made us wear collars, didn't you Mam?

PAUL: Oh God she did – sure she still makes me wear one. I wasn't allowed on the plane without scrubbing up properly.

CHARLIE: You scrub up well Paul, let's be honest.

DEAN: Charlie.

CHARLIE: I mean he could be a model Annie, for Marks or someone.

PAUL: Don't be daft. Annie's sister did some modelling for a bit in her day – proper swimsuits, the whole shebang. Though I always said Annie would have worn them better.

JACK: Ew, Dad.

ANNIE: Paul, honestly.

PAUL: What?

ANNIE: Could we change the subject please?

PAUL: So yes, this is a grand place. You've done well.

JACK: Thanks. We got a good deal on the mortgage – and it's a good area.

PAUL: Right.

JACK: Bradley's new school is only fifteen minutes by bus, and we've the tube station just on the main road too. So yeah. Six months in anyway, everything's grand.

PAUL: Right.

ANNIE: Who are your neighbours?

JACK: What Mam?

ANNIE: I said who are your neighbours?

BRADLEY: There's a young couple with a baby to the left – the Ramsays – they're nice, we see them a lot. It's an older man on the other side, he's a bit.

JACK: We don't think he likes us very much.

PAUL: Why doesn't he like you?

BRADLEY: Well. You know.

–

We're young people.

–

DEAN: There building going on next door?

BRADLEY: In his place.

DEAN: What's he doing?

BRADLEY: We don't really know.

DEAN: Probably subsidence, looks like it. You've got it too at the back.

BRADLEY: Do we?

PAUL: You'll want to get that looked at.

DEAN: Some idiots don't bother til it's too late Paul.

ANNIE: You can't leave that to chance Jack. You need to sort out stuff like that. You probably know someone, do you Dean?

DEAN: Sure.

BRADLEY: Well, the scaffolding's been up for weeks.
But it's fine. Well, the banging and the drilling can be a bit distracting. It's annoying if we want a nice lazy lie-in, isn't it?

–

DEAN's phone rings.

He takes it and exits.

CHARLIE: How long are you over for then guys?

PAUL: Well our flight back is the evening of the 28th. My sister Margaret lives in Putney so we'll get down to her too.

CHARLIE: Oh yes! I've met Margaret! She's the spitting image of you, isn't she?

PAUL: I'm sure she wouldn't be too happy to hear you say that.

CHARLIE: Oh now you be nice to yourself!
They are though, aren't they? Alike.
Aren't they Annie?

ANNIE: Paul and Margaret? Yes very alike.

PAUL: The stockings – if we're – while I see them there. I mean, tradition and all, / can't be forgetting them.

ANNIE: / That's not Darren's stocking too is it?

JACK: No. Mine. Bradley has his own.
You can do them later Dad.

PAUL: Not at all, I'm sure Charlie wants to see me being Santa.

CHARLIE: Absolutely.

PAUL: An orange in the bottom. Bag of sweets – he was a mad sweet tooth when he was young. Pair of socks – Christmas wouldn't be the same without them. A pencil. I found this little pig stress-ball in the pound shop – you'd know better than anyone Charlie, he's a worrier. And this wee torch too, just thought it was handy to have – and he was scared of the dark as a kid.

JACK: Dad.

PAUL: Batteries not included so I bought some to go with it.
And a nice shiny coin.

JACK: Thanks Dad.

PAUL: You have pretty much the same Bradley, sorry.

BRADLEY: No that's great, thanks. Really thoughtful.

CHARLIE: We left our present for you under the tree.

ANNIE: Thank you, you didn't need to do that.

CHARLIE: Rubbish! Couldn't forget the Murrays! Now it's nothing exciting, whiskey – the boys are only getting wine of course, but I thought I'd splash out on something a bit nicer for you.

ANNIE: Paul, did you give her ours –

PAUL: / No, hang on.

CHARLIE: / You shouldn't have.

ANNIE: / I'm sorry I didn't know about –

CHARLIE: Dean.

ANNIE: Dean. He seems a grand fellow.

CHARLIE: Oh he is – oh that looks BEAUTIFUL – I'd nearly be happy with just the wrapping paper! And the little ribbons! – Wow, I'm very touched. Here, give it here, I like to give it a good shake –

BRADLEY: I do that too.

CHARLIE: It's pretty quiet, is it clothes no don't tell me, I'll save it for tomorrow. I'll put it on the doormat right in front of the door so I'll remember to take it with us when we go. Don't want to forget – this is the first pressie I'm opening tomorrow morning! Cheers, ta so much. You're the best – kiss? and kiss. Oo, I'm SO glad I get to see you both. Thanks a million.

ANNIE: Don't mention it, it's just a little thing.

CHARLIE: It's the thought that counts though Annie, isn't it though? Little gestures mean so much. To my Irish family – CHEERS! Merry Christmas.

ANNIE: Merry Christmas.

PAUL: Cheers.

CHARLIE: *(Spilling wine on the carpet.)* Shit sorry.

BRADLEY: Woops.

JACK: Move move, don't step in it.

CHARLIE: Sorry Jack.

JACK: It's fine.

ANNIE: Don't rub it, dab it.

PAUL: Can I – ?

JACK: No. Bradley can you get the kitchen-paper and the Vanish? Under the sink.

BRADLEY exits.

ANNIE: You just want to soak it up.

JACK: I know.

ANNIE: Don't rub it.

CHARLIE: I'm sorry Jack I'm a twat.

ANNIE: Here, let me.

JACK: It's fine Mam.

ANNIE: No look, move and I'll pour some of this on it. *(Pours her white wine onto it.)*

JACK: What are you / doing?

ANNIE: It helps. Just dab it, stop rubbing it.

JACK: How does it help? I'm not rubbing it.

BRADLEY re-enters.

ANNIE: It just helps. Do you have salt?

CHARLIE: Oh your lovely carpet.

DEAN re-enters.

JACK: We have Vanish Mam.

DEAN: What happened?

ANNIE: Salt is really good for red wine.

CHARLIE: I spilt wine.

JACK: The Vanish – careful Brad – it'll do well enough.

DEAN: Fuck's sake Char.

PAUL: Did it go anywhere else?

CHARLIE: It was an accident.

BRADLEY: I think that's it.

DEAN: Still, enough.

ANNIE: There's a spot there.

PAUL: Mind your step everyone.

CHARLIE: It just splashed Jack.

JACK: Honestly it's fine.

ANNIE: I'll get that bit, give me the towel.

JACK: Leave it.

ANNIE: Honestly –

JACK: No –

ANNIE: Let me do it.

JACK: I can do it myself.

ANNIE: Jack –

JACK: Seriously Mam, fuck off.

Silence.

PAUL: Jack. Apologise.

JACK: Sorry.

ANNIE: Honest to God –

CHARLIE: Guys I'm sorry it was my fault.

PAUL: It wasn't.

CHARLIE: No, I feel awful.

DEAN: Seriously –

CHARLIE: It just splashed.

DEAN: Charlie stop talking.

ANNIE: Can we forget it now?

PAUL: Good idea.
   Can we – did you say there was food?

BRADLEY: Oh yeah, is that pie ready to go, do you think Jack?

JACK: It should be.

BRADLEY: Well why don't we head inside and eat?

CHARLIE: Are we not – ?

BRADLEY: No, kitchen. There's a bit more room inside.
   Alright?

DEAN: I think we should head – before it gets late.

BRADLEY: That's a fair point.

PAUL: Not a bit of it, you'll have to eat.

CHARLIE: Exactly. I'm starving. You come with me now Paul.

PAUL: Right.

   CHARLIE, PAUL and DEAN exit. BRADLEY exits.

JACK: Are you not too warm now Mam?

ANNIE: No.

JACK: In that jacket.

ANNIE: No.

JACK: Are you going to be like this all week?

ANNIE: What?

JACK: Are you going to sit hid away in corners with your lips
all – all – thin and trying to ignore – everything?
Because Charlie and Dean are going after dinner. It'll just
be the four of us.

ANNIE: I know that.

JACK: So are you just going to keep acting like this is the worst
situation you could possibly be in in the whole world?
Or will you at least pretend you don't mind staying with
your son and his boyfriend.

ANNIE: I don't –
That's hardly fair.

JACK: What's not fair? It's what you've done so far.

ANNIE: If this is how you're going to treat me –

JACK: How I treat you?
What about you? You're acting like we don't exist.

ANNIE: It's –

JACK: You're more interested in cleaning the bloody carpet
than in the / man I love.

ANNIE: / I'm just trying –

JACK: You've paid more attention to Charlie and to HER
boyfriend than you have to your own son and his.
You even said his name. You've never used Bradley's
name.
How do you think that makes me feel?

ANNIE: You said – you said you wanted us to come spend
Christmas with you, so we did. I'm here.

JACK: Yes, spend Christmas with us, spend, not – fucking – freeze us to death. I had to drag you out of that chair to hang up a fucking decoration your sons made for you. Look at you – you're not even here yet, you're still in your bloody coat, all wrapped up, all set to just go.

BRADLEY and PAUL enter.

ANNIE: You don't need to swear.
You never used to swear.

JACK: –

BRADLEY: Babe.

PAUL: Come on the both of you, let's have some food.

JACK: Ask me how I am.

ANNIE: What?

PAUL: Come on Jack.

JACK: Ask me.

ANNIE: What do you mean?

JACK: ASK ME: HOW ARE YOU?

ANNIE: Don't shout at me.

JACK: You haven't asked. You haven't asked me How I Am. How I'm Feeling. Nothing. You haven't engaged, you you you don't want / to know.

ANNIE: / Jack –

JACK: It's the same if I phone you – nothing, nothing beyond 'what have you been up to, what will you be doing'. Nothing emotional. Nothing unp – God forbid nothing UNpredictable. The less you know the less you have to – to even – Do you talk to your friends about me? Do they ask you how I'm doing? It drives you mad – but you probably don't, right? Move on, change the subject – switch lanes. Just avoid it.

ANNIE: I'm here aren't I?

JACK: Same old story – not talking about it makes it not exist, yeah.

ANNIE: Don't you dare –

JACK: Yet here I am. You're burying your head and it's, it's, it's cowardly. We're too fucking scared in this family. If you, if one of us had been brave enough to talk about ourselves four years ago, Darren / might –

ANNIE: / Ah Jesus, why –

JACK: Darren might still be alive.

PAUL: Jack.

Silence.

ANNIE: –

Why did you have to go and say that?

PAUL: That's out of line.

JACK: Well you didn't – no one wanted to talk about it – no one ever talks about problems do they?

ANNIE: If you want to – ask me how I am then?

JACK: Clearly fucking miserable.

PAUL: Christ –

ANNIE: Can you blame me?

JACK: I just want you to look at us and talk to us like we're not total fucking strangers.

ANNIE: Stop swearing at me!

Don't speak to me like that – I am your mother. Whether you like it or not.

And I did everything for you and your brother. Don't suggest –

Don't you ever think – do you think I've not had those
same thoughts? Do you not think I blame – every day?
Your Dad and I have spent the last four years wondering
just what we did wrong. What did we not do well enough
to make him happy or secure?

JACK: You should have talked and listened more.

ANNIE: DON'T TELL ME WHAT I SHOULD HAVE
DONE!

Don't you dare. Don't you dare. Don't you ever dare.
There's no right answer and that's the worst part of it.
How do you talk about things like that? How were we – I
mean we never knew, no one thought that would happen.
I didn't –
I was brought up a certain way and
and when you think your life, the life you have – is going
one way and then it doesn't, it's
bloody
hard.
When you and Darren were little boys –
this – this isn't what I saw –

JACK: It's what is though.

ANNIE: That doesn't make it any easier.

JACK: You have to face up to things / Mam, that's the only
way –

ANNIE: / I face them every day!
I know what people think when they see me and they talk
about me. It's awful.

JACK: Try being gay Mam.

PAUL: Don't be so flippant.

ANNIE: You ran away.

269

JACK: I couldn't stay there. I couldn't just be stuck at home
– where we JUST COULDN'T talk about things. In that,
that scared repressed half-life I'd been living.

ANNIE: Stop.

JACK: I died four years ago too and thank God I went to
Heaven – to my English Heaven.

ANNIE: You left us.

JACK: Of course I did – I'm in Heaven here. In this house, in
this country, with my Bradley.
He welcomed me with open arms. He said yes, from the
start. So why would I go back? This is my home now.
All I wanted was for you to come here and see it and be
happy for me.

PAUL: Can we please come and sit down and eat as a family?

ANNIE: How can I be happy?

JACK: What do you mean?

ANNIE: You just left almost as soon as Darren was buried.
You told us you were gay and you went off to London and
suddenly my house was empty. Both my sons were – . You
acted like you were the only person who –
lost.

JACK: I couldn't stay.

ANNIE: Why not? You didn't have open arms in Ireland?
We were still there. You ran away just when we needed
you. Not just away but far away. When we needed you.
And I needed you to need me. For a while.

JACK: I do need you – I need you to be okay with this.

ANNIE: You yell and and – and abuse me and blame me for
not – how? How could I? That was my whole life – from
under me – in a month. How could I be okay with it?

JACK: You've had four years!

ANNIE: You can't put a time limit on me! You can't – I can't
flick a switch.

I tried to do my best with you both.

JACK: I need you to try harder.

Silence.

JACK: Bradley.

BRADLEY: Yes?

JACK: Will you marry me?

BRADLEY: What?

ANNIE: Jesus.

JACK: I love you. Will you marry me?

PAUL: Son –

BRADLEY: Why?

JACK: What?

BRADLEY: Why?

JACK: Because I love you.

BRADLEY: Why are you asking now?

JACK: Because I want to marry you.

BRADLEY: Really?

JACK: Yes.

BRADLEY: No.

JACK: What do you mean?

BRADLEY: You're not asking because you want to, /

JACK: / I am

BRADLEY: you're asking because they're here.

JACK: No I'm not.

BRADLEY: You are. And I'm not – Christ – fuck – I'm not a fucking prop Jack. / Sorry.

JACK: / Bradley –

BRADLEY: You can't just use me to make a point. How dare you – of all the – *(Exits)*
(Offstage.) – Why the fuck are you still here!? *(Back door slams.)*

ANNIE: You're just like your brother.

JACK: I'm just what?

ANNIE: Both of you, hotheads – rushing into things. Why can't you just slow down?

JACK: There's no time.

ANNIE: I think it would be best if we went to Margaret's –

PAUL: Annie.

ANNIE: I'm going to the car.
Some of us can't run Jack. Some of us have to walk.

ANNIE exits.

PAUL: Christ almighty Jack, what are you at?

JACK: She's burying her head –

PAUL: What in the name of God are you thinking?

JACK: What is she thinking?

PAUL: Now lookit.
Whatever about her. What on Earth – Jack.
What are you doing?

JACK: I don't know.

PAUL: Excuse my language but are you trying to piss everyone off?

Cos it looks like it.

My son is smart and meticulous and you have been neither of those things tonight.

JACK: I know.

PAUL: Proposing? I mean –

what? What sort of flippin' head-case are you?

She's barely arrived and you've turned her world upside down and shook it for good measure.

And putting Bradley on the spot like that?

You can't do that to people.

JACK: I was –

PAUL: I love your Mam to bits.

I'm annoyed with her for being – well she was being rude.

And I asked her to – to talk to you and to give you and Bradley a chance.

JACK: Well / she

PAUL: / Now. Wait.

You had to give her a chance too.

You shouldn't have – I know it's –

it's not easy.

Don't ever speak to her like that. Or to anyone. That's not who you are or who we raised you to be. We're doing our best. That's not your best.

Barreling into things, head down. Like a bull in a china shop. Or like your brother. He was always the hothead.

You think we don't – I mean I could have thumped you.

When your Mam brought me home to meet her parents for the first time, your gran didn't think I was up to much. I had long hair for a start – hard as that may be to believe. And I was in a band and I had a motorbike. I was not what she was hoping for. And after I left she told your Mam as much. And your Mam said, 'I know what I'm doing. So butt out.'

And when you told me you were gay, yes I was a bit surprised. And a bit disappointed, I'll admit. And then when you told me you'd met Bradley – do you know what? The thing I most worried about wasn't that he was a man. It was whether he was the right person for you. But I remembered what your Mam told your gran. So I butted out.

But I'm butting back in for a second to tell you this – if you want us to trust you to know what you're doing, do it right. Alright?

She needs – your Mam – she. Right. No one likes to be pushed.

And I've been trying to talk to her and – you're not the only one – it's.

It's hard. Right? Yeah?

I've told her. And we've argued about it. We've had a lot of – and there are nights I can't – sleep – or whatever. And I'll go lie down in your room. Or in Darren's. And it's. Yeah.

JACK: Dad.

PAUL: Seriously. It's. Yeah, fine. It's fine. It is what it is.
You'd know all this if you called more.

–

Look – we'll, we'll go and stay with your Aunty Margaret tonight.

JACK: Right.

PAUL: You can talk to me you know? I'm your Dad. And a teacher. Sometimes I know stuff.
Check that stocking – stress-ball. Because I know what you're like.
Pound coin. Sterling. Because I know this is your home now.
And a torch. Because you still don't know where you're going, apparently.

JACK: I'm sorry.

PAUL: We haven't made it easier.
But you shouldn't have just run away.
We've got more time than we think.

JACK: Yeah.

PAUL: Right. Good.
Are our bags – ?

JACK: I'll get them.

Exits upstairs.

PAUL alone.

PAUL sees ANNIE's card. Reads it.

JACK re-enters.

PAUL: Read that.

JACK: 'Darling Jack and Bradley, merry Christmas, with love, Mam'.
I'm a dick.

PAUL: Last plate in the china shop.
And language. She's right, you never used to swear.
I'll call you tomorrow.
Let me know – yeah.
Merry Christmas son.

JACK: Merry Christmas Dad.

PAUL exits.

JACK alone

CHARLIE and DEAN at the door. JACK sees them.

CHARLIE: Jack, we'll
we're going to –
Dean.

DEAN exits.

CHARLIE: Look I'm sorry – I don't even know but – cos I love you – both actually. Don't fucking – you know – don't – go – fucking it up. Even if I tried to – and I'm sorry. She's your mum and – and Bradley is –

DEAN: *(Offstage.)* Charlie.

CHARLIE: Fucking wait.

   –

Fix it.

CHARLIE exits.

JACK alone.

*

A bench in a London park. It is spring. Four years before.

BRADLEY: She sighed with relief because finally she was certain about the one thing she had never been certain about: She had been right all along.

What? God I'm sorry, it's not that bad is it?

JACK: No.

BRADLEY: Then why are you crying?

Oh fuck, have I broken you?

JACK: –

My brother killed himself last month. I told my parents I was gay last week. I moved here on Saturday and I am living with three people I don't know in a flat I hate – I thought I had a plan –

– and now I have literally no idea what I'm doing. I have no idea where I'm going. I want to be something but I have no idea what that is or where I can go to be the thing so if you have any hints please fucking tell me because. I am fucking lost.

BRADLEY: Wow.

> That's.
>
> A lot of things.
>
> In one. Chunk. To process.
>
> I've. I don't think anyone has ever – I mean. Whew.

JACK: Sorry.

BRADLEY: Don't be.

JACK: You're the first person I've talked to in four days.

BRADLEY: Well yeah. I feel – honoured. Really.

> That's – what you've – that stuff is precious.

JACK: It's yours. Have it.

BRADLEY: I. Well.

> Look.
>
> If it makes you feel any better – though why would it – anyway –
>
> I just got dumped.
>
> I've also had to move back in with my parents.
>
> And – look – my notebook is empty.
>
> So I don't really know where I'm going either. Or what I want to be when I get there. But it sounds like you're heading the same way. It could be fun to go there. Together. For a bit.

JACK: Yeah.

> That could be good.

BRADLEY: Drink?

JACK: Christ yes.

BRADLEY: Cigarette?

JACK: I don't.

*

JACK and BRADLEY's house. Four years after. JACK still as before.

BRADLEY enters smoking.

BRADLEY: I hide them in a flower-pot.

JACK: Oh.

Clever.

BRADLEY: Not really.

Silence.

BRADLEY: Your Dad was nice.

JACK: I'm sorry.

BRADLEY: You should be.

JACK: I am.

BRADLEY: You bloody – fucking – bloody should be.

Was that spontaneous?

JACK: I'd planned to – it was meant to happen tomorrow.

After dinner.

BRADLEY: And were you going to propose to me because it

was the right time to propose to me or were you going to

propose to me because your parents were here?

JACK: It's the same.

BRADLEY: No it's not.

That – of all ways – was the single worst possible way you

could have asked me that question.

JACK: I thought it was –

BRADLEY: I would never say yes to a proposal that was meant

as a – gesture to somebody else.

JACK: Bradley –

BRADLEY: Never in a million years. I told you, I'm not a prop.
Or a weapon in a war. Your parents don't need shock
therapy.

JACK: That wasn't why –

BRADLEY: You say that – you might even think that, but it is
why.
You pulled a stunt. With me as your, your plant.
No way. No fucking way. Don't ever do that again.

JACK: I just want us to be together –
and I want us to be happy –
and them to see and accept that. We're happy.

BRADLEY: Jesus Jack – serious?
Okay. Listen right.
I'm going to tell you something you need to get your head
around.
You don't need your parents – or anyone else – to think
you're happy just to make it true.

JACK: It's easy for you, your parents are fine.

BRADLEY: Would you rather I'd had a harder time coming
out? You think I've had it easy?

JACK: You haven't had it as tough as this.

BRADLEY: Fuck off Jack. You're not special. Not in that way.
My parents didn't like my first boyfriend and I desperately
wanted them to, but I got tired of feeling sorry for myself.
So I just got on with it.
You want her to see us as normal – you just need to – be
normal.
I mean – I was here too. It's not like it was just you. On
show.

JACK: She didn't give you a chance –

BRADLEY: You didn't give her the space to. You don't –
sometimes –

JACK: What?

BRADLEY: You want things too fucking much.

You fucking grab things. And hug them too hard.

It's – I mean. It's like trying to breathe in a smoke-filled room, it's suffocating – I could murder you and claim self-defence, seriously. And I think, fuck me it would be so much easier not to be with you, with your family and your friends and your fucking aeroplane-load of baggage. You're not a bluebottle you're a fucking mosquito – nnnnggggg – stuck in my brain and you can't keep your worry to yourself, you pass it on like bloody malaria. Having to care for you is so – Jesus, it's never-ending. – you go on and on and on. You! Everything has to be just – massive. You can just Be Everywhere. And there there's suddenly no space anymore – I can't exist because there's so much YOU.

I just want there to be – nothing. For – for for however long. Just: *(Breaths)* huh – huh –huhhhh.

You know? That.

Quiet. White and quiet and empty of anything, except me – and a a vast, endless Nothing Else.

I need – to be 3D – 4D. Space and time.

JACK: I – I mean – now? Everything we have with each other and the house and – the bits of the jigsaw – coming together.

BRADLEY: Yeah. But you can't cut the last bits up to try make them fit into place.

JACK: –

    I'm such a dick.

    I've ruined –

    I fucked it with – and I treated you like –

    –

    Break up with me.

BRADLEY: I thought I did.

    That's where I went.

JACK: So why are you here?

BRADLEY: It's cold outside.

    Silence. Lots of it.

    JACK starts to tidy the room.

    BRADLEY helps.

    They sit. JACK's head on BRADLEY's lap, crying quietly.

BRADLEY: Honestly. I know – I don't know what alternative there is.

    You can't sit still or calm down or let go. And it's infuriating and you – buzz buzz fucking buzz – drive me mad. You've proved it Jack – no one else could love me as hard as you do. You don't need to try any harder. You silly prick.

    If there's one person I would want to drown me, or who I would want, holding my head under water, you know – squeezing the life out of me – well it's you.

    It's you.

    Silence.

JACK: I'm sorry.

BRADLEY: I know.

JACK: I'm sorry I'm killing you.

BRADLEY: There are worse ways to die.

More silence. BRADLEY stands. He throws a blanket onto the table and stands on it.

BRADLEY: Let's get out of here.

JACK: What – ?

BRADLEY: Magic carpet.

JACK: Are you mental?

BRADLEY: Come on princess.
 I'll take off without you.

JACK: –
 Alright Aladdin. *(Climbs on.)*

BRADLEY: Hold on tight.
 Okay.
 Here.
 We.
 Go.

They take off.

Up up up between a streetlamp and a tree up into the sky snow streaking white, a broken TV of static, as evening falls past us drowning the day. We fly over London, spiral round Nelson's Column, wave to Big Ben, in and out of the London Eye and then up up higher higher until the city is just a sprawl of distant lights beneath us and England is a vast dark body with roads for veins and cities for organs and it all breathes deeply in a sleep with no more dreams because we've taken them all.
 Where to now, princess? Ireland?

JACK: No. Not Ireland.

BRADLEY: Where then?

JACK: Somewhere
 new.

Somewhere new and wonderful. Somewhere we'll visit
together some day.

BRADLEY: Right-o.
We head south

JACK: towards Kent

BRADLEY: towards the Channel Islands

JACK: towards the equator!

BRADLEY: Over France

JACK: Bonjour!

BRADLEY: over Spain

JACK: Hola!

BRADLEY: over Morocco

JACK: Hi Morocco!

BRADLEY: onwards south, across the desert and out into the
Atlantic ocean.

JACK: Can we drop down?

BRADLEY: Yes! Swoop!

JACK: Just above the surface,

BRADLEY: the ocean is dark and the waves are crashing

JACK: and we can reach our hands down into the water

BRADLEY: splashing cool and silver

JACK: and our hands make rippling Vs behind us as we fly!

BRADLEY: A school of dolphins leap past us.

JACK: It's getting warmer and warmer

BRADLEY: Tropical!

JACK: and the moon is glistening on the ocean

BRADLEY: water-diamonds!

JACK: water-diamonds!

BRADLEY: and on the horizon an island appears.

JACK: Is it a desert island?

BRADLEY: Yes. It's the sort of island a child would draw

JACK: with a hump of yellow sand

BRADLEY: and a lone palm tree

JACK: a single rock

BRADLEY: a mountain

JACK: a volcano!

BRADLEY: and a jungle covering its slopes

JACK: and a thin plume of smoke piping from its crater

BRADLEY: We're hovering just over the beach now

JACK: we can grab the sand and let it run through our fingers

BRADLEY: It's moonlit and quiet and warm. Like the air is hugging us.

JACK: Bradley – is this our island?

BRADLEY: This, Jack, is our island.

JACK: –
    It's quiet.

BRADLEY: Just the sound of the waves on the shore.

JACK: Shall we explore?

BRADLEY: No. Not in the dark. It's Christmas Eve.

JACK: Santa's going to deliver to our island!

BRADLEY: He bloody well is. So we better get into bed.

JACK: Where is it?

BRADLEY: The carpet floats over to the palm tree and – oh, we need two palm trees –

JACK: They're right there!

BRADLEY: the carpet floats in between the two trees and ties its corners up around the two trunks and we are in a magic-carpet-hammock, sleeping under the stars on our tropical island.

Silence.

JACK: I really do / –

BRADLEY: / Yeah. I know.
Open your present.

JACK unwraps a little stuffed Martian.

JACK: You are – just – bloody – beautiful.

BRADLEY: Irresistible.

JACK: And you are kind. And funny. And careless. Which I love.

BRADLEY: Yeah?

JACK: It all reminds me of – us. Together.

BRADLEY: Yeah.

JACK: Open yours.

BRADLEY pulls out a small ring box from his oversized present box.

JACK: I got you two presents.
The second was going to be the question I asked when you opened the first. But. I have to save it for the right moment.

BRADLEY: –
Idiot.

JACK: Twat.

BRADLEY: Loser.

JACK: Dickhead.

BRADLEY: Feckin' eeeeejjjiiittttt!

JACK: Racist.

BRADLEY: Boyfriend.

JACK: Fiancé.

BRADLEY:

–

END

HALF LIGHT

BY MOLLIE MOLUMBY

IN COLLABORATION WITH RICHARD DURNING,
MARTHA GRANT, KERILL KELLY, CAMILLE OSWALD
AND COLM SUMMERS

MUSIC AND LYRICS BY FIONN FOLEY

Half Light by Mollie Molumby in collaboration with Richard Durning, Martha Grant, Kerill Kelly, Camille Oswald and Colm Summers. Devised with Ursula McGinn and Tilly Taylor. With special thanks to contributors Catherine Bell, Juliette Crosbie, Fionn Foley, Catriona Moloney and Briony Morgan. Music and lyrics by Fionn Foley.

Half Light was first developed with the support of Trinity College Drama Department and performed in the Samuel Beckett Theatre, 17-19 February 2016.

ROBIN – Colm Summers

GUITAR MAN – Richard Durning

INNKEEPER – Martha Grant

CROW – Camille Oswald

HERBERT – Kerill Kelly

Half Light was further developed and premiered at The New Theatre as part of Dublin Fringe Festival, 12-17 September 2016.

ROBIN – Fionn Foley

GUITAR MAN – Richard Durning

INNKEEPER – Martha Grant

CROW – Juliette Crosbie

HERBERT – Kerill Kelly

Directed by Mollie Molumby

Set and Costume Design by Ursula McGinn

Lighting Design by Ellen Gorman

Stage Managed by Tilly Taylor and Catriona Moloney

Production Managed by Dara Ó Cairbre

Music Composed by Fionn Foley

Sound Design by Richard Durning

Props Managed by Luke Casserly

Dramaturgy by Briony Morgan
(Samuel Beckett Centre Production)

Produced by Mark Ball and Iannis Barron
(Samuel Beckett Centre Production)

Jimmy Kavanagh and Michael Stone
(The New Theatre Production)

Pine Trees and folk music. A band station where CROW, HERBERT, GUITAR MAN and INNKEEPER sit on logs playing music. ROBIN hides behind a tree, wearing pyjamas and a woolly hat.

The house lights go down. ROBIN walks out.

ROBIN: Hi … hello, how's everyone doing tonight? Is everyone well? Yeah? Very cool. Me too. Welcome to the show. Thank you for coming. We're really excited to get going. Let me introduce you to the band. We've got Innkeeper on the flute. Herbert on the piano. Crow on percussion. And Guitar Man on the guitar.

So, what we really wanted to do here tonight, with this show, is to take you on a journey. It started off as an emotional journey, like "an experience." A voyage from one state to another. But somewhere along the way we… that got a little convoluted.

So today we're gonna take you on an actual journey. Up a mountain. But in your minds. Or at least we're going to try to do that…

It's a story about a boy. A true story. This may sound far-fetched at times, but we'll need you to believe us when we say that it is true: as true as it is untrue. Or as untrue as it is true. Simultaneously fact and fiction. For the purposes of this, we're going to need you to really imagine it. To visualise. To *see* with your eyes, *without using your eyes.*

Do you understand? Great! Ok. So here's the story-

But first, every good story needs a good beginning. And every good beginning needs music.

Music.

Okay, imagine this: You're walking. You are walking through a forest of pine trees. You're trying to find your Dad. To save your Dad. He's been taken by a monster. You're walking uphill. This forest is on a mountain. And it's his Birthday.

And you are walking. You're walking up this hill towards the monster and your Dad. And it's cold! It's really cold, and the wind is blowing into your face and your eyes are watering from the wind and it's so chilly that there are tears running down your face and they freeze as they run along your face and turn into icicles and these icicles get absorbed into your eyes and they freeze and explode. Explode into tiny pieces of tiny eyeball –

GUITAR MAN: Wait, wait, wait, wait. Calm down. You're getting very caught up in the emotional detail. I mean, you're very involved. Are you sure we shouldn't start at the beginning?

INNKEEPER: Yeah, I mean you just sort of jumped in. We have to create the world, you know? We should tell them where the boy was before this.

CROW: This might be a bit confusing.

HERBERT: You've skipped way ahead.

ROBIN: Fine, guys. Fine.

ROBIN starts to leave stage.

CROW: Yeah, take ten.

GUITAR MAN: No worries, man.

HERBERT: Yeah we got this.

INNKEEPER: You did really good.

ROBIN sits in auditorium and watches the following.

GUITAR MAN: So this is how it happened.

INNKEEPER: Let us paint the picture for you.

CROW: You are a young boy. Ten. Ten or ten and a half. And your name is Robin.

HERBERT: You live in a cosy house on a quiet street, in a quaint village next to a dark and scary forest. You live with your parents.

GUITAR MAN: Your mum and your dad. You are a happy kid. Very. As children tend to be.

CROW: You have won the creative writing competition in class two years in a row. Your 'Bert the Frog's Goes Camping' was described as a delight.

HERBERT: You have also written three academic papers, including 'What makes a hero? Counter Culture and the Lone Ranger in Adventure Films of the Mid 1980s.'

GUITAR MAN: You are a clever kid. A writer and illustrator just like your Dad.

CROW: Your Dad writes children's books.

INNKEEPER: He used to work for a successful company for children's literature but he lost his job. Financial crisis. Circa 2008. He doesn't have an office anymore so he writes and illustrates his books from home in his shed in the back garden.

HERBERT: You love his stories.

CROW: Every night Dad reads you one before bedtime. Usually something new he's been working on. He likes to hear what you think. Sometimes your Dad gets stuck for ideas and you help him. But recently, story time with Dad hasn't really been the same.

INNKEEPER: Sometimes he gets distracted. He starts looking around the room and forgets where he is in the story.

CROW: Then you have to remind him and he has to stop and go back.

INNKEEPER: And the dramatic tension is lost.

GUITAR MAN: Until one night Dad doesn't turn up for story time at all. It was his birthday. His fortieth Birthday. And he had been acting funny all day.

INNKEEPER: He stayed in bed really late in the morning. You didn't see him before school so you had to wait until dinner to give him his card.

HERBERT: Dad was acting really strange at dinner too. He hardly said a word during the whole meal. Mum bought him a big chocolate cake for dessert but he didn't eat any of it.

CROW: Later that night, you put on your pyjamas, hop into bed and wait for Dad to come in and tell you a story. Mum pops her head round the door to say there will be no story time tonight. Dad has some work to do and he'll be in his writing shed until late.

GUITAR MAN: You imagine your Dad in his shed. Sitting at his desk, looking around the room and stuck for inspiration.

GUITAR MAN: You have an idea.

CROW: You will wait until it gets really late, and then you will sneak out to help Dad finish the story.

HERBERT: So when Mum has gone to bed and turned off the light, you put on your boots and hat and venture out towards the garden.

ROBIN makes his way back on stage.

GUITAR MAN: You creep across the floor. You creek open the door. You tip-toe along the landing. You sidle up to your mum's bedroom door and press your ear against it.

Snoring.

CROW: The coast is clear.

GUITAR MAN: Now the hard part: the stairs. You scuttle down the first flight, then leap and slide down the banister. You crawl across the hallway floor like a soldier through mud.

Quietly, you slink into the kitchen and gently peer out the back door.

HERBERT: There is a light coming from the Dad's shed. He must be in there.

CROW: Dad's rusty old lantern is hanging on the porch wall beside you. You grab it and begin your journey through the garden and over to Dad's shed.

INNKEEPER: You step over the rake. Then go round the pond. Round again. Then scramble through the bushes until finally you are at the door of the shed.

HERBERT: You knock on the door of the shed three times and listen. No answer. You knock on the door of the shed three more times and listen. No answer. You knock on the door of the shed three more times and –

CROW: You have had enough. You throw open the door. You duck as something rushes towards you.

HERBERT: You turn and look behind you to see a bird flying out into the open night sky. The crow that nests in the corner of Dad's shed.

INNKEEPER: But where's dad? His big brown jacket is there on his chair. And his special pen is sitting on his drawing pad. But these don't look like Dad's drawings.

HERBERT: They're dark and really sketchy and rough, not like the cleanly-inked drawings you are used to.

GUITAR MAN: You start to flick through the pages and see a forest of pine trees under an icy blue sky, an old wooden cottage with a bunch of balloons tied to the lintel, a big marquee, snow-covered mountain tops and a ramshackled old hut.

HERBERT: Some of the pictures are a little frightening. Men and women with their eyes and mouths sewn shut. A crow with piercing red eyes and coal black feathers.

INNKEEPER: And on the corner of every page, dark ominous shadows which could only belong to some sort of beast.

CROW: You get to the last page and in the picture, you see a tiny, solitary light way off in the distance. You look at it and you are transfixed. It is an amazing swirl of colour and as you peer closer and closer, you can see the brush strokes of a hundred different pigments in it.

INNKEEPER: You stare and the strokes seem to move and envelop you, swirling around, changing shape and colour, flashing and then fading.

GUITAR MAN: You try to look away. You close your eyes and shake your head, but the colours keep swirling and moving around you –

HERBERT: You stumble forward and hear an ink pot smash as it tumbles to the floor.

GUITAR MAN: You feel like you are falling. You *are* falling. You close your eyes and turn around to look back at the –

INNKEEPER: – But Dad's shed has disappeared.

ROBIN makes his way back to the stage.

ROBIN: And you are in a forest. A forest of pine trees.

HERBERT: And you are at the foot of a mountain, a mountain covered in fir and larch and pine. The mountain stretches up for miles and miles and you cannot see the top.

GUITAR MAN: You hear a scratching. A pen scratching against crisp parchment. The sound is so light you can only just make it out. You wander uphill and you follow the sound.

GUITAR MAN: Pine trees tower over you.

CROW: Branches come at you from out of nowhere. They poke at your arms and scratch your face. Twigs and pine cones snap and break on the ground beneath you. A flutter of wings makes you spin around as a crow flies over your head and out of sight.

ROBIN: And it's cold. It's freezing cold. You can see your own breath as it crystallizes in plumes of pale grey in front of your face. Your foot catches a snake of root and you fall onto the ground. The palms of your hands meet a damp bed of mud and pine needles. You are cold, you are alone, and you are lost.

HERBERT: A new sounds catches your ear. A faint murmur, winding its way out of the breeze. You hear it grow louder. It changes into voices and laughter.

GUITAR MAN: You pick yourself up, and you follow the sound. You scramble through the thick forest and come across a strange winding path through the trees. You follow the path and the voices grow louder and louder. And so you begin to pick of speed. You run and you follow this path and then suddenly you come across an old wooden cottage with a bunch of balloons tied to the lintel. A sign above the door reads 'The Beginning of the Story Tavern'. So you go inside to ask for directions.

ROBIN knocks on an invisible door.

INNKEEPER: Who could that be?

ROBIN knocks again.

INNKEEPER: Hello! Come on in you poor thing. Whatever were you doing outside in that cold weather? Why I would throw you in the fire just to keep you warm! Come inside. Come inside.

ROBIN: Oh, I can't stay long. I'm just looking for direct –

INNKEEPER: Sit down, sit down. You're just in time for the party.

ROBIN: Party?

INNKEEPER: Why, it's the illustrator's Birthday! Come join us, celebrate! Have some cake, take this noise-making thingy!

ROBIN: Look, I'm sorry but I really shouldn't stay, I'm –

INNKEEPER: Oh, but of course you can stay here. This is
'The Beginning of The Story Tavern,' where everything is
always warm and cosy and everyone is always happy. Sure,
any young adventurer could save him or herself a lot of
hardship if they'd only stay here! Can I get you something
to drink? How about something to eat?

ROBIN: No thank you, I'll be fine, really. I just –

INNKEEPER: "You'll be fine!' oh what a brave boy. Such
positivity! Why, you remind me of my husband. Herbert!
Herbert! This is Herbert, my darling husband. Well he
used to be not so darling let me tell you that, wanted to
leave here, brave the outside world, and all that. Ha, what
a messer. He walked through the forest for miles and miles,
until eventually he came across a clearing bathed in a
ghostly mist with these awfully strange floating lights that
said terrible terrible things. Things he couldn't forget…
So I sewed up his ears so he couldn't hear those things
anymore! Oh just you wait! You're going to fit in so well.

ROBIN: But my dad –

INNKEEPER: – Now let's meet the others, they're great.

Enter CROW as See-No and GUITAR MAN as Speak-No.

Meet this young boy. See it was just after I solved Herbert's
little problem, they came knocking at the door. They'd had
a run in with the monster, you see.

ROBIN: Monster? What monster?

INNKEEPER: Oh you know the one with the big teeth, red
eyes, five sets of claws, two sets of whiskers, sucks all the
life out of the world. That one.

ROBIN: But what if he's got my dad?

INNKEEPER: Oh don't worry he never eats anything with a
tail.

ROBIN: What do you mean tail? My dad doesn't have a tail.

INNKEEPER: Oh I thought you said dog. Yeah, he'd eat your dad.

ROBIN: What?

INNKEEPER: Moving on. He doesn't always eat them. Take See-No for example. After she had a run in with him, she couldn't stand the sight of the world anymore. And Speak-No. Sure he used to be a poet. But after the monster he just couldn't write or speak like he used to. It was terrible to see them that way. I wished they could see the world how I do! So it was decided, I would make them happy just like I made Herbert happy. I closed her eyes and closed his mouth and sewed them up so they didn't have to see anything sad or say anything unhappy ever again.

CROW: Oh yes life is so much better now I can see no evil...

INNKEEPER: Sure speaking no evil's great isn't it?

GUITAR MAN: *(Mumbling, barely audible.)* Yeah it's fucking great.

INNKEEPER: So you see. You'll just *have* to stay.

ROBIN: But my dad! If this monster –

INNKEEPER: There will be no talk of monsters here. You see, here, we have a certain way of dealing with things...

IGNORE IT

IGNORE IT
THE WORLD IS SCARY, WHY WOULD YOU
EXPLORE IT?
STAY INSIDE, IT'S GUARANTEED
THAT YOU'LL HAVE EVERYTHING YOU NEED
THERE'S REALLY NO GOOD REASON WHY
YOUR MIND SHOULD HAVE TO INTERCEDE
SO BLOCK THOSE FEELINGS OUT
SHUT YOUR MOUTH

AND JUST IGNORE IT
IGNORE IT
PACK-IT-UP-AND-SEND-TO-SINGAPORE IT
SOON ENOUGH, YOU'LL FIGURE OUT
THAT IT'S NOT WORTH THE FIGHT
SO BLOCK THOSE FEELINGS OUT
WHIST YOUR MOUTH
AND JUST IGNORE IT

(Spoken.) Did I ever tell you about my cousin who refused to ignore it and instead took his chances and braved the outside world? No?

Whispers into ROBIN's ear.

AND NOW HE'S GOT NO KNEECAPS
WHISHT YOUR MOUTH AND
JUST IGNORE IT
IGNORE IT
A SONG'S AN EASY WAY TO
METAPHOR IT
INTERNALISE THOSE GLOOMY EYES
THERE'S SWEET FLIP ALL FOR YOU OUTSIDE
SO FOLD YOUR CARDS, YOU'RE OUT
WHISHT YOUR MOUTH
AND JUST IGNORE IT

During the song CROW and GUITAR MAN give ROBIN three balloons which he uses to hide behind and escape.

INNKEEPER: Huh! Where did he go? You're all bloody useless.

ROBIN: You've escaped! You've escaped from the clutches of the Innkeeper. Now, with balloons in hand, you realize that although this may once have seemed like a practical escape plan you hadn't the time to consider the true gravity of the situation.

The balloons in ROBIN's hand begin pulling him upwards.

Or rather, the lack of gravity. And now you're going straight up. Up, up, up and away! Over the tavern, over the twisting path, over the pine woods, over the mountain. And you keep floating.

ROBIN begins to ascend up through audience seating.

Down below you can see the little tops of the pine trees shrinking smaller and smaller as you wonder where in this forest your father could be. You worry that you might float up here forever and ever and never see him again. But then, you have an idea! Hey, excuse me, could you please pop this for me.

ROBIN offers an audience member a pin to pop one of his balloons. Feel free to ad-lib here.

Choose your weapon. Thanks! And this one. Great. Not in my face!....And this one.

ROBIN moves back down through audience.

And then, slowly, very slowly, in a totally risk assessed way, with what might be your last drop of courage, with one eye open, and one eye closed, with only one balloon left unpopped, you begin to glide gently, gently down.

ROBIN returns to the stage.

GUITAR MAN: You drop and dip ever so lightly. You are scared that you might hurt yourself when you hit the ground, but instead, you feel the tip top branches of pine trees as they tickle the soles of your feet and gently break your fall. And you slip and slide from branch to branch, ever so slowly, until you find yourself on the floor of the forest once more.

Guitar music.

INNKEEPER: You rest for a moment. And as you sit and catch your breath you see a shadow emerge from the bushes in front of you. A crow with feathers as black as coal. At first you are frightened but then she speaks to you. She says:

CROW: You look shaken
    You say you don't recognize
    That there is no sense of ownership
    And your sense of self, taken
    That you can feel your mind drift
    And wander
    And slow
    And it's about to take flight
    Like a murder of crows

    A murder
    Those birds as harbingers of death
    A murder

    But I want to remind you that
    Crows are just birds
    And birds migrate to where it's warm
    And birds mean freedom
    And birds mean peace
    And birds mean hope
    Maya Angelou said it, Emily Dickinson too
    I know it's cliché, but I also know that it's true

    And I want to remind you to look at your hands
    Those tiny paws, seemingly clutching at nothing
    But those hands have ten fingers
    And if I could
    I would take you in my arms
    And stretch you as far as the sky
    Until you could reach the stars
    And fit each tiny piece of light inside your palms
    Circled safely by your ten narrow digits

    So, when your mind feels cloudy
    And something's not right
    And you're worried that murder of crows might take flight,
    Think of the birds, and think of your paws,

And just try to remember we're the same stuff as stars.

ROBIN: I'm sorry have we met somewhere before?

CROW: I'm not sure. That depends what you mean by met?

ROBIN: I saw a crow earlier today…

CROW: Yes?

ROBIN: The bird in my father's shed… It is you.

CROW: Mmhmm…

ROBIN: What are you doing here? Why would –

CROW: I am a creation of your father's. I was one of the first drawings in this book. I understand how scary it can be when you feel alone. Know that I'm here to help.

ROBIN: I could really use some help. I've been wandering through this forest. I'm trying to find my dad. Have you seen him?

CROW: I'm sorry I haven't seen your Dad at all today. But I do have an idea of somewhere he could be. I've been watching him in his shed for a while now and I've noticed that when he's sad he draws these scenes, these party scenes. A big marquee. It's right at the peak of this mountain. Maybe he's there? It's worth a try. If you'd like I could bring you there? Would you like me to?

ROBIN: Sure, it's worth a try.

INNKEEPER: So you hop on the crow's back and she takes flight, diving and cutting through the air as if it were nothing. The crow flies up and up, towards the peak of the mountain. You feel totally weightless but safe, like you're floating in the sea. You swoop and you soar for what feels like mere seconds before the crow says:

CROW: There it is!

GUITAR MAN: You look down and see that you are headed towards a big marquee full of strange lights. The place is hopping with people chirping and chatting, laughing and lounging.

CROW: I'll have a look around.

CROW joins INNKEEPER, GUITAR MAN and HERBERT, now performing as party guests.

ROBIN: Beyond the marquee and partially hidden through misty skies, you can just make out an even higher slope, covered in icy snow and you realise that where you are standing isn't the summit of a mountain at all and then… music starts to play.

Spanish music.

And you feel yourself, being taken over by a jazzy beat.

CROW: I can't find your Dad anywhere. But do you wanna stay? We could have a little boogie and look for him later? Let's stick around. I'm being taken over by the jazzy beat.

INNKEEPER: Hola! Come here. This will be fun.

HERBERT: Why worry about your Papa? What you need is a night off. Come on. Vamanos.

INNKEEPER: Take this.

HERBERT: Drink this.

CROW: Try this.

INNKEEPER, HERBERT and CROW: It'll be fun.

ROBIN: And you think to yourself, 'maybe I will stick around, just for a little while.' Then, suddenly, there's loads of really good looking people out there in the clearing in front of you. They're all sitting together and smiling and having a really good time. And you're looking at them and they're looking at you. And you are looking at them, looking at you, looking at them and they're looking at you, looking at them, looking at you. They're all being taken over by the jazzy beat too and they're all nodding their heads. Yeah, just like that! They're all nodding their heads up and down and you're nodding your head up and down and then, suddenly...you see her!

ROBIN locks eyes with an audience member and falls in love, instantly. ROBIN slowly, very slowly pursues audience member dazzled. GUITAR MAN follows with rose in mouth. HERBERT sings the following. CROW and INNKEEPER provide backing vocals.

HERBERT:

MI AMORE

MI AMORE
MI ADORE
MI AND YOU, EH?
PA FAVOUR-AY
ESTOY FINITO
MI BURRITO!
MI AMORE
MI DORITO
MI AMORE
MI AMORE, MI AMORE AND MORE AND MORE, EH?
MI ADORE, AY CARUMBA, MI AMORE
MI AND YOU-EH?
MI AND YOU-EH MY TEQUILA MI AMORE
PA FAVOUR-AY
PA FAVOUR-AY, PAR PINATA, PA FAVOUR-AY
ESTOY FINITO
MI BURRITO
MI AMORE
MI DORITO!

ROBIN: And even though you are only ten, you know that you have just fallen madly in love. Real love. And you may never experience this kind of real love ever again. And you're looking at her and she's looking at you.

And you say 'hey'.

And she says:

Wait for response.

And you say "come here often?" and she says:

Wait for response.

And you say "it's cool, isn't it?"

Wait for response.

Yeah, trendy. So, I brought you this.

Offers the rose.

So eh… I'm sorry I don't really know what to say. I'm only ten, and this is all very new to me. Maybe I'll eh…catch you later, alligator? Cool…

End Music.

So you rejoin the party and have a dance with the people there for a little while. For a while it's great. But as the night wears on you stop enjoying the party. It's all too much. Everyone is dancing and you're trying to bop along but you felt like an idiot no matter what. You find yourself just smiling and nodding, smiling and nodding.

The truth is you can't stop thinking about Dad. It's his birthday. You miss him and you miss home, or at least what home used to be like. And you feel guilty and horrible for having a good time when you know Dad's not. You wish you could be there for him but you don't know how, and you wish you could tell him it's gonna be ok but you don't know if it will. How can you look after someone when you can't even take care of yourself? You don't really want to be alone but you don't want to bring anyone else down either. And there is nothing worse than feeling alone in a crowd, feeling like everyone's looking at you.

HERBERT: So, you leave the party and you get back to your climb up the mountain. As you ascend it gets steeper and steeper and colder and colder. Your teeth chatter. Your

bones shiver and quake. The wind bites your face. Your
toes turn purple and numb. Frost forms on your boots. You
worry you might freeze but still, you keep walking.

HERBERT: It's cold
But it's winter
It's cold
But it's night time
It's cold
But it's not like that
Hands shake as eyes water and the cold clutches my chest
Stopping my lungs from breathing deeply
Breathing
Deeply
Breathe
deeply

It's cold
But I can do this
It's cold
But I'll try not to feel it
It's cold
But no one notices
With a defiant step and a blazing smile I kick start my
numb body,
Push it down
Lift it up, up, up
Until no one can see
Just see what I want you to see
What I can make you see
The light bubbly person
I can be
But sometimes the mirror can crack and a
Streak of something hidden can be seen...
But it's okay
Because

"How are you today?"
Can always be
It's cold.

INNKEEPER: You walk for miles and miles until, eventually, you come across a clearing bathed in a ghostly mist. Something about the place doesn't feel right. You wonder if you have been here before. You set forth…wearily, carefully.

GUITAR MAN, HERBERT, INNKEEPER and CROW as Will of the Wisps.

GUITAR MAN: You're not going to find what you came here to find.

ROBIN's lantern goes out.

ROBIN: Hello?

HERBERT: What's the point in continuing?

ROBIN: Who are you?

CROW: You're not getting anywhere.

ROBIN: What?

INNKEEPER: You've failed at everything you have ever wanted to do.

ROBIN: What are you talking about? That's not true.

HERBERT: You're useless.

ROBIN: No I'm not.

INNKEEPER: You're old

ROBIN: I'm ten!

GUITAR MAN: Happy Birthday.

ROBIN: It's not my… what?

CROW: What's the point?

ROBIN: Point of what?

HERBERT: Your life is half over and you haven't done anything valuable with it.

ROBIN: I told you, I'm only ten! Who are you?

GUITAR MAN: Your son is going to make the same mistakes as you and there's nothing you can do to help him.

ROBIN: Son? I don't have a son.

HERBERT: Forty wasted years.

ROBIN: Forty? I told you I'm ten. My dad's forty. Dad…

CROW: You're pathetic as an artist.

ROBIN: My dad is a great artist. He can draw better than anyone I –

GUITAR MAN: It's your fault your family is struggling.

ROBIN: Hey! That's not true. We're just fine.

HERBERT: They're ashamed of you.

ROBIN: No, we're not. I'm so proud of my dad and so is Mum!

CROW: Your son hates being around you.

ROBIN: I love spending time with Dad.

HERBERT: Your wife is sickened by you.

ROBIN: My mum loves my dad.

GUITAR MAN: You cannot support your family.

ROBIN: Yeah he does support us. And we support him too!

CROW: Your family are better off without you.

ROBIN: That's not true! Of course we wouldn't be better off without him. Who would I go to when I was sad? Who would tell me stories and teach me things and spend time with me? My dad's always there for me. Stop saying these horrible things. They're all lies. I love my dad and that won't ever change no matter what!

Will of the Wisps disappear. The stage is almost completely dark.

GUITAR MAN: And suddenly you are in total darkness. You cannot see anything at all.

ROBIN:
HALF LIGHT

ALONE AGAIN
AS NIGHT DESCENDS
WITHOUT A FRIEND
I HEAR YOU SPEAK
THEN DISAPPEAR
A COLD FRONTIER
AND I..
OH I
I KNOW THAT I WILL FIND YOU
EVEN IF IT TAKES A LONG, LONG TIME
BUT YOU
OH YOU
YOU DON'T SMILE THE WAY, OR LAUGH THE
WAY
OR TALK THE WAY YOU USED TO DO

BUT IF LIGHT IS IN YOU
LIGHT WILL FIND YOU
AND YOU HAVE GOT THE BRIGHTEST LIGHT OF
ALL
SO WHAT COULD EVER MAKE YOU FEEL SO
SMALL?
OOH OHH OOH
AHH
YOU DON'T SEEM LIKE… YOU?

(WEIGHT ON YOUR SHOULDERS I HAVE NEVER
SEEN YOU CARRY)
WHAT CAN I DO?
(DO ALL THE THINGS I CAN DO TO MAKE YOU
HAPPY)
IF I KNEW..
AHH
MAYBE THEN
(THINGS WOULDN'T SEEM SO STRANGE AND
YOU'D BE FEELING ALRIGHT)
YOU'D COME HOME AGAIN
(INSTEAD OF WALKING THROUGH THE FOREST
IN THE HALF-LIGHT)
...IT MUST BE WAY PAST TEN...
AHH
BUT THE NIGHT
IS GETTING COLD AND GREY
AND I DON'T UNDERSTAND WHY YOU WOULD
WANT
TO MAKE YOURSELF A CASTAWAY
WHATEVER PAIN, WHATEVER STAIN, WHATEVER
MARK
IT WILL WASH AWAY AND YOU WON'T NEED
TO STAY FOREVER IN THE DARK
BECAUSE IF LIGHT IS IN YOU
LIGHT WILL FIND YOU
AND YOU HAVE GOT THE BRIGHTEST LIGHT OF
ALL
BUT NOW I CAN'T SEE ANY LIGHT AT ALL
OOH OHH OHH
AHH
SO WHAT COULD EVER MAKE YOU FEEL SO
SMALL?

ROBIN sits and tries to light his lantern.

INNKEEPER: Do you remember the night that our rabbit Bella passed away? I'd never experienced that kind of sadness before. I woke up in the middle of the night in floods of tears. I cried and cried. I'd never experienced death before and I couldn't comprehend it. I was heartbroken. I cried so loudly that I must have woken you up. You came into my room and I thought you'd be annoyed or you'd ask me to explain but you didn't. Somehow you just knew. You knew what to do. What I needed. You lay down beside me and put your arms around me. You told me everything was going to be okay. This too shall pass. And amazingly, I did feel better. I cried a little bit but eventually I fell asleep. In your arms. With you beside me.

ROBIN's lantern begins to flicker back.

Sometimes I think about that and remind myself to bring it up. To ask you. Do you remember? Because I do. Thank you for that. I don't think I say that enough. Thanks.

GUITAR MAN: A light switches on. In the distance you can just make out the outline of a shed.

CROW: Your dad's shed? Could it be? You walk up the last stretch of snowy mountain.

GUITAR MAN: You are nervous as you take the very last step toward the door.

CROW: It seems to tower above you. It's like nothing you've ever seen before.

GUITAR MAN: This isn't much like Dad's shed.

CROW: You think to yourself.

GUITAR MAN: It's bigger, older, ramshackled. You reach for the ancient brass knob. It's rusted and stiff.

CROW: You twist it but it doesn't move. You tug it but it doesn't budge. You put down your lantern and you pull with all your might. You hear the latch go and stand backwards, as the door blows open all by itself. Something blasts past you.

GUITAR MAN: A shadow?

CROW: And then –

GUITAR MAN: A torrent of paper bursts out through the door. The room is a hurricane of pages being tossed around by the wind. You raise your hands to shield your face and you march into the fray.

CROW: Dad must be close but it's dusty in here and dark like tar.

GUITAR MAN: It's sopping with ink. Out of the infinite blackness, you hear the scratching of pens.

CROW: Your instincts kick in as the dark gathers round. You reach out with your lantern and the black is forced back by a brave beam of light illuminating the stairs all the way up. A trail of ink and dust lead to a desk at the top of the steps and behind it sits…

GUITAR MAN: …two dark silhouettes. Within the dark, you can just about make out a figure on a chair. Scribbling wildly. Bent over a desk. Haggard, but familiar.

CROW: Your dad.

GUITAR MAN: Your dad in his checked shirt and paint-splattered jeans. His hair sticking up in tufts. But even though he's there, he isn't really *there*. And there is a figure standing over him like a shadow, or maybe just a twisted up, rinsed out, inky old scrawl.

CROW: Other stories have monsters with fangs, claws and wings but the scariest thing about Dad's monster was…

CROW and GUITAR MAN: …that it looked just like him.

CROW: But you know that you have to keep going.

GUITAR MAN: Or soon Dad will be gone. Sucked into the leathery black. You follow the trail of ink to the top. You slip and you fall...

CROW and GUITAR MAN: ...but you don't stop.

CROW: Moving through the half light with the bright guide of your lantern.

GUITAR MAN: Until you arrive at the desk.

CROW: The figures that seemed so big from down there now seem much smaller. You notice the paper, the pens, the ink puddle all around the desk.

GUITAR MAN: You notice your dad's chest heaving. The monster stands motionless, as if somehow...

CROW: ...at rest.

GUITAR MAN: Wading through a mass of pencil shavings, you know you have to reach him. You call out for your dad, but nothing calls back. In a roar of ink and paper the shadow stretches out, crosses the walls, and scurries down the stairs to meet you. A shadow? A beast? You don't even flinch as the 'something' slips past you.

CROW: You approach the desk and you hear your dad cry. And slowly you reach out. You touch the back of your father's head and you say:

ROBIN: It's okay Dad. It's me. It's Robin. I've come to save you.

CROW: And you look Dad in the eye for the first time in what feels like forever. And you wait for Dad to speak, and then he says...

GUITAR MAN as Dad.

GUITAR MAN: Robin.

CROW: His voice is nothing like you've heard before, a gravelly murmur.

GUITAR MAN: I come here myself, I'm not captive to anything. This is just life. The monster is just, it's just.

ROBIN: I know Dad.

CROW: Said Robin.

GUITAR MAN: You know Robin.

CROW: Said Dad. And he puts his arm around you.

GUITAR MAN: You look into Dad's eyes again. They are dark, and deep and cold. But soft, and kind and flecked with gold. You reach down for the page. You hold your father close then and whisper into his ear.

ROBIN: Can we go home now?

GUITAR MAN: His hands are shaking, and yours are too. And he puts his hand in yours, and drops his pen. He stands up. The storybook world shrinks away. It seems to get smaller and Dad looks as big as he used to. Wow, the shed, the shed seems –

CROW: Normal. As it was before. The darkness ebbs away. You see sunlight, coming to meet you as if from a distant place. You pull your head off the desk, and Dad squeezes your shoulder. And he says…

GUITAR MAN: How are you?

CROW: And you say…

ROBIN: Good.

CROW: Dad laughs.

GUITAR MAN: Shouldn't you be in bed?

ROBIN: Yes. I couldn't sleep. I'm sorry about the mess.

CROW: Dad smiles as he wipes ink from your face.

GUITAR MAN: We'll clean it up in the morning.

ROBIN: Happy birthday, Dad. I'm glad you're back.

CROW: Said the kid.

GUITAR MAN: Thanks, Robin.

CROW: Said his dad.

GUITAR MAN: But what do you mean? Sure I've been here the whole time.

CROW: And with that Robin and Dad left the shed.

Closing music. ROBIN lowers his lantern.

BRISEIS AFTER THE BLACK

BY
DYLAN COBURN GRAY

Characters

WRITER

ACTOR

Briseis After The Black was first performed as part of Tiger Dublin Fringe 2016. Production team was as follows:

WRITER – Dylan Coburn Gray

ACTOR – variable

Stage Manager/Co-Devisor – Ursula McGinn

Dramaturg/Co-Devisor – Molly O'Cathain

Producer/Publicity/Marketing – Carla Rogers

Development ACTORS – Aisling Flynn, Danielle Galligan, Fionnula Gygax, Mary Lou McCarthy, Áine Ni Laoghaire, Siofra O'Meara, Hannah O'Reilly.

With thanks to: Claire O'Reilly, Brian McMahon Gallagher, everyone at Fringe.

Special thanks to Breffni Holahan, patient zero, for shambling with me through the first shamblethrough.

– **ACTOR reads lines in bold.**

– WRITER reads lines not in bold.

The script from which ACTOR reads is partitioned between three locations onstage:

LOCATION ONE, downstage right or left. Pages 325 to 347 and 368 to 374.

LOCATION TWO, upstage seated at a table. Pages 347 to 358 and 375 to 382.

LOCATION THREE, downstage right or left. Pages 361 to 366 and 383 to 387.

How the script should be presented is up for grabs. Our production had straightforward folders with script in them, but also hid prompts in the mess in Maria's apartment, as referenced in the text. The governing thought was that the stage is a bit like a filmset for an actor who refuses to learn their lines, *à la* Brando in Superman, reading his lines off his fake baby's face. Ideally, though, prompts aren't just fun gimmicks, but serve to remind the audience of the live dynamic between ACTOR and WRITER even as the text wanders into other layers of the story. Instantiate that using your own criteria of instantiation.

This masterscript contains two types of stage directions, those for the reader and those used by ACTOR to navigate the play in realtime. The latter are given in *(ITALICISED CAPS)*, the former in *(Italics but not caps.)* Any text of WRITER's that is not needed to cue ACTOR can be omitted from ACTOR's working script, ditto all non-ACTOR-specific stage directions.

The following two pages are a test script, used to familiarise ACTOR with how the script will function. WRITER and ACTOR should go through it together before the audience arrive.

– If you look you should see what I'm saying now in the script, and what you should say back to me.

– I am the actor, I read the lines in bold.

– I am the writer, I read the lines not in bold. Could you read the following stage direction please?

(THIS IS A STAGE DIRECTION IN BRACKETS/ITALICISED CAPS. CLAP THREE TIMES.)

– How was that?

– That was great NAME, and as you can see that's what your name will look like written down.

– Anything else I need to know?

– It might help to know that Briseis is pronounced Briseis.

– I knew that Briseis was pronounced Briseis.

– Did you know Achilles is pronounced Achilles?

–I knew Achilles is pronounced Achilles.

– Wow. And that brazier is pronounced brazier?

– Yes.

– Wow.

– You're actually being really condescending right now.

– Sorry about that.

– Sometimes I might not know why I'm saying something.

– And that's okay.

– **I might not even know what it means, and you might be talking about something else entirely.**

– The rain in Spain falls mostly on the ground.

– **Calling non-linear studies 'non-linear studies' is like calling zoology 'the study of non-elephant animals'.**

– Newton invented the Jovilabe.

– **But it's okay, because there's no wrong way to speak the script.**

– Which used a body of mercury as a kind of damper.

– **If in doubt, a matter-of-fact tone will do just fine.**

– But what about your character?

– **What about my character?**

– Yes, are you going to speak as yourself or as the person you're playing?

– **Yes.**

– Which?

– **Either is fine. What's important is for them to hear me speak, no matter how I speak. Which is exciting! I'm looking forward to experimenting. Playing around.**

– Oh, okay, I suppose that makes sense.

– **Question.**

– Yes?

– **Should I talk to the writer?**

– People sometimes find that hard to understand, that non-linear systems don't actually necessarily have anything physical in common, it's partly a language artefact.

– **Or should I talk to the audience?**

– Yes.

– It's all good?

– Whatever you choose, NAME, I can roll with it.

– I'd like to leave pauses. Space.

– That's fine, I'll talk fast because I have all the long technical bullshit lines, but that doesn't mean you have to.

– Isaac Newton was kind of a dick.

– Feel like you've got the hang of it, NAME?

– Yes!

(WRITER WILL PROMPT YOU HERE.)

Briseis After The Black

(Both ACTOR and WRITER are onstage. They are seated at a table, covered with stuff whose relevance remains to be established. Markers, stickers, a polaroid camera, three cups full of torn paper, three sketchpads, envelopes, books, a corkboard on which the photos of past ACTORs are displayed. Downstage of the table, there are two locations at which segments of the script are preset, plus a tape player and an assortment of tapes, plus three cups full of water placed on coasters. The play begins with WRITER visibly reading the following from a piece of paper. Thereafter, unless otherwise specified, WRITER speaks their lines from memory.)

– This is the prologue.
Thank you for coming. You were always going to.

This is a performance of a play called Briseis, written by Maria Black, edited for performance by Bea Moore, subsequently dicked around with for performance by me. Hence the title in any promotional material you will have seen, *Briseis After The Black*. It's not exactly the play she wrote, and I'm not allowed say it is. So I'm not saying that. I will say that it is a sincere attempt on my part to capture the spirit if not the letter of a play which I totally fell in love with the second I saw it.

Maybe you didn't see any promotional material. If you didn't, thank you for coming anyway.

Even though you were always going to.

(Pause.)

In addition to the legalities, I chose the title with a sense of poetry. Since Maria Black's suicide in 1995 her work has fallen into a public obscurity completely at odds with the cult enthusiasm it inspires in those who've been lucky enough to see one of the regrettably few performances.

All of which is by way of saying that the title *Briseis After The Black* is, of course, a functional acknowledgement of my edits. But it is also expressive of my hope that Black's work can and will endure and be appreciated beyond her tragic early death. And a final big thank you to Bea, without whose permission and active involvement none of this would be possible.

Thus ends the prologue.

(At this point WRITER introduces ACTOR, asks them are they nervous, reassures them, says thank you for participating, asks if it's alright if WRITER takes ACTOR's photo, takes their photo on a polaroid camera, puts photo on corkboard with all other participants' photos, asks them to tear up the piece of paper WRITER just read the prologue from as a warmup, asks are they ready to begin.)

– If you look you'll see what I'm saying now in the script, and what you should say back to me.

– **So we're starting?**

– We're starting. I thought it might be nice to begin with a little background on the play, if you don't mind?

– **Not at all.**

– One other thing I forgot to say till now, I took a photo of you a minute ago, would you mind if I took another a little later on as part of the performance?

– **Not at all.**

– Wonderful. This is Briseis by Maria Black.

– **Edited for performance by Bea Moore.**

– Subsequently dicked around with for performance by me.

– **Tonight I am Achilles.**

– And I play Briseis.

– **I also play Maria Black herself.**

– And I also play Bea Moore, her friend and collaborator.

– **Imagine I'm twenty-four years old.**

I have dark hair, which I cut myself, never shorter than my shoulder.

I wear men's shirts which are too large for me, you wouldn't catch me dead in a dress.

People often think I'm a lesbian, which says more about them than it does about me.

(During this text WRITER gives actor a Nineties-ish oversized shirt to put on, not dissimilar to the one WRITER is already wearing.)

– Imagine I'm twenty-four years old.

I have dark hair, which I most recently got bobbed but regret.

I have a second-hand motorbike jacket I'm very proud of, which is my only secondhand piece of clothing.
I also wear men's shirts which are too large for me.

People often think I'm a lesbian which I find obscurely flattering.

– **We met at university.**

– Undergraduate drama, I then went on to do a masters in playwriting, which I got a first in.

– **I just wrote plays.**

– In which I got a first. I liked you instantly.

– **I thought you were a twat.**

– I liked how not likeable you were.

– **You wanted everyone to like you.**

– I learned to enjoy being mean from you.

– **You were alright one-on-one.**

– You were so funny about people or plays you hated.

– **You were more yourself when you let yourself be mean.**

– You were a miserable woman who hated plays by miserable women.

– **You hated your own writing, but you hated everyone else's more.**

– You hated a movement you helped define.

– **You hated watching plays and feeling like you could have written them better.**

– One of many contradictions that defined your brilliant, frustrating, contradictory personality. I added all this bit.

– **Which bit?**

– The bit where we play Maria and Bea.

– **Based on Bea's memories of her friend.**

– I'd like to just reiterate my thanks for her permission to do this show in this way.

– **It's strange to see her face in photographs.**

– And my gratitude that she was willing to share the details this text depends on.

– Writers never look like their work, if you know what I mean.

– And my gratitude that she was willing to let me play her, she's much better looking than this. It's supposed to serve as a kind of frame.

– Obviously it's a fiction.

– We can't choose to not know what we know about Maria's death.

– Who remembers the exact words of a conversation twenty years ago?

– And what we know can't not inform how we watch her work.

– You remember the gist, maybe a memorable phrase.

– We can't not engage, only engage intelligently.

– I had a knack for phrases.

– It's impossible to not see her life in the play.

– The writing of this play and its role in her death.

– It's impossible to not see the play in her life.

– Bea's efforts to bring Maria's work to production.

– But this is still – in spirit if not letter – a performance of Maria Black's *Briseis*.

– It's representative of her style.

– For which she personally favoured the term 'deliquescence'.

– She knew it was pretentious.

– She enjoyed the pretention.

– **"When people call you pretentious, they mean you're not actually as clever as you think you are."**

– "It's no coincidence that every woman who writes gets called pretentious."

–**"You might as well embrace it."**

– She said that.

– **And she did.**

– Embrace it, in lots of ways, amongst them using the word 'deliquescence'.

– **That means ragged edges.**

– Sudden slips of time.

– **of character.**

– of register.

– **Unanswered questions.**

– An assault on unity.

– **on logic.**

– Refusing the tyranny of plot.

– **Neither real nor unreal –**

– But abreal, refusing any distinction between the two.

– **Not dream logic.**

– A fruitful reconciliation of the poetic and the post-modern.

– **Nightmare logic.**

– Poetry for those who've got the memo it's barbaric.

– **Edward Bond wrote her a nice letter after seeing her perform a monologue she wrote as a student.**

– Bond is a playwright famous for having last enjoyed himself sometime in the late fifties.

– **Celebrated playwright Caryl Churchill refused to see any of her work.**

– Black claimed this was because she spilled a drink on her at an opening night party in 1992.

– **Bea Moore says she was very proud to have once called one of the Spice Girls a cunt.**

– She was passing a signing or something, she didn't go specifically to call one of them a cunt, that would be a bit much.

– **She doesn't know which one.**

– Bea Moore doesn't, presumably Black did, you can make up your own mind, I like to think it was the ginger one.

– **All her friends say she could be very charming when she wanted to be.**

– Very funny.

– **In very few words.**

– A unique laconicism.

– **You can see it in her writing.**

– Laconicity?

– **This play was begun in 1994. She was twenty-four years old.**

– Annoyingly young to have written what she wrote.

– **Sad when you think about what she could have done if she'd lived longer.**

– Even just as long as Keats.

– **or John Kennedy Toole.**

– or Kurt Cobain.

– **or Jeff Buckley.**

– or Emily Brontë.

–or Sylvia Plath.

– She could have been Sarah Kane, if Sarah Kane weren't Sarah Kane.

– **But she wasn't, because she didn't.**

– Live longer that is. Cut shorter than the cut short.

– **But maybe if she'd lived she couldn't have done what she did.**

– She committed suicide in February 1995, shortly before her twenty-fifth birthday, ten years after being diagnosed with major depressive disorder, aged fourteen, following a profound catatonic episode.

– **It was an overdose, if you were wondering.**

– I took the last photo of her. *(WRITER at this point indicates the photo earlier taken of ACTOR.)*

– **I'm smiling in it.**

– We're both overexposed by the flash, I'm in it too, so that's about all you can see, that you're smiling in it.

– **We're in a club.**

– It makes me think of Walter Benjamin, the face as the last refuge of cult value, I know that that's pretentious.

– **Embrace it.**

– The only place where the depicted still matters more than the depiction.

– **I hated having my photo taken.**

– That's what I try to create in my writing.

– **And you loved taking photos.**

– Portraits uncanny but comforting.

– *Briseis* **was unstaged at the time of my death.**

– You'd only finished it a few days before. It's a two-hander, the characters are Achilles and his lover Briseis.

– **His slave Briseis.**

– His lover and his slave, it's complicated.

– **True love is impossible without freedom.**

– It was a different time, not the 90s, Ancient Greece I mean.

– **The action unfolds over a single night.**

– in Achilles' chambers.

–**I am Achilles.** *(At this point WRITER gives ACTOR a nametag on which is written Achilles.)*

– Son of Thetis.

– **Greatest of the Greeks.**

– Destined to die but be sung of forever.

– **Sort of.**

– It's been 3000 years so it looks like he's right.

– **But we won't know for sure until after forever.**

– Which will be at least a little while longer.

– **Tonight Achilles reads his lines from a script.**

– I added this bit.

– **His actions are as fixed as a ballroom dance.**

– The original only specifies two performers, presumably with a normal amount of rehearsal behind them, but I think this says something interesting about fate.

– **He was always going to do what he did.**

– And the gender flip is deliberate, it's to redress the power imbalance between me and NAME here.

– **He was always going to die as he did.**

– But this is still – in spirit if not letter – a performance of Maria Black's *Briseis*.

– **What happened was always going to.**

– I play Briseis.

– **I love you.**

– And I may love you.

– **You're my lover.**

– and I'm your slave.

– **You grew up in the temple of Apollo with your father.**

– Whose name was Briseus.

– **Until I stole you.**

– Which is confusing, objectively, but don't worry about the Greek names, the only ones that matter are Briseis and Achilles.

– **I was inspired to write the play by my worst ever acting job.**

– The part of Lavinia in Titus Andronicus.

– **Two hours of screaming every night.**

Two hours of pretending to have no arms.

Two hours of pretending to have no tongue.

Two hours of spitting fake blood everywhere.

– The reviews were good, pay was good, but still not much fun.

– **Is that what success looks like?**

– Is that what success feels like?

– **I was tired of being paid to suffer.**

– She was tired of playing a receptacle for pain.

– **A bleeding trophy.**

– *Briseis,* the play, grew out of that frustration.

– **She was the first.**

– Briseis, the slave, the earliest work of literature's earliest victim.

– **The first woman no one cared about.**

– Everyone else in the Iliad is someone's son or daughter.

– **That's why it's sad when they die.**

– Except for Briseis.

–**She doesn't even get to die. She just disappears.**

– She only exists to motivate Achilles to sulk and stop fighting when she's taken from him.

– **A favourite toy with nipples.**

– After that she's never mentioned again, save in passing to say she mourned Achilles' death.

– **Which I don't buy.**

– Maria set out to explode that myth.

– **I wanted to make her matter.**

– The first draft was completed in just under two weeks.

– **I wanted her pain to matter.**

– She would sit at her kitchen table drinking huge quantities of shit coffee or shit wine, depending on the time of day, writing furiously.

– **If they wanted pain, I'd give them pain.**

– Sometimes I'd come to visit and it'd look like she hadn't moved since I'd left.

– **Until they choked on it.**

– Sometimes I'd arrive at ten in the morning and she'd be pissed having worked and drank through the night.

– **Until they started to think about why they liked watching pain.**

– When the play starts, Hector's rotting corpse is here, downstage, in view.

(At this point WRITER writes BRONZE in one of the sketchpads, and places it visibly where the notional corpse notionally is, for reasons that become clear later on.)

– **Death casts a long shadow over this play.**

– The first full staging in Germany used an actual pig corpse.

– **This play shows the first of our last nights before I die.**

– Seven different pig corpses over the run, what can I say, it was the Nineties in Germany.

– **Winedark nights.**

– The insurance was crippling and stage management nearly quit.

– **Bronzebright days.**

– Also it smelled.

– **Now that I've rejoined the fighting.**

– I wasn't there, but Bea – who I'm playing – told me it smelled.

– **I am rough with you.**

– The violence is abstract.

– **Passionate.**

– It would be impossible not to mention distasteful to represent it literally.

– **That's what you like.**

– That's what I know.

– **There's nothing either good or bad but thinking makes it so.**

– Which is what the play is about.

– **Lots of the reviews couldn't get past the first scene.**

– It opens on what looks like a rape.

– **It turns out it's much more complicated than that.**

– The second scene begins with a question which turns everything upside down.

– **Was that what you wanted?**

– No.

– **It was the same.**

– It wasn't.

– **I said everything I said before.**

– Yes.

– **I did everything I did before.**

– Yes.

– **It was the same.**

– It wasn't.

– I crossed the beach and followed the path.

– The day was bright but the temple was dim.

– I came to the doorway and saw you standing there.

– I saw your long shadow from the morning sun behind you as it stretched across the floor.

– You looked up and ran.

– I could hear your following footsteps between mine and my heartbeat.

– You crashed into a standing brazier and it fell.

(WRITER indicates but does not knock over one of the chairs at the table.)

– I knocked a second over on purpose to try and slow you.

(WRITER indicates but does not knock over the other.)

– I didn't slow.

– I fell. *(WRITER kneels by the BRONZE sign.)*

– I looked at you.

– I looked at you.

– I smiled.

– The action the two simulate is undeniably assault.

– I did not hurry.

– But the simulation itself is undeniably consensual.

– I came and knelt in front of you.

– Are we to assume that Briseis has managed to fall in love with her abuser?

– I waited.

– If real then can her consent be meaningfully considered informed given the trauma she suffered and now relives at his hands?

– **You waited.**

– Or is Achilles simply the only available instrument in her volitional attempt to relive – and in reliving so reclaim – that trauma?

– **It seemed as if the world stopped.**

– Equally, what are we to make of Achilles' seeming subservience which so belies his very real authority as a vector of socio-structural coercion?

– **The temple was silent.**

– He keeps telling her he loves her.

– **Save for your breath.**

– He seems to believe it, and she seems to believe him.

– **And mine, and my heart.**

– The ensuing action of the play is an iterative process, re-enacting this moment with telling differences.

– **I love you.**

– Ringing the changes on a sequence.

– **I wish you would love me.**

– Irish playwright Enda Walsh has acknowledged the enormous influence Briseis' cyclical form has had on his writing.

– **But love is not water in a jug.**

– Sometimes Briseis' consent or even control is explicit, sometimes it is not.

– **And I am not a crow.**

– A theme emerges by virtue of its commonality to each revolution.

– **Love cannot be made to flow by so many deeds of love, dropped like stones.**

– Love is both irreducible and invisible.

– **Love cannot be made to flow by smashing the vessel.**

– Nothing in a physical action *per se* can determine if it is consensual or coercive.

– **You either love me or you do not.**

– What appears to be one may in fact be the other.

– **I am your slave and only your love can free me.**

– A theme that only grows more pressing in the age of internet pornography.

– **I obey you in everything in the hopes that you will love me.**

– Which just goes to show how prescient Maria's writing was.

– **But you cannot love me as long as you are my slave.**

– What would she have written if she'd lived to see the internet?

– **Maria's death aside, it's no wonder it was controversial.**

– Is Briseis defined by her pain?

– **or does she define it?**

– Yes.

– **Is this real?**

– or is this simulated?

– Yes.

– Is this feminist?

– or misogynist?

– Yes.

– Is this love?

– or is this rape?

– Yes.

– It's a dark play.

– It's a beautiful play.

– Darkly beautiful.

– The reviews were polarised to say the least.

– "With *Briseis,* Black announces herself as a fierce and wholly original talent."

– "An original and searingly poetic voice."

– "*Briseis* herself reinvented as an anti-Echo or anti-Philomel, in revolt against the millennial silencing of women."

– "A writer who refuses to play Penelope to any man."

– "Shows suicide as an expression not of despair, but the only rational response to a pathological world."

– "A brutally honest look at powerlessness and power, from a writer intimate with both."

– "*Briseis* unfolds in a bleak existential plane where to be a woman is to be subject to brutal exigency but, most unsettlingly, the action – which recalls recent stories from the Bosnian war – is perhaps not so removed from the world we live in as we would like to think."

– "So much self-indulgent tearing out of hair."

– "Refuses the supposedly bourgeois comforts of narrative and structure, touting its failure to offer anything more satisfying in their place as a political victory. Its artistic failure is presumably a non-issue to the artist, if she even claims the title."

–**"Feminist bullshit. Pornographic. Vomit-inducing. You can smell the dungarees off it."**

– It's impossible, now, knowing what happened, to experience that first scene the same way they did then.

– **You wish you could not know what the critics had said.**

– You wish you could experience it completely fresh.

– **As a total mystery.**

– You wish you could watch Briseis die not knowing that Maria died.

– **You wish you could not wonder about the link between them.**

– But you do wonder, all those things and many more too.

– **How free is free will?**

– Was what happened always going to?

– **Yes.**

– Was love as we understand it possible for a slave?

– **There she is!**

– And if not what of Achilles, fated to do what he did?

– **Woman of the hour!**

– Can you hate an abuser who has no choice?

– **Pleased with how it went?**

– Achilles didn't choose to be born as he was.

– **Hard to watch.**

– Maria Black didn't ask to be born as she was.

– **I saw some people crying.**

– Was that her?

– **The writer?**

– Yes.

– **Yes.**

– Did you mean any of that?

– **Fuck no I thought that was awful.**

– Really?

– **Piece of fucking shit.**

– Here's your wine.

– **Thanks.**

– Did you really hate it?

– **Did you really like it?**

– I thought parts of it were very affecting.

– **Like the monologue about her suicide attempt?**

– Visceral, yes.

– **It made me wish she'd gone through with it.**

– I know you don't think that.

– **Ten minutes in and with no end in sight I did.**

– It wasn't ten minutes.

– **Porn.**

– Honesty is porn now?

– **It is when it's porn. You really liked the writing?**

– God no she can't write for shit.

– **But it moved you.**

– The facts are powerful.

– **It's a shame about everything else.**

– You're a much better writer than she is.

– **I know.**

– Well that's blunt.

– **Should I pretend I don't think so? Both of us are much better writers than she is.**

– Thank you.

– **It's not a compliment.**

– The reviews are good.

– **Of course they fucking are.**

– Maybe we should just give up.

– **Maybe.**

– Be cab drivers.

– **Fuck you too.**

– What?

– **My dad's a cab driver.**

– Good one.

– **Really.**

– You're winding me up.

– **I don't want to shock you, but some dads AREN'T lawyers.**

– Well how was I to know if you never talk about him?

– **It's not my fault no one wants to talk about my family.**

– I don't not want to talk about your family.

– **I'm used to having a dead mother, it's other people who get awkward and change the subject.**

– Oh fuck off I never did that.

– **Is apologising that hard?**

– Sorry then.

– **There we go.**

– Don't be a bitch about it.

– **I'm not!**

– I didn't mean anything.

– **I know. What were you saying before?**

– The reviews are good.

– **She should start thinking about what she'll do.**

– For her next play?

– **For her next suicide attempt, or she won't have anything to write about in her next play.**

– I know you're more sympathetic than you're sounding.

– **Love the sinner but hate the sin.**

– You've written about your problems.

– **I've written characters with problems like my problems.**

– What's the difference?

– **The difference is characters do things. Characters don't almost kill themselves. Characters just kill themselves.**

– You don't think almost killing yourself is interesting?

– **Almost doing anything isn't interesting.**

– I write from my life.

– **And?**

– Is that what you think about my writing?

– **Would we be friends if I did?**

– The door was open. *(WRITER goes and sits at the table at this point.)*

– **You're right, I'm sorry.**

– Tea please.

– **You write beautifully. I wish I had your economy.**

– Under the weather?

– **Be fair Bea, what am I supposed to say?**

– Sorry, I should have known.

– **I think you confuse your life with your talent.**

– Do you want me to go?

– **They're really not.**

– You're sure?

– **A sculptor runs out of clay, but he doesn't run out of hand.**

– If you change your mind …

– **I love you.**

– Why not grapefruit?

– **Calm down, I do, I love you.**

– I didn't know that.

– **Are you getting the tube or are we saying goodbye?**

– I'll have to be careful if I'm making you sangria.

– **Alright then, I love you.**

(GO JOIN WRITER AT THE TABLE)

– I brought your post up. *(ACTOR is prompted by written stage direction to leave the first music stand and go to the table here. Switch from Location One script to Location Two script, contained in one of two envelopes preset on the table.)*

– **Thank you. Sweet.**

– Who's it from?

– **My dad, checking in on me.**

– Who's going first or are we reading at the same time?

– **Script is on the table.** *(WRITER at this point writes WINE on another piece of paper, and places it on the table.)*

– With the wineglass on it?

– **Yes.**

– This is your Greek rape play?

– **If you want to call it that. This is your abusive boyfriend play?**

– If you want to call it that. Finished draft?

– **Sort of.**

– Sort of?

– **All the action is there. The arc. I might add some text. But then again I might not.**

– So the play is finished, you just haven't written all the lines yet?

– **Yes.**

– And you'll put the spaghetti on after we've had dinner, will you?

– **That's not as clever as you think it is.**

– Would you mind if I took a photo from your window?

– **Why would I mind? Why do you want to take a photo of shit apartments and a chip shop?**

– It's a description exercise.

Take photos of things or moments, write descriptions of them periodically and as heterodoxically as you can manage. Practise versatility, plurality of perspective, an unsentimentality about any given metaphor no matter how good. Build an inner index of visuals and affects, wage war on the war of attrition that is clichéd idiom, or that's what Derek's course outline says anyway.

–**Or you could write a play.**

– I don't rip the piss out of your exercises.

– **I don't do exercises.**

– You just drink shitloads of wine.

– **And it works.**

– You've left a big ring on the script. *(WRITER draws a big ring on the WINE sign.)*

– **How will you ever forgive me.**

– Here's mine, I'm finished, AND I've written all the lines as well. The arc is there. The thought. It says what I want it to say.

– **Will I bother reading it or do you just want to tell me?**

– Kettle's boiled. Is there milk?

– **On the floor over there.**

– In that pile of dirty clothes?

–**Yes.**

–The fridge is more traditional.

– **The fridge is full of mould.**

– Also you'll break those books' spines leaving them like that. Also I don't know how you don't step on all those tapes.

– You can tidy my apartment if you want to. I won't stop you. Or you can start reading.

– Is this the end?

– **Which?**

– She says "yes"…

– **And he says "no".**

– Yes.

– **Yes, that's the last line before the stage directions.**

– What's with the stage directions?

– **What about them?**

– Bronze? Wine? Black?

– **What about them?**

– What the fuck is an actor supposed to do with that?

– **It's a Greek thing.**

– Pretentious.

– **Embrace it.**

– "The stage directions of *Briseis,* to paraphrase Lyotard, occupy not the end but the nascent state of dramaturgy."

– **You know they described the sea as wine and the sky as bronze?**

– "A non-indexical qualifier such as *bronze* or *wine* is only negligibly more absurd than Eugene O'Neill's specification that Burke should be 'too in the seventh heaven of bliss to truly understand her."

– **The colour didn't matter, it was the degree of intensity.**

– "Neither can be instantiated without the reader supplying their own criteria of instantiation."

– **I sometimes feel like that's a lesson for playwrights.**

– "Their total abstraction is not creative nihilism, but an acknowledgement and freeing of the interpreter's own faculties"

– **Right and wrong are for a court of law. The stage isn't for pastels.**

– "Theirs is an illusive and elusive didacticism."

– **Write it so they perform it the way you felt it. Why shouldn't stage directions be poems?**

– SO fucking pretentious.

– **It's only pretentious until you're taken seriously.**

– Your finished play has no ending.

– **Okay then.**

– This is just a load of words that don't mean anything.

– **They don't mean anything specific.**

– Very Dada.

– **Good to know.**

– I don't see why you're being coy when everyone knows they die.

– **She doesn't.**

– In the original I mean.

– **She doesn't.**

– She doesn't?

– **She just disappears because she's not important.**

– So have something happen to her. Give us her ending.

– **The Iliad ends right before everything happens.**

– You're not Homer.

– **Neither was Homer when he wrote the end of the Iliad.**

– Stop being quotable for a minute and just tell me honestly how you imagine the ending. They swap roles.

– **Yes.**

– Then they play the story again.

– **And she says yes.**

– And he says no, and then they have to somehow 'do' bronze, 'do' wine, and 'do' black, which means…?

– **Something else happens.**

– It's not inherently artistic to be mysterious.

– **I don't care about the action, I care about the feeling.**

– "Where her contemporaries specified poetic impossibilities, the transformation of an actor into a bird or the sudden growth of a sunflower up through the stage, Black is concerned with the impossibility of action itself."

– **If I told them what to do and they did it without the feeling, that wouldn't be the ending I wanted.**

– "This shift is analogous to that between classical musical notation or tablature and the bounded freedom of a jazz chord-chart."

– **You can't not interpret.**

– "Regulative rather than constitutive, end rather than means."

– **You just have to interpret intelligently.**

– Look, the play is obviously about free will.

– **Good to know.**

– Achilles is just as much a victim as Briseis.

– **Is he?**

– He knows he's going to die.

– **Everyone knows they're going to die.**

– He knows when and how and there's nothing he can do because he's trapped in his role as a great hero in the meantime.

– **Poor rapist. He had a choice.**

– Did he?

– **Yes.**

– Between what and what?

– **Between going home and dying at Troy.**

If he goes home, he lives a long and happy life.

If he stays at Troy, he dies young.

But he will never be forgotten.

– So he chose to die young?

– **If he doesn't die young, he doesn't become famous. If he doesn't die young, he doesn't become Achilles.**

– So why don't you show that?

– **Because I'm not interested in him almost doing something. I'm interested in what he does.**

– To this woman.

– **Yes.**

– Over and over.

– **Yes.**

– Don't you think that's a bit gratuitous?

– **Probably.**

– Porn, even?

– **Probably.**

– She should die.

– **That's the easy answer.**

– She should kill herself.

– **The one thing I am absolutely sure about is that she doesn't kill herself.**

– She would kill herself.

– **Good to know.**

– *(Pause.)* Are you sure the choice between family and glory isn't interesting?

– **No, because for most people it's not a difficult choice.**

– No?

– **No. Would you kill yourself tomorrow if it meant your plays would be famous forever?**

– *(Pause.)* No.

– **Are you sure?**

– Would you?

– **No.**

– You sure?

– **Absolutely.**

– "As radical as Black's waspishly defiant Briseis is, her feminised Achilles is at least as noteworthy."

– **I don't want to be a myth.**

– "Where Briseis grasps for the authority not mandated to the women of the *Iliad*, Achilles willingly renounces and subjects himself to it."

– **I love myth.**

– "Power destroys the possibility of understanding and – with it – the possibility of love."

– **But I don't trust myth.**

– "He suffers so that a sufferer can love him."

– **Myths are simple stories for a cruel world.**

– "A secular nihilist Christdom."

– **If we ever want to live in a less cruel world, we have a duty to be more than myths.**

– "This inversion of the original is revealed to be no such thing."

– **We have a duty to not be Achilles.**

– "The attainment of immortality or Briseis' love both require Achilles not just to be destroyed, but to destroy himself willingly." Shit.

(WRITER at this point overturns a cup full of paper on the floor, without any pretense that it was accidental.)

– **I'll get you a teacloth.**

– Thank you.

– **What were you saying?**

– I wasn't, you were.

– **About fate, yes.**

– Whether what happened was always going to.

– **Yes.**

– Any questions or comments for me?

– **How harsh am I allowed be?**

– How harsh do you want to be?

– **You know I don't like a mix of monologues and scenes.**

– And I know you're wrong.

– **We've done this before.**

– Is some constructive criticism too much to hope for?

– **Why aren't the scenes monologues and why aren't the monologues scenes?**

– The monologues express what she can't express quotidianly.

– **You could just say 'in real life'.**

– You don't like it.

– **There's feeling, but no insight.**

– A vivid description of a feeling can be an insight to someone who's never had that feeling.

– **He punches her in the face. Then you give her a monologue so she can tell us what she thinks about being punched in the face.**

– And?

– **We just saw it happen.**

– And?

– **All she really tells us is that pain is painful.**

– Well what should she tell us?

– You tell me what she should tell us.

– No you tell me what she should tell us.

– I don't think she should tell us anything, I think she should decide something.

– There are stories that disappear if you try to tell them through action. Their reality is internal. If you externalise it you coarsen it. What do you want her to do, kill him?

– Or kiss him.

– That would normalise abuse.

– Don't flatter yourself. Abuse doesn't need your help. Abuse IS normal, here and everywhere.

– Good to know, any further sermons?

– It's very obviously based on you and Mark.

– Only if you know me. Only if you knew Mark.

– Even if I didn't. Even if I hadn't. I'd know.

– How?

– It's very obvious that the things she knows are things you know.

– Like?

– Like what it feels like to be punched in the face.

– If you didn't know me you wouldn't know.

– I would.

– How?

–Because every time she talks I can tell I'm supposed to be impressed.

– And?

– **And I'm not.**

– That's just you. Someone else might find it interesting.

– **You're not talking to someone else.**

– So you think this scene is just completely and categorically devoid of interest of any kind to any possible viewer.

– **No. I think it makes YOU more interesting. I think it makes your play less interesting.**

– *(Pause.)* You could have just said the exposition needs to be smoother.

– **I could have.**

Look.

I think the language is great.

I think the action is great.

But the emphasis is wrong.

Go ahead and put your bed in a gallery.

Go ahead and charge people admission to see your knickers full of discharge.

Go all the way and kill yourself, be the martyr they want you to be.

Show them you're a fuck-up.

Be the most fucked-up fuck-up they've ever seen.

They'll love you for it.

But you're a woman.

It's what they expect from you.

Men become writers because they have talent, women become writers because they have pain. Right?

Some day, when you're famous and adored and dead, little girls will look at you and think

that being a fuck-up is the best they can do.

They'll think: "When I grow up, I want to put MY head in an oven!"

We have a duty to each other.
We have a duty to be more than our pain.
We have a duty to not be Achilles.

– I think you're wrong.

(WRITER WILL PROMPT YOU HERE)

(WRITER at this point prompts the ACTOR to go put a tape on the tapeplayer, and to start playing it immediately even if WRITER is still speaking.)

You know what they say, the show begins the first time you hear about it and it ends when you stop thinking about it, which means everything you know about the show is part of the show.

Like it or not, real life is part of the art and the art is part of real life, the ground is the figure.

Artists don't have a monopoly on art, art is all around us.

Memories are stories we tell ourselves.

Stories are the memories of people we aren't but could be.

"Don't tell me the moon is shining: show me the glint of light on broken glass."

Why shouldn't I use my broken glass to make my writing more vivid?

Vivify, right.

You write your sensibility, but seeing as your sensibility's a symptom of your entire life you can't help but reveal yourself.

You can't help but be part of the story.

Why not embrace it like you're always telling me to do?

If you don't want your audience to know who you are, why do you write for them?

How can you write for them?

(Pause.)

I think you're in denial.

You don't want to bejust another depressed woman, but you are.

You should have been that you are had the maidenliest star in the firmament twinkled on your bastardising.

You're the one who's always telling me to embrace pretentiousness.

Pretention, whatever.

(WRITER switches on the lamp on the table and overhead light goes to blackout. Under the music, they prompt the ACTOR as follows.

PROMPT AUDIBLE TO THE AUDIENCE: WRITER asks ACTOR how they're doing. Explains that this music is a way of letting everyone know we're in a club now. We're using a tape player because it's more Nineties appropriate, even if the music isn't the music you would have heard in a Nineties club and the club wouldn't have been playing tapes. Please imagine it's trendy Nineties dance music, and now let's dance, even calmly, but let's dance so everyone knows in reality we were dancing our socks off. Now WRITER has a private prompt for ACTOR.

SECRET PROMPT: After each of WRITER's lines, ACTOR should say "please don't take my photo". When WRITER says HERE WE GO and claps, ACTOR will go open the as yet unused script at Location Three.)

– DO YOU WANT A DRINK

ARE YOU SURE
BECAUSE – WHAT? – OH, RIGHT

I'LL HAVE ONE IF YOU'RE HAVING ONE

DO I NEED TO –
CHEAP!

SHOULD I TAKE TWO AS WELL?

OF COURSE I HAVE I – WHAT

WHAT

OKAY THAT WAS A LIE I HAVEN'T EVER BUT I
DIDN'T – WHAT

OKAY

OKAY

THANK YOU
OKAY

HERE WE GO

(WRITER claps and ACTOR goes to Location Three)

– I THINK I'M FEELING IT

– **VIVID**

– ARE YOU?

– **UGLY**

– I'M DEFINITELY – WHAT

– **GLORIOUS**

– ARE YOU?

– **INTIMATE**

– NO I'M DEFINITELY – WHAT

– **CLENCH**

– OH MY GOD

– **CLASP**

– WAIT CAN I TAKE A PICTURE

(WRITER stops dancing here and looks at ACTOR. They begin to write BLACK on a sign)

– **BUCK AND BUCKLE**

– TO REMEMBER

– **FLESH GIVES**

– I DO FUCKING INSIST

SPASM

– PLEASE

UNDER MY HANDS

– PLEASE

JUMP OF MUSCLE

– PLEASE

PALSY

– LOOK ISN'T THAT LOVELY, THE TWO OF US, AND YOU'RE ACTUALLY SMILING

NOT MINE

RABBITRED

I TASTE BLOOD

CRUEL ARCH AND STRETCHED MOUTH

BITTEN TONGUE

MINE
SWEAT SLICK
HEAVE
SPIT SALT

RED MASK GAPPED WHERE I FILL HIM
NOTCHED

HAND CROWN

MILLENIUM GLIMPSE OF THORNS

(FADE MUSIC)

BLEEDING SAVIOUR HAND

PRICK CIRCLE OF FRANTIC TEETH

VOWEL SPEECH

IDIOT FRENZY

HIS TONGUE GESTURES

ACROSS THE FIST COLONY

MINE
PUSHED PAST HYSTERICAL IVORY

HIS SMASHED PORTCULLIS

SOFT AS LOVE IN A CRABCLAW

HIS CHEEK IN MY HAND

AND WORDS ARE ALMOST

ALMOSTING

FROTH OF MEANING BLOWN FROM HIS GAPE

I TORQUE IN HIM

GRIPPED AND ANGLING

FLESH GIVES

– Maybe we should take a break.

– **Instant animal discord**

– Check in with one another.

– **Silk silence of blood as it crowds**

– Before we go any further.

– **Liquid rasp of his throat filling**

– Because the next bit's worse.

– **I am most myself in these moments.**

–How are you doing NAME? *(WRITER turns off lamp and overhead light returns.)*

– **Mad stuff, isn't it?**

– Are you finding it too much?

– **Not at all. I really enjoyed that last bit.**

– Achilles' war monologue, it's a favourite of mine.

– **I really enjoyed the juxtaposition.**

– Of dancing and violence?

– **Yes, showing they're connected.**

– Yes.

– **It's kind of sexual as well.**

– Yes, Dionysiac pleasures, not exactly immoral but –

– **Amoral.**

– Couldn't have put it better myself. You can't choose not to enjoy something you enjoy.

– **You can't choose not to be something you are.**

– You don't think it's too clever clever?

– **Not at all.**

– I mean the hope is that it accesses something really fundamental to the play, even if it's a creative liberty.

– **What even is a creative liberty?**

– I like to think that's what she'd have thought.

– **Spirit not letter.**

– Exactly. And just to warn and maybe reassure you in the next bit we're going to show one of the scenes where Achilles pursues Briseis, but it's okay because it's one of the ones where the preceding text indicates her explicit consent.

– **I appreciate the warning.**

– Although seeing as it would be dramaturgically redundant to show that scene, now that I've told you it happens, we're not going to do it.

– **Wonderful.**

– And obviously I also consent to having you chase me.

– **Cool.**

–And you're sure you're not finding it too disturbing so far?

– **Not at all.**

– You sure?

– **It's just strange knowing what eventually happened.**

– What she eventually did.

– **Yes.**

– The number of jokes she makes.

– **Yes. Do you think that she...?**

– What, knew she was going to do it then?

– **Yes.**

– Couldn't say.

– **She talks about it so much.**

– Yes.

– **And it doesn't sound like she was going to.**

– *(Pause.)* No.

– **Is her father still alive?**

– Yes, he's been to see the show, he's lovely, super supportive.

– **But her mother died?**

– When she was three.

– **That's hard.**

– It goes without saying.

– **Quick question.**

– Yes?

– **I wondered about the art piece she mentioned there.**

– That you mentioned.

– **Yes, that I mentioned. It's *My Bed*, isn't it?**

– Well spotted!

– **Thanks, I actually know a lot about art.**

– I don't doubt it, sorry, did I sound condescending just there?

– **That's not it, but I wondered about something.**

– I try very hard not to mansplain.

– **You're fine.**

– You're sure?

– **Yes, but can I check something?**

(WRITER opens the other envelope on the table, inside which is the game text beginning 'Consequently the play's triumph')

– The problem of female sexuality and agency in *Briseis* is
irreconcilable with facile binarism of the sort that defines
a work as either unarguably empowering or irredeemably
problematic.

–She did the tent before the bed, didn't she?

– Indeed, the fundamental subject of the play is the
collision between unstoppable force and immovable
object; Briseis' undeniable agency in a world which cannot
countenance it.

**– *Everyone I Ever Slept With* in 1995, and *My Bed* was
1998, wasn't it?**

(WRITER WILL PROMPT YOU HERE)

*(WRITER prompts ACTOR to stand stage left in preparation for the
following game:*
*when WRITER claps the ACTOR is going to chase them, grab this
piece of paper off them and keep tearing it up into smaller and
smaller pieces until told to stop. At the point at which they lose the
paper, WRITER returns to speaking their lines from memory at the
point indicated below.)*

– Consequently the play's triumph is to maintain a constant
awareness of – and singing dissonance between – consent
and coercion.

Briseis consents in a world where meaningful consent is
impossible.

Achilles coerces in a world where coercion is the only
possibility.
(Game starts here.)
Briseis foregrounds the mechanism of tragedy as much as
it depends upon it, and few plays strike so fine a balance
between the invocation and subversion of their constituent
tropes, or indeed expose so incisively the cruellest irony
of the 'Apollonian' artform; the gesture which allows us to
most strongly experience our own humanity as audience
members – namely the entropic winding down towards

inevitable destruction – is precisely what robs the tragedy's subjects of their humanity. What meaning can their self-determinism have in a deterministic universe?
Seen through this lens, Black's re-interpretation or, alternatively, creative misprision of, Greek schema is not simple revisionism or pastiche, but an attempt to manifest the latent nihilism of the Greeks, as articulated by Silenus the forest spirit and subsequently quoted by the young Nietzsche in the Birth of Tragedy. "The best thing for man is not have been born, the second best to die soon."

This is, of course, the inevitable conclusion for both Achilles and Briseis.

(When game ends, WRITER skips to this point.)

Black's own premature and volitional death, while not part of the text *per se*, is certainly apposite or at least –

I mean of course I miss her, she –

people always say this, I know, but hardly a day goes by –

really –

that I don't think about her.
Afterwards, I remember right after there was this –

she'd done this ad voiceover and it was still on telly and it was so strange –

I'd hear her voice saying –

in that cheerful voice, you know –

but she'd I don't actually remember what the ad was for but –

And I'd always sort of laugh because –

if you knew her it was very funny and I'd think –

I'd be laughing and planning to tease her and then I'd remember.

Every time all over again.

(WRITER prompts ACTOR to return to location one.)

I felt the only thing we could do was stage it.

Interest but no pressure, is what the theatres –

considering the circumstances –

interest, in the play, but no pressure –
With that and then there was some German money there
to be had –
Germans love weird shit, in exchange for a commitment,
the money was I mean –

I say that with love, obviously I – love for her –

"Weird bitch" was sort of a, I don't know, an affectionate
thing, back and forth.

She'd call me a weird bitch and I'd call her a –

you get it.

– I wish I could see my father again.

– The only issue was the ending.

– It's been years.

– "Abstract is fine, but this isn't abstract."

– Is he an old man yet?

– "This is a narrative you can't possibly access."

– Does he now look like my grandfather used to?

– "It's inconsistent if not disingenuous to say it's abstract
when you know she had a right answer in mind."

– Do I now look like he used to?

– They had a point.

– There is no return voyage from this furthest shore.

– Much as I loved her, she was full of shit sometimes.

– I wish I could speak to him.

– Those ridiculous stage directions.

– Even just once.

– There's pretentious and then there's annoying.

– I don't know what I would say.

– And we'd spoken about it less than a week before.

– I love you.

– And she had said she was going to add more spoken text.

– I'm sorry.

– And I was the one who found her.

– I might say nothing and he might understand anyway.

– The door was open it was always open and she was just, her mouth was full of –

– I have loved and been loved.

– Pale in the gloom, bright as – she might say, like her Greeks, I'd gone to apologise, we'd had this fight, but who else could it have been?

– I have lost more than some will ever have.

– It was there on the table with that big ring of wine on it and – her spirit is in it.

– I have lost love by dying, but I was always going to.

– If it were a screenplay I wouldn't get a named credit.

– But my love will be remembered because I will be remembered.

– Less than 33%.

– **Better to be dead than to be forgotten.**

– And it's only the truth that the work was largely editorial.

– **I am both, wiped away like a spilled drink.**

(WRITER overturns one of the cups full of shredded paper.)

– The ending has sparked as many critical outpourings as the start.

– **Briseis still hasn't found what she is looking for in their games.**

–And Achilles' obedience hasn't made her love him as he loves her.

– **Neither wants to be themselves anymore.**

– And so they swap roles. *(WRITER and ACTOR at this point swap shirts, with nametags attached.)* Achilles plays the slave girl stolen from her father.

– **And Briseis plays the hero of the Trojan war.**

– They trade lives and powers and live the story one more time.

– **Moore remembers Black describing the process as "wiping your hand across a charcoal drawing".**

– "The skeleton is clear but the detail is diffused throughout the frame."

– **Love is a becoming.**

– I am suddenly, finally, strangely, submissive.

– **I am suddenly, finally, strangely, dominant.**

– Is this a game where we become the things we've never been?

– **Or is this what we've been all along?**

– Yes.

– **Now that the roles are reversed, the loop suddenly breaks.**

– The action can continue.

– **It is now.**

– It is here.

– **This is happening right in front of you.**

– Hector is dead by Achilles' hand.

– **Achilles knows his name will live forever.**

– And he cannot make Briscis love him as he loves her.

– **There is nothing left to win.**

– No one left to fight.

– **Why not die now?**

– Suicide is the only means by which Achilles can exercise control over his destiny.

– **If he must die young, he can at least choose when and why.**

– But a gentle and willing death is the only kind he knows nothing about.

– **And so Briseis shows him.**

– Briseis dies at Achilles' hands.

– **In order to teach Achilles how to die himself.**

– They unlive the unhappy past they were trapped in, and the new past becomes their future.

– **She asks him is he ready. Are you ready?**

– He asks her is she ready. Are you ready?

– **She says yes. Yes.**

– And he says no. No.

– **And this time Briseis strangles Achilles.**

– Which means Achilles, playing Briseis, strangles Briseis.

– **Briseis, playing Achilles, is strangled by Achilles.**

– Don't worry, it'll be less confusing when we do it in a minute.
He finally sees himself without the power he never wished for.

– **She finally sees herself with the power she always wished for.**

– Her character is a fiction but her consent is real.

– **He strangles her.**

– She is not Achilles but she is happy to die.

– **He sees that in her and he wonders.**

– Did she love him that much?

– **Or hate life that much?**

–Yes.

– **No.**

– It's impossible, now, knowing what happened, to experience that last scene the same way they did then.

– **You wish you could not know what the critics had said.**

– You wish you could experience it completely fresh.

– **As a total mystery.**

– You wish you could watch Briseis die not knowing that Maria died.

– **You wish you could not wonder about the link between them.**

– But you do wonder, all those things and many more too.

– Just like Achilles.

– Is that the ultimate despair?

– Or the ultimate gesture of love?

– Yes.

– No.

– It's an astonishing ending.

– Hello then.

– I find it very hard to watch, speaking as her friend just thinking about it makes me cry.

– It's always open.

– "He gripped her hard so that life should not drag her from that moment."

– Me too.

– But love was not enough.

– How many times is that you've called now?

(GO JOIN WRITER AT THE TABLE.)

(ACTOR is prompted by stage direction at this point to return to the table, and resume the use of the envelopescript.)

– Nothing could hold her when she wanted to go.

– I thought it was something like that.

– You disappeared.

– I didn't think you'd miss me, you looked like you were having fun.

– Were you not?

– I felt sick.

– I worried.

– **You managed.**

– You could have said.

– **I thought I'd leave you to it.**

– Were you not having fun at all?

– **Nothing happened.**

– With the Es?

– **I took them and nothing happened.**

– Why?

– **Probably all the other stuff I'm taking.**

– What are you taking now?

– **Will the names mean anything to you?**

– Just curious.

– **All you need to know is they took me off twenty milligrams of one thing and put me on twenty milligrams of this thing.**

– That's a lot.

– **That's the most.**

– And it's making you worse?

– **No.**

– But you feel sick.

– **I'm adjusting. You feel sick when you're adjusting.**

– Is that normal?

– **Yes.**

– So how do you know if they're working?

– **I don't know.**

– You don't know?

– They keep changing my prescription, so I keep having to adjust.

– So you just feel sick all the time?

– Yes.

– Is that better than just being off them?

– Yes.

– How?

– For my dad.

– For your dad?

– Yes.

– How?

– Because getting a phonecall saying I'm in hospital again upsets him.

(Pause.)

– Has that happened a lot?

– Bea, I say this with love.

– You say what with love?

– You're exhausting.

– I'm just trying to understand.

– You don't need to understand.

– I can't help if I don't understand.

– I don't need you to help.

– I'm your friend.

– You are.

– Friends help.

– You can help by listening.

– I am listening to you.

– You're not.

– I am listening, but you're not explaining.

– You want me to explain?

– Yes.

– Sometimes just existing is exhausting.

And people make it worse.

If you phone I might not answer.

If we make plans I might not turn up.
If you knock on my door I might not answer.

That has to be okay.

– So you do whatever you want to do and I have to be
okay with that?

– Yes.

– How is that fair on me?

– None of this is fair on anyone.

– Am I important to you at all?

– I don't need you to be important.

I need you to be my friend.

– What is that supposed to mean?

**– Sometimes you seem more interested in saving me
than talking to me.**

– What is that supposed to mean?

– You want me to be blunter?

– Yes.

– **I think you need me to need you.**

– I don't.

– **I think you think life is a soap opera sometimes.**

– I don't.

– **I think you think my life is a juicy storyline sometimes.**

– I don't.

– **And I worry that my life is going to turn up in your writing.**

– It won't.

– **And sometimes I feel like I'm Kurt Cobain, and you're waiting for me to die so you can write *Who Killed Kurt Cobain*.**

– Wow.

– **Is that blunt enough?**

– *(Pause.)* I was thinking the other day you're never kind to me.

– **So why do you want to be my friend so much?**

– I was thinking the other day that if I was more successful than you we wouldn't be friends.

– **Yes.**

– That's all you have to say?

– **I'm not going to be your villain, Bea.**

– You're so fucking condescending.

– **Yes.**

– If I had your career and you had mine, I wouldn't be your friend just to make myself feel big.

– **If I had your career and you had mine, I wouldn't be your friend just to make myself feel less small.**

– I'm as good as you.

– **You're not.**

– Fuck you.

– **That was predictable.**

– What makes you think you're so great?

– **I'm not the one who thinks that.**

– You want me to think you don't care what I think or what anyone thinks but the truth is you care more than anyone what everyone thinks, you're terrified we'll work you out, you're terrified we'll think you're as small as you think we are.

– **Okay then.**

– And you think I'm a boring writer.

– **Yes.**

– Fuck you.

– **What do you want?**

– Your Greek rape play is shit.

– **Probably.**

– You wish that the things that had happened to me had happened to you.

– **No.**

– You shit on me for writing about my shit of an ex-boyfriend because you wish you'd had one.

– **No.**

– You wish you'd even had a boyfriend.

– **Really no.**

– Yes, because then you wouldn't have to be 'abstract' to hide the fact you don't know what the fuck you're talking about.

– **I know everything I need to know.**

– You wish, how?

– **Because you fucking love telling me.**

– And you love to be told but you'll never admit it. You say you find misery boring but only because you're always miserable for no reason. You're jealous because I have something to be miserable about.

– **I'm not the one who wants to be miserable.**

– So I am?

– **He hit you once and then you left him. Get the fuck over it already.**

– *(Pause.)* I think you're a deeply selfish person.

– **Good to know.**

– In that last moment.

– **Storm out if you want to, but I'm not going to call you back.**

– Spastic terror.

– **That's not what's going on.**

– Intimate crepitus of the straining neck.

– **That's not the story we're living.**

– Abortive suck.

– **We're not living a story at all.**

– Crippled and purpling.

– I thought this was the only way.

– Abrupt rupture.

– She didn't love me.

– Desperate upward rut.

– Or so I thought.

– I drown in myself.

She put on my skin.

I put on hers.

Because love is a becoming.

My hands are not my hands now.

My face is not my face.

I speak someone else's words with someone else's voice.
I don't know why I'm saying what I'm saying.

Am I saying this right?

I'm worried I'm fucking it all up.

I don't know how to pronounce this word.

Or this one.

Or this one.

Or this one.

I don't know what to do.

Someone just tell me what to do.

Please.

Am I saying this right?

(WRITER WILL PROMPT YOU HERE.)

(WRITER switches the lamp on as this text ends and overhead light goes off. They turn on the tapeplayer. They tear up the BRONZE sign which has been indicating Hector, and ask ACTOR to lie on the floor amongst the tearings with a larger piece of the sign protruding from their mouth.)

Maria?

The door was open so I

Maria?

Maria? Maria?

Jesus.
Shit.

(WRITER takes three steps one way, then three steps the other. They tear the WINE sign out of the book and pocket it. They take ACTOR's photograph with the polaroid camera. They turn the tapeplayer off. They help ACTOR up, give them the polaroid to put in their pocket, and quietly prompt them to go read the text on the coaster under the rightmost downstage cup of water. They write YES and NO on their hands while ACTOR speaks the following tabletext, revealed as each cup is lifted and drunk.)

– **Imagine this is whiskey, or vodka, or rum.**

(DRINK THE WHOLE THING AND GO PICK UP THE NEXT ONE.)

– **I don't know for sure, I wasn't there.**

(DRINK THE WHOLE THING AND GO PICK UP THE NEXT ONE.)

– **And imagine I'm a much smaller woman than I am.**

(DRINK THE WHOLE THING AND WRITER WILL PROMPT YOU HERE.)

(ACTOR drinks the glass of water and is prompted to location three. WRITER turns off lamp and overhead light returns.)

– Still doing alright, NAME?

– **Yes.**

– Not finding it too weird?

– **Not at all.**

– You sure?

– **I do kind of need to wee.**

– After drinking all that water, of course, sorry about that.

– **What was that about anyway?**

– One of the factors in Maria's death was a blood alcohol of .35%, which is very high, nearly as high as Amy Winehouse's upon her death.

– **I thought overdose meant sleeping pills or something.**

– And you're sure you're not uncomfortable with having to say some of the things she says?

– **I wish you'd stop asking that.**

– I know I find her dismissal of Bea's past abuse particularly uncomfortable, but Bea felt and I felt that it's important to acknowledge her more problematic opinions, that and some of the things she says about other women, I personally give her the benefit of the doubt because she was herself a woman.

– **Do you think it's a problem that you're a man and you're presenting this version of the play?**

– I see what you're saying and I take that as a potential criticism very seriously but no, I don't think it is a problem, why would it be when the play itself is ultimately by a woman?

– **So women can't be misogynist?**

– It's not for me to pass judgement on her experience of womanhood.

– **Are some of your best friends women?**

– I try very hard to respect the source text.

– **Were those her exact words?**

– You can't not interpret, you can only interpret intelligently.

– **You said you added Bea and Maria to the text.**

– And after all the research I really feel I know her.

– **The Spice Girls had their first single in 1996.**

(WRITER upturns a cup full of paper.)

– Shit.

– **I remember it coming out, it was Wannabe.**

– Don't worry about that, NAME, I have a spare.

– **And Who Killed Kurt Cobain wasn't written until 1999.**

– What was I saying?

– **She said Achilles had a choice.**

– I feel like I knew her, like I know her, I do know her through her work.

– **He chose the myth.**

– She had a beautiful mind, too beautiful to be durable.

– **or the myth chose him.**

– "Who shall measure the heat and violence of the poet's heart when caught and tangled in a woman's body?"

– **My mouth is full of blood and my tongue is gone.**

– Bright flames burn briefest.

– **I have been turned into a swallow.**

– I do see where you're coming from about some of the things she says.

– **I am graceful but my hands are fans of agony.**

– Bea says she was actually much harsher than this.

– **I cannot speak.**

– The things that she says, that you say, about women and pain could be seen as internalised misogyny, a patriarchal discounting of the lived experience of other women.

– **I cannot write.**

– But I like to think she's making a much subtler point about the naivety of first world choice feminism which doesn't acknowledge the ways in which choices that are personally empowering can entrain conditions that leave other women worse off.

– **"Most women can't write."**

– But yes, Bea says she usually wasn't even that multivalent.

– **But I am writing.**

– But it was the Nineties, you have to make allowances.

– **I am a character traced on the sky.**

– Yesterday's radicals are today's reactionaries, just look at Germaine Greer.

– **I mean only myself.**

– As a feminist ally or just a feminist if no one minds me calling myself that – do you mind NAME? Are you sure? – it behooves me not to misrepresent her through manipulative editing.

– **I cannot be interpreted.**

– She was a more brilliant thinker than some of the things she said made her sound.

– **Are you serious?**

– I know her well enough to say that with confidence.

– **You want me to say that?**

– It's not what she said, but it's what she would say today.

– **I'm not going to say that.**

– Ultimately her father saw where I was coming from.

– **That's disgusting.**

– I understood why he was upset, but she's not just his.

– **This is fucked.**

– She belongs to everyone who discovers her work.

– **Totally fucked.**

– He knew her longer, but did he know her any better?

– **Help me.**

– Can he confidently say she was never like this?

– **Bronze.**

– Can he confidently say she didn't mean this?

– **Wine.**

– No, so this is still – in spirit if not letter – a performance of Maria Black's *Briseis*.

– **Black.**

(WRITER WILL PROMPT YOU HERE.)

(WRITER tears the BLACK sign from the book and gives WINE from their pocket to ACTOR, prompting them that they are about to play the game they played last time. This time they're both trying

to destroy the other's sign, and whoever grabs the other has to tear up both.)

I suppose that's a no, since I did the last edits for publication –

I haven't –

It's too real still –

The violence of the language is too close to how she was when she –

during the bad times, she would –

And the ending, I still wonder –

was it some kind of –

almost, I mean we can't know, rehearsal or –

I think she knew even then and –

it makes me so angry that she –

Speaking as her friend just thinking about –

So that's a no.

I have our photos at least.

People have asked for them but I said –

for an archive, but I didn't want that.

They're too personal.

They're mine.

She's mine.

(ACTOR should rush forward expecting a chase, but WRITER offers no resistance. There may be a still moment that lasts until ACTOR realises the show cannot continue unless the game plays out. They may just grab the sign. Either way, WRITER directs ACTOR to put their sign – saying BLACK – in their pocket, to tear WINE to pieces, and to go to their location for the finale.)

Why won't you speak?

You scare me when you won't speak.

I know you didn't speak before, but I can't remember it on my own.
I crossed the beach and followed the path.

(ALL OF THESE PROMPTS ARE DELIVERED USING THE WORDS WRITTEN ON WRITER'S HANDS.)

– **Yes.**

– The day was bright but the temple was dim.

– **Yes.**

– I came to the doorway and saw you standing there.

– **Yes.**

– You saw my long shadow from the morning sun behind me as it stretched across the floor.

– **Yes.**

– You looked up and ran.

– **Yes.**

– You could hear my following footsteps between yours and your heartbeat.

– **Yes.**

– You crashed into a standing brazier and it fell. *(WRITER knocks over the first chair earlier indicated.)*

– **Yes.**

– You knocked a second over on purpose to try and slow me. *(WRITER knocks over the second chair earlier indicated.)*

– **Yes.**

– I didn't slow, and you fell.

– **No.**

– No?

– **No.**

– You knocked a second over on purpose to try and slow me and it did.

– **Yes.**

– I fell. *(WRITER kneels where ACTOR died.)*

– **Yes.**

– I looked at you.

– **Yes.**

– You smiled.

– **Yes.**

– You came and knelt in front of me.

– **Yes.**

– NAME, will you do me a favour?

– **Yes.**

– Will you come and kneel in front of me?

– **Yes.**

– You said "This is what you want more than anything."

– **Yes.**

– I said "This is what I want more than anything."

– **Yes.**

– NAME are you finding this disturbing?

– **Yes.**

– It'll all be over soon, will you do me a favour?

– **No.**

– Would it help if I said this is the hardest part?

– **No.**

– Would it help if I said we're about to change scenes?

– **Yes.**

– Will you take the photo I took of you out of your right breast pocket and arrange my body so I'm lying on the floor like you are in the photo?

– **Yes.**

– Now will you put your hands on my neck like you're strangling me, but don't actually strangle me, if you need to sit on my chest or stomach to do that that's fine.

– **Yes.**

Tom I'm so glad you came!

It really means a lot!

Not that I thought you were going to –

But then that's what opening night is for, it's so nice to see –

It's probably the same for you, it definitely is, all the friendly faces who care so deeply.

The outpourings.

Moving. It's moving. I find it moving.

Do you have a drink, can I, do you, let me buy you a drink?

– **No.**

– How's the cab business, still driving the cab, I suppose London being London, busy as ever?

– **Yes.**

– Please, let me buy you a drink, it's no trouble, don't just be polite, after everything that, I mean, are you sure?

– **Yes.**

– Powerful isn't it?

– **Yes.**

– The show? Astonishing, the –

Sorry were you going to say something?

– **No.**

– Sorry, she was an astonishing writer wasn't she, you must be so proud.

Did you enjoy it?

Not enjoy it, that's the wrong word, did you –

I feel I should say it's been an absolute honour. Is that inappropriate?

– **No.**

– I'm so glad it happened.

That the show got to happen, that we got it made, that I was able to play a part in making sure people got to –

Sorry I just wanted that to be clear.

Hot isn't it?

All these people.

So wonderful.

Is something wrong?

– **No.**

– Do you have to go?

– **Yes.**

– Are you sure there's nothing wrong?

– **Yes.**

– Because I have this feeling, please, if there's anything, maybe this is the wrong thing to say but I'd rather know if there's something I've done or –

NAME will you lean down so I can whisper in your ear?

– **Yes.**

– Yes, I did do something, inadvertently or, either way I'm sorry Tom, please just tell me, let's not let it, I suppose, fester.

(Whispered prompt to ACTOR to say the following.)

All they said was they couldn't rule it out.

She tried before and –

She'd drunk that much before.

– and that time she –
You should know, you'd seen her drink that much before.
But you said in the paper she killed herself.

You know she didn't listen.

They said she choked.

She didn't listen when they gave her big lists of things to remember.

She wasn't supposed to drink.

She's not a character Bea.

She was my little girl.

She was real.

All she did was fall.

And you you just

You just

Bronze.

Wine.

Black.

(WRITER directs ACTOR to take the BLACK sign out of their pocket and tear it in half. As they do so, blackout.)

TRAITOR

BY

SHANE MAC AN BHAIRD

Traitor will be performed from the 20-24 September 2016 at The Project Arts Centre as part of Tiger Dublin Fringe by That Lot theatre with the followed cast and production team.

BANNION: Aonghus Og McAnally

FINBAR PLUNKETT: Jamie Hallahan

FRANCES PLUNKETT: Gillian McCarthy

GRACE MEEHAN: Roseanna Purcell

LIZARD: Kevin C. Olohan

Director: Shane Mac an Bhaird

Producer: Alan Mahon

Set Designer: Cait Corkery

Costume Designer: Amy Hegarty

Sound Designer: Rob Moloney

Lighting Designer: Cillian McNamara

Production Manager: Barry O'Donovan

Dramaturg: Maureen White

This play was commissioned by Rough Magic Theatre Company as part of the SEEDS Programme.

A massive thank you to
Lynne Parker, Darragh Kelly, Gina Moxley, Jennifer O'Dea, Margret McAuliffe, Shane Lennon, Rob Malone, Geoff Gould, Jen Coppinger, Clare Robertson, Bébhinn Cronin, Diego Fasciati, Caroline Williams, Ferdia Lennon, Des Ward and Sinead Hogan.

Scene

The play is set in a park commemorating Finbar Plunkett which was once the site of a protest camp against the fire sale of an old public mental hospital to a foreign hedge fund.

Time

The play is split between two moments, the first, late in the day in February 2026, the second is ten years previously and spans a few crucial days surrounding the Dublin riots in 2016. The time period shifts back and forth during the play, the actors moving in and out of the different times as required, sometimes observing events in the past from their position in the future.

February 2026. Night of the election results.

A small, commemorative park in the shadows of high-end apartment blocks.

The statue is covered by a sheet and a speaking plinth is set up next to it.

The sound of a huge crowd cheering and singing can be heard in the distance.

ENTER LIZARD. He is completely covered in tattoos (pictures of wires, mathematical formulas, geometric shapes, electrical circuits). His face has been altered and his eyes tattooed.

He is carrying bags and drops them in front of the statue. He circles it. He spits.

LIZARD: Ha!

Nah.

Ha?

You're a statue now Finbar, that's the latest.

LIZARD spits.

LIZARD starts unpacking his things.

LIZARD hears the crowds in the distance, singing 'Wild Mountain Thyme'…

Hear them singing? There's a huge rally in the city today. They've set up a podium on O'Connell Street and it's full, end to end, stuffed with thousands and thousands of people, waving flags and singing. They think they're going to win the election.

First chance they get they'll be tearing at each other like rabid dogs. Marching together now. Spite and 'ating each other tomorrow. Law of the creature. Like gravity.

LIZARD slaps his hand to his neck.

Still haven't… There. I'm sure there's still a part of my neck I haven't finished yet. I can feel it.

LIZARD takes out a mirror from one of his bags.

I need to finish my neck…

LIZARD checks the tattoo on his neck.

Chants of "change, change, change" in the distance…

LIZARD: *(Mocking chant.)* Change. Change. Change.

There are fireworks.

Fireworks. I hate fireworks. A flash of colour and a fizzle and that's that. Nothing but darkness after that! Pop. Flash. Fizzle. Darkness.

LIZARD takes out a Lizard mask out of one of his bags and looks at it.

Sounds from behind. LIZARD spins around.

BANNION: *(From off.)* Friend Meehan! Grace! Slow down!

LIZARD throws the mask back in one of the bags and hides under the sheet over the statue.

ENTER GRACE. She paces about stopping every few paces, shivering.

BANNION: *(From off.)* Friend Meehan!

Sounds of chanting in the distance.

GRACE listens to it.

LIZARD spits under the sheet. GRACE looks around to see where the sound came from.

Enter BANNION. He is out of breath.

BANNION: Grace! Have you gone completely mad?!

You just insulted one of the most powerful bankers in Europe!

GRACE: Mr. Gonzi is now aware how seriously I take his advice.

BANNION: He turned to his aid and demanded to be taken straight to the airport. You've made an enemy.

GRACE: You know you're getting things done when you're making enemies.

BANNION: We're going to have to patch this up. The man is on the board of the Federal European Bank. You don't piss him off.

GRACE: He shouldn't have been granted access to me, not today.

BANNION: You can't just…

GRACE: But I did.

BANNION: You can't is what I'm saying.

GRACE: You enjoy scolding me don't you? It gives you a little flutter of pleasure.

BANNION: He's an enemy we can't afford to have.

GRACE: There it is! A little flutter. Is it a kind of sexual thing? Discipline. Order. Rules. It really gets you going doesn't it?

Don't look at me like that, you were a little impressed. The car was moving about ten miles an hour and out I leap and hit the footpath walking at a clip. I should get an award.

BANNION: What if someone caught you on camera?

GRACE: Snubbing Gonzi? My popularity ratings would jump another ten points in the polls.

BANNION: He looked vicious.

GRACE: You loved it.

BANNION: They're meeting us because it's dawning on them that we have a chance of winning. You have to be more careful now than ever.

There are certain facts…

GRACE: I find if you just do a thing you can sneak out ahead of the facts. It's why I'm in charge and you're chasing around after me.

BANNION: Philippe Gonzi…

GRACE: Gonzi can suck in his cheeks and toddle off. I'm in charge and I couldn't give a fuck.

Now. I think we should add that to our manifesto.

Today is our day.

BANNION: And what if tomorrow is his? *(Pause.)*

GRACE: I haven't been back here since the protest camp. Two thousand and sixteen. Can you believe it… Ten years ago. It's where we first met.

BANNION: The source of most of my suffering.

GRACE: It was good place to be young.

BANNION: It was a good place to descend into alcoholism, depression, and madness.

GRACE: Sometimes it's the same thing.

Back then if I had found myself sitting in a government car with a suit like Gonzi I would have slapped him across the face.

BANNION: Congratulations on your personal development.

You have to talk to him, he's going to report to the Commission tonight.

GRACE: He wants me to run the country on the whims of an algorithm.

BANNION: We have to keep sight of the challenges…

GRACE: I'm aware of the challenges. We're all numb from the challenges.

Ecological catastrophe, vast human migration, robotics creating mass unemployment, proxy wars, potholes in North Tipperary…

BANNION: We're a small country, we need to do everything we can to survive.

GRACE: Have we drafted a statement about North-Tipperary? We have to be cast-iron on our position for that one.

BANNION: Gonzi is letting us know how precarious our situation is.

GRACE: He believes his mathematics are a universal truth. It makes him incredibly dangerous. He's a fanatic.

BANNION: Exactly. And if we don't play ball they'll collapse our economy the moment we get into government.

Your job will be to manage the people's expectations.

GRACE: You want me to pacify them.

BANNION: Yes.

GRACE: To betray them.

BANNION: You don't have a choice. *(Pause.)*

I'll ring and reset the meeting. I'll explain you needed some air… that you are considering his advice.

GRACE: His threats.

There are ten million citizens I have to listen to. He can get to the back of the fucking line.

BANNION: No, I won't tell him that…

BANNION walks away on the phone.

GRACE: Well tell him I saw him eyeing me up when I got into the car. All the suits and algorithms in Frankfurt won't disguise the fact he's a sleazy prick.

GRACE walks up to the statue.

BANNION: He's not answering.

They're unveiling the statue at four tomorrow. The Youth Wing of the party. We have to keep them on side. Their support is wavering already.

(Pause.)

We need to go. They're expecting us on O'Connell Street in the next hour.

GRACE: Do you ever lose faith Friend Bannion? There've been times over the last few days...

You never get a chance to think. All these huge events are happening and you don't get a chance to wonder at it. At yourself.

Do you feel like you've abandoned a part of yourself along the way?

(Pause.)

BANNION: My hair.

GRACE: What?

BANNION: A part of me I've abandoned along the way...

I'd a fine mop of sleek black hair. They called me the Hugo Chavez of Coolock.

GRACE: You never had much hair.

BANNION: That's a lie. I'd a fine mop.

Never mind what we were. We were irrelevant. Now we have an opportunity to get power. Limited power. But we'll have it...

Cheers in the distance.

Listen to those people, thousands of them... Hundreds of thousands. Cheering, chanting, expecting. Waiting for you to lead. Listen to them.

They adore you.

GRACE: Do you make your flattery obvious to conceal something else or are you really just thick and obvious.

BANNION: You're too astute to manipulate.

GRACE: You're just thick and obvious. It's your technique.

(Pause.)

I'm going to have to lie to millions of people.

BANNION: You'll lose everyone's confidence if you start telling the truth.

Sounds of cheering in the distance.

GRACE: It must feel incredible to be in that crowd cheering. They must feel free.

Keep trying Gonzi. I'll talk to him again.

BANNION nods.

Give me half an hour.

BANNION: We should go...

GRACE: I need half an hour.

BANNION: I have some calls to make. I'll be waiting at the gates.

Don't lose your nerve now. I couldn't bear to see them tear you to pieces.

Exit BANNION.

Sounds of singing in the distance.

GRACE: I'm not the person you want me to be….

LIZARD spits.

GRACE walks to the statue. She pulls off the sheet. LIZARD is standing there. They stare at each other.

Behind LIZARD is a life-size statue of FINBAR. His head is bowed and the palms of his hands are facing upwards. His feet are surrounded by heather.

GRACE: I can't believe it. It's you.

LIZARD: Got to go. Got to keep moving.

GRACE: Lizard?

LIZARD starts throwing his things back into his bags.

GRACE: Wait. What are you doing here?

It's me. Do you remember me?

LIZARD: I remember you.

GRACE: Lizard…

Look at you. You look…

All those tattoos, I remember you working on them, but this…

You've completely changed.

LIZARD: So have you.

GRACE: Not like this…

Can I…?

LIZARD steps backwards.

No. I'm sorry. What are they?

LIZARD: Mathematics. Equations. Laws of science… Look…

LIZARD uncovers his arm, points at a tattoo.

Second law of thermodynamics. Delta S equals Q over T. Five symbols. Five. Means the universe tends towards disorder and chaos and will wind up a flat grey sludge.

GRACE: That doesn't sound very hopeful.

LIZARD: It's not.

LIZARD uncovers his other arm.

V equals X to the power of 4 plus A X cubed plus B X squared plus C X.

GRACE: What does that mean?

LIZARD: It's going to happen much sooner than you think.

GRACE: You're completely covered.

LIZARD: There's always more space between the lines and once you've filled that with finer, smaller lines there's space between those lines too. Smaller spaces. Finer lines.

GRACE: I was just thinking of you… You and Finbar.

Do you like our statue to him?

They turn and look at the statue of FINBAR.

LIZARD: Not much.

GRACE: No? Me neither. There's something missing.

LIZARD: He was shorter than that.

GRACE: That's not it.

GRACE inspects the statue.

LIZARD: I've been watching your speeches. In the welfare camps dependents share them around like contraband.

They believe in you.

I don't.

When you talk your eyes are empty. There's nothing behind your eyes.

GRACE walks up to the statue.

GRACE: They've made him too glum. He could hardly look at me without flushing red and losing the run of himself.

GRACE takes her glove off, and then touches the statue's crotch.

Nothing stirring. Not a tremor... What's the point in commemorating someone if they leave out the life?

LIZARD: Do you ever think about what he did? I think about it all the time.

(Pause.)

GRACE: They want me to mention Finbar in my speech tonight. I came here because... maybe I wanted to get his permission. Why are you here?

LIZARD: I might share this place with Finbar for a while. Sleep under the sky like we used to.

GRACE: You were in the welfare camps?

LIZARD: OB Enterprises in the Curragh.

GRACE: How was it?

LIZARD: Mostly homeless and the New Poor. People unemployed since the crash. Some migrants. Travellers. There's clinics for old people. You survive. You get a weekly allowance... just less than enough for food, water, clothes and to pay rent for the shelters. Everything is on credit from the company. They give you just enough of everything so you have nothing.

You can get along there. But you don't live.

You promised to get rid of them if you get elected.

GRACE: I don't know if we can… Almost a third of the country depends on the camps. There's a lot of money being made. Powerful interests.

LIZARD: I guessed not. Don't worry, I wasn't going to vote for you anyway.

GRACE: It's getting cold.

LIZARD: If it doesn't rain tonight it won't be so bad…

GRACE: You said I've changed. How?

LIZARD: You used to glow Grace. You were a kind of strange sun.

Now.

Something else has taken hold of you.

More fireworks go off.

GRACE: Fireworks.

I hate fireworks.

They look up, their faces lit by colour, the air filled with explosions.

The statue of FINBAR comes alive. He moves around them, stretching and groaning as they watch.

SCENE 2

FINBAR walks towards a large tent.

It is a hot morning during the summer of 2016.

GRACE and LIZARD watch him from ten years later.

FINBAR: Neck is stiff.

FINBAR stretches.

Slept strange last night. Whole shoulder – down my arm, fused, like someone poured concrete through it.

FINBAR twisting from side to side.

GRACE: He looks slight. Like a boy. I remember him being older.

LIZARD: We were all young. Where are you Finbar?

FINBAR: In the protest camp. I'm sleeping in a tent on the grounds of the old mental hospital in Stoneybatter. There's about a hundred of us sleeping here, activists and drifters suffocating in the heat.

LIZARD: What year is it?

FINBAR: Two thousand and sixteen.

LIZARD: You look happy.

FINBAR: I suppose I am. I'm in love.

LIZARD: Is that your tent?

FINBAR: No. I sleep in a little pop-up closer to the food-bank.

This is Grace's tent. I've been doing some work on it.

LIZARD: Why are you fixing Grace's tent?

FINBAR: She's always busy.

FINBAR starts to sing "Wild Mountain Thyme".

FINBAR: And we'll all go together/ to pluck wild mountain thyme / all around the blooming heather…

FINBAR picks up some cardboard lying against the tent and starts to make a placard. He cuts out a rectangle with a knife and tacks it to a piece of wood.

LIZARD: What are you doing Finbar?

FINBAR: Making a sign for the march later.

GRACE: It's the day of the riots.

LIZARD walks away from GRACE into FINBAR's space. As he walks his movement becomes looser. Less coiled.

LIZARD: This heat. I'm sweating something unnatural.

FINBAR is whistling.

What are you so happy about?

FINBAR: Lizard. What a beautiful day!

FINBAR hums Mountain Thyme.

LIZARD: What's wrong with you?

FINBAR: What do you mean?

LIZARD: You've a strange look on your face. You're singing. You never sing. Something's up.

FINBAR puts his finger to his lips. He winks.

LIZARD: Was that a wink?

FINBAR: It was.

FINBAR winks again.

LIZARD: Two winks. Something is definitely up.

FINBAR: All I can say is… I am the man.

LIZARD: You are not the man.

FINBAR: I don't know about that… I think I might be…

LIZARD: No. I've decided I'm better not knowing.

FINBAR: Fine so.

But I am.

FINBAR winks.

Sound of drums from off.

LIZARD: The hippy from Belmullet is drumming. He won't stop now until the march is over, beating away… ME. ME. ME. ME. ME. ME. The ego of it.

FINBAR: You want me to make you a sign for the march?

LIZARD: I'm not going.

FINBAR: You always throw a strop on the day of an action. We've been working towards today for weeks.

LIZARD: They kicked me out of the committee meeting this morning.

FINBAR: Again?

LIZARD: Our objectives are too narrow.

FINBAR: I thought nobody knew what our objectives were. It's why everyone is happy and getting along.

LIZARD: No. We're all about social housing all of a sudden. I told them, I'm a techno-ecologist, it's inconsistent for me to agitate for a future with an increased amount of human beings in it.

FINBAR: Human beings aren't so bad.

LIZARD: You're sentimental.

They can't keep excluding me, it's against the rules.

Is Grace…

FINBAR: Grace? What about Grace…?

LIZARD: What…?

FINBAR: I didn't say anything about Grace.

FINBAR winks at LIZARD.

LIZARD: Is…

FINBAR winks again. Nods.

What are you winking for?

Is Grace around? She normally intervenes when they try to exclude me. She knows I'm the only one with anything interesting to say.

FINBAR: She wasn't at the meeting?

LIZARD: No and she's supposed to be speaking at the march later.

FINBAR holds up the placard.

FINBAR: "Bring us your love, we'll build a better world with it."

LIZARD: What are you on?

FINBAR: Grace said it in a podcast.

LIZARD: Love is a game we amuse children with so they don't go mad thinking about death.

FINBAR: You're not going to put me in a bad mood. Not today.

LIZARD: In the future we'll care for each other rationally. We won't waste so much energy on it.

FINBAR: Look at you. You're dying to know my secret.

LIZARD: I have no idea how you got that impression.

FINBAR: Myself and Grace kissed. *(Pause.)*

LIZARD: So?

FINBAR: So?… So? What do you mean so? We kissed.

LIZARD: How long did you kiss for?

FINBAR: What? Why does that matter?

LIZARD: I'm interested to know.

FINBAR: Is that your only question? How long we kissed for?

LIZARD: Okay… wait. I get it. You want me to ask how it happened don't you?

So… how did it happen?

FINBAR: It was yesterday. We'd been cycling all over the city hanging posters. It took hours and by the time we were done, the two of us were exhausted and we sat resting on a bench in Clontarf by the bay…

Grace had a bottle of wine in her bag and we drank it right there by the water, passing it back and forth, draining it with big gulps. She was talking and talking. You know how she lights up when she gets like that.

She asked me if I'd go away with her. Imagine that, just up and leave the country with Grace.

LIZARD: Grace won't do that...

FINBAR: I said I'd do anything with her. Anything at all as long as I can do it with her. I told her that.

She looked at me strangely, poked me in the chest, laughed and then we kissed.

Electricity.

I told her I'd been besotted by her since the moment I saw her.

LIZARD: You used the word – besotted?

FINBAR: I have no idea where it came from. I've never said it before but it felt like the right word.

LIZARD: Besotted? I don't think it was.

FINBAR: She laughed and looked at me like I was ridiculous. I suppose I was a little ridiculous. Then we cycled back here, weaving through the traffic. I kept repeating to myself, don't get knocked down, don't get knocked down now you're finally happy.

LIZARD: You're experiencing a chemical delusion designed to make reproduction tolerable.

Still. I'm happy for you.

FINBAR: Thanks.

I feel a part of something here. It's exciting. We're going to make the world a better place.

I've wasted the last few years. Miserable and lonely and thinking I couldn't do anything. Unemployed, no money, no prospects, sleeping in my mother's house, draining my days into computer screens.

I finally feel like I'm fit for life. I can't go back to the way it was before.

LIZARD: Here she comes.

FINBAR: What?

LIZARD: Grace. Grace!

You should tell her.

FINBAR: Tell her what?

LIZARD: That you're in love with her.

FINBAR: Are you insane?

LIZARD: I'll tell her if you want.

FINBAR: Wait, hold on a…

GRACE walks into the scene.

GRACE: Have you seen them? They're gathered and dancing by the main gates. Banners, drums, whistles. A rabble. The most hopeless eight-rate revolutionaries every mustered.

There are too many people in this protest camp content to squat and grow beards. We need to keep up our energy up. Constant change.

Lizard. Let me guess. Your ear?

LIZARD: No.

GRACE: Your back?

LIZARD: No.

GRACE: Foot?

LIZARD: Not even close.

My eye.

GRACE: Go away! Let me see.

GRACE looks into LIZARD's eye.

It's completely black.

I love it. You're an inspiration. Change everything. Throw it all out. Beautiful new forms and shapes and elegant wonders. Don't you think Finbar?

FINBAR can't speak.

Finbar is a little conservative. He's not comfortable with your extravagance.

What the Lizard has Finbar, and it's the most important thing to have, is a passion. One central passion that makes sense of everything else. He wants to become something else. He wants to change. And he devotes himself to that totally.

LIZARD: I hear you kissed Finbar.

GRACE: Did you?

FINBAR: I should…

FINBAR stands up quickly.

No.

He sits down again.

GRACE: I feel like everything is filthy here. I'm starting to fantasise about having a bath. Does that make me bourgeois? Or does it make me bourgeois to associate having a bath with being bourgeois? I think I'm bourgeois.

Finbar, why are you looking at me like that?

LIZARD: I'm formulating the theory that he's fallen in love with you.

FINBAR: *(Standing up.)* It's time for the march.

LIZARD: He's worried you won't feel the same. People are completely odd.

GRACE: You said you're in love with me?

FINBAR: The most important thing, that we can all agree on, is that the lack of social housing being built in this country is a complete bloody disgrace. Am I right? Yes. Am I right?

GRACE: Yes, that is important isn't it?

FINBAR: You were saying that the other day Grace, that, that you could build enough houses on these grounds alone to cut the Dublin housing list by a third. Instead they're flogging it off to a hedge fund for next to nothing...

I mean it's a land grab...

(Laughing.)

Isn't it? Isn't that what you said? It's a land grab.

GRACE: So then, if that's how you feel, what are you going to do about it?

FINBAR: About what? The housing list. Are you talking about the housing list?

GRACE: Okay. Let's talk about housing if you want to...

FINBAR: *(To LIZARD.)* She was talking about housing wasn't she?

LIZARD: You never can tell, can you?

GRACE: International capital created the crises, then colonised us while we were reeling from the blow. What are you going to do about it?

FINBAR: I'm… we're going to the march. Aren't we going to the march? I'm confused.

GRACE: Disappointing.

FINBAR: What should I do?

GRACE: I spent last night in jail. *(Pause.)*

FINBAR: Are you alright?

GRACE: Of course I'm alright.

LIZARD: What did you do?

GRACE: I caused a public disturbance.

FINBAR: Did they hurt you?

GRACE: I don't need you worrying about me. I can look after myself.

FINBAR: I know you can. That's not what I meant.

GRACE: I was talking to Meabh Kelly from Belfast – she's fascinated by the body and the terror Irish people have of it – we decided right there and then we should do an action. Why talk about it? You should just do something about it. So we infiltrated a late mass in the Pro Cathedral, marched up the centre of the aisle and jumped on the altar in the middle of the mass…

FINBAR: I can't believe you…

GRACE: And I was topless and had "I am God" painted across my chest.

(Pause.)

LIZARD: Did you cause a stir?

FINBAR: You weren't wearing any clothes?

GRACE: I was wearing a long red skirt and I had a crown of flowers on my head. Hyacinths I picked from the walls of the hospital.

LIZARD: In the future we'll have technology that controls our body heat. Clothes will be considered a form of barbarism.

FINBAR: What did they do?

GRACE: Nothing at first. I was shouting, "I have eaten your god. I have eaten your god." I don't know why. It just came into my head when I got up there. Everyone was stunned. There were only about twelve people at the mass and most of them were looking at the ground trying to pretend I wasn't there.

Finally an old woman in the back row of the church roused into life, stood up and screamed "you dirty, raunchy harlot." People started shushing her. It was really odd. Still, at least she had a bit of spunk.

FINBAR: You were topless?

GRACE: For Godsake Finbar, they're just boobs.

LIZARD: What did the priest do?

GRACE: He just stood there. He looked sad.

FINBAR: You frightened the life out of him.

GRACE: Do you know, while I was up there, I felt holy.

Maybe the Church has just lost its edge. People weren't as shocked as I thought they'd be. It was disappointing.

Taking out her phone and showing it to LIZARD.

Meabh took photographs. She got some good ones.

LIZARD: That's impressive clarity you achieved with the letters.

GRACE: What do you think Finbar?

LIZARD: That's not easy on a curved surface. Very impressive.

GRACE showing FINBAR the phone.

FINBAR: No, I'd better not.

GRACE: They're just boobs!

FINBAR: I know they are. I just think… you know. I just think it would be safer if I don't look.

GRACE: Unbelievable.

LIZARD: Did the guards arrest you outside the church?

GRACE: No. The arrest wasn't anything to do with the action in the church.

We put back on our tops and on the way back to the camp I spotted two guards outside a chipper. They were standing there, leaning against the car and one of them said something. The other laughed and they both looked me up and down. So I knocked over their chips…

FINBAR: Grace.

GRACE: And kicked their car.

FINBAR: Grace!

GRACE: Whose side are you on?

FINBAR: Yours but…

GRACE: Slam! I'm against the bonnet of the car and they're handcuffing me. One of them, this fat little red haired man is pressing heavy into my back and breathing over my neck. The stink of grease off him. "You've kicked a cop car, you're in trouble now," grunting as he got on the cuffs. The other stole the crown of flowers off my head threw them on the ground and stamped on them…stamped on them like a child throwing a tantrum.

They were enjoying it.

They brought me to Kevin street barracks. They took my shoes, forced me to remove the strap from my skirt – I had to hold it up with my hand to stop it from falling around my ankles – and then they threw me into a freezing cold cell for hours.

There was a little slit in the cell door that would slide open every hour or so and the red haired one would shout, "you've done it now, you're in deep shit now," and then slam it shut again. They wanted to frighten me.

We need to have courage. That's the only thing that matters. Make a mark and move on and make another mark and keep turning and twisting and becoming more incredible people.

Look at you Lizard. You're beautiful. When I look at you I feel like anything is possible.

FINBAR: I am besotted by you.

LIZARD: No, it's definitely not the right word.

GRACE: We shouldn't have any loyalty to people, only to ideas.

There is already a revolution underway, but not the one we all hope for… it's a revolution led by corporations and conservative politicians. The entire structure of our world is being altered, traditions erased, cultures flattened. All in the name of profit, enterprise, power.

But we can change this. We get in their face and refuse to be obedient. That means acting now. And again. And again. And letting nothing get in your way. Because if we don't act, then the slide will continue. We'll live in their world instead of our own.

Pure life. That's our weapon.

We need to put saddles on our dreams and ride them like big dragons through the streets.

We don't know where we're going and that's the way it has to be. Everything is going to change… Everything!

SCENE 3

Commemoration Park 2026.

LIZARD goes to one of his bags and takes out a pair of clear plastic gloves.

GRACE's phone rings. She answers it. LIZARD takes out the tattoo gun. He starts to tattoo his foot.

GRACE: *(On phone.)* What?

Who leaked that? Never mind… I think I know… They threatened me…. With everything… They'll stop funding the private welfare contracts, they'll close banks, introduce tariffs on our exports.

Everyone is getting ready to celebrate but we're perched on the edge of an abyss.

Get Friend Hughes to send me a breakdown of the figures. I want to know exactly how long we can hold out if they come at us…

Well then get the figures.

Take volunteers off the election. This is more important.

I don't care what Bannion says… He's trying to set up another meeting with Gonzi now.

Have you been going through his papers? Well?

Keep checking. I'm sure there's something there.

Who's speaking before me?

Change the speaking order. I want to be introduced by Friend Kinsella instead.

Your job isn't to criticise, it's to keep the party united behind me.

She hangs up.

LIZARD: It used to be… even if you were doing the wrong thing… you would have known it was the right thing.

It wouldn't have surprised me if you'd set up a charity or started kidnapping financiers… But I was sure that whatever you did, you'd do it like you were possessed.

It's strange to see you uncertain.

GRACE: When I get elected, everyone will expect there to be change. That's why I'm going to win. They want me to make the country the kind of place they can bear to live in. I have to do something.

But the second I act, the second I use that power and start to change anything, that power will be taken away by Gonzi, the FEB, the markets.

I can't turn back and I can't go forward. I'm stuck.

LIZARD: Trust in mathematics. There's always a process… a predictable pattern.

GRACE: Not with this. There's no certainty with this…

LIZARD: There is. You're just not able to see it yet. *(Pause.)*

GRACE: Why do you do the tattoos?

LIZARD: They put a kind of order on me.

Sailors in the navy got ink so that if their ship was blown up they'd be able to tell who owned which body part by the tattoos.

GRACE: Does it hurt?

LIZARD: It's like being bitten by a line of ants.

GRACE takes the tattoo gun off LIZARD.

It's a beautiful machine isn't it?

This one runs on battery. There's a rotation, a magnetic coil that drives the action. It pumps the needle there… you see?

You attach a tip to the needle… there. See how it's split in two? It traps the ink between the two points and jabs in and out puncturing your skin about five times a second. It leaves tiny droplets of ink behind under the surface of your skin.

GRACE presses the trigger of the tattoo gun.

You poke through. Jab. Jab. Jab. Jab. Jab. And the outside seeps in.

GRACE: What do you think I should do?

LIZARD: It doesn't matter in the long run. We're not the stuff of the future.

GRACE: You've written us off completely?

LIZARD: Haven't you?

Can you imagine the world a thousand years from now with human beings in it? After the damage we've done in the last twenty years…

A hundred years from now… Maybe I can imagine that. But in that picture, most of us are miserable and poor.

Now imagine the world in a thousand years without human beings in it. Serene. Perfect. Blue oceans and clean air.

GRACE: There are things that redeem us.

LIZARD: Like what?

GRACE: Isn't there anyone in your life that you're close to?

LIZARD: No.

Even when I was young, I'd make whole groups of other children go quiet just by walking near them. There is something about me that always put people ill at ease.

GRACE: You don't put me ill at ease.

LIZARD: You must be always surrounded by people. Crowds of admirers.

GRACE: I live alone in a massive empty house in Malahide.
I'm hardly ever there. Normally I sleep in hotels.

Last year I offered the spare rooms in my home to people
from the welfare camps. It was a publicity stunt Bannion
dreamed up.

I took in a young mother and her child from Tallaght, a
family of seven migrants from the floods in Bangladesh
and one of the New Poor who lost his job during the
closures at the start of the twenties. All stage-managed for
optimum effect.

Be the change you want to see.

The thing was I started to loathe them.

That isn't a very humanitarian thing to say is it? They
were guests in my home. And polite too. Considerate. But
the more they tried not to be a hassle to me the more I
hated it. I could hear them moving about in the rooms, the
children pattering on the floorboards with their feet, the
old man clearing his throat and turning the pages of his
book. I was disgusted by the smells of their food, of their
nappies, driven to distraction by the sounds of their voices.

Every movement or noise felt like an intrusion. I started to
lash out at them for the smallest things. And they started to
fear me. To hate me. When I got back to the house I could
hear the parents whispering to their children to be quiet. I
resented that too. I resented that they made me aware of
my power over them.

After a few weeks I paid for their rent in a house somewhere
else. I don't know where. It didn't matter as long as I didn't
have to see them. Someone else organised it.

What's happened to me?

LIZARD: It's the way we are. We have to turn to mathematics.
Code. Universal eternal forms.

GRACE traces the lines of LIZARD's tattoos with her finger.

No greed, no violence, no need.

No despair.

GRACE: Pictures you've drawn on your skin.

LIZARD: More than pictures.

(Pointing at tattoos on his body.)

That formula traces the arc the earth takes around the sun, this… this is the process of nuclear fission. Nuclear fission… the engine of the sun… it unfolds according to those symbols etched on my skin.

Every apparent innovation of nature, every curling fractal, every radiating ion, it's all obedient.

Look. The Mandelbrot set. $Z = Z$ squared plus C. An unimaginable interplay between order and chaos. That formula iterated generates a model of such complexity that it outstrips reality itself. I have seen forests in it, oceans, insects, whole mountain ranges unfolding with precision.

Is there anything in your life that could match the beauty of that? Is there anything anyone could give you that will be as true?

GRACE: Will you do one for me?

LIZARD: What?

GRACE: A tattoo. Down my spine.

LIZARD: Why?

GRACE: I want to feel something.

LIZARD: What do you want me to draw?

GRACE: Anything. It doesn't matter. Don't tell me what it is. Just do it.

LIZARD takes the tattoo gun off her and changes the needle.

LIZARD: I'll use the three-tip needle.

I'll start from the base of your neck and work down into the small of your back.

I'm going to have to shave it.

GRACE: What?

LIZARD: I'm going to have to shave your back.

GRACE: You really know how to charm me don't you...

LIZARD: I have to. Any little hairs on your back will interfere with the line. I'm serious. I won't do it any other way. I'm going to have to shave it.

LIZARD takes out a razor.

GRACE lifts her top at the back. LIZARD puts the razor to her back.

GRACE: Stop. Hold on...

Okay.

LIZARD: You'll feel it just there.

LIZARD touches the back of GRACE's neck.

SCENE 4

2016: On the street at the protest march. FINBAR and GRACE are dressed for the march; masks, backpack, flag. It is really loud. Music. Drums. Whistles. They are speaking loudly.

GRACE: You have the megaphone?

FINBAR: Got it.

GRACE: The banner?

FINBAR: Got it.

GRACE: Look at you. You look great. Like a proper anarchist.

FINBAR: I do, don't I? I feel a little pumped.

GRACE: Me too. I think there's something erotic about protests.

FINBAR: Sorry?

GRACE: I said I think there's something erotic about protests.

FINBAR: Erratic?

GRACE: Erotic!

FINBAR: Oh…

Is there?

GRACE: Breaking rules… breaking down boundaries. I want to touch everybody.

FINBAR: I never thought about it like that.

GRACE: It's exhilarating. *(Pause.)*

You pack the vinegar?

FINBAR: Sorry?

GRACE: The vinegar

FINBAR: Vinegar?

GRACE: For pepper-spray. For your eyes.

FINBAR: No.

GRACE: I'll get some. On the way.

FINBAR: How many of us do you think there are?

GRACE: A few thousand.

FINBAR: Do you think they'll listen to us?

GRACE: Who?

FINBAR: The government.

GRACE: God no.

FINBAR: What do we have to do to make them listen?

GRACE: Have a whistle.

GRACE hands FINBAR a whistle.

FINBAR: I'm not sure this is going to work.

GRACE: Have you tried it yet?

FINBAR blows the whistle.

FINBAR: You think they heard me?

GRACE: No. Do you feel better?

FINBAR: A little.

GRACE: They think they can keep us quiet. They won't.

FINBAR: We need to let them know that we're serious.

GRACE: Enjoy yourself. They hate it when we have fun. It makes them furious.

Go on. Blow your whistle. I'm serious. Blow it.

FINBAR blows his whistle.

That's the spirit.

FINBAR: What about physical action?

GRACE: Dancing?

FINBAR: Violence.

GRACE: You don't want that…

FINBAR: Something real.

GRACE: This is real. You're real. I'm real.

FINBAR: But they just ignore us. Nothing changes.

GRACE: What do you want to do?

FINBAR: I don't know. Throw a brick?

GRACE: Isn't there something you'd rather do than throw bricks?

FINBAR: Is there?

GRACE: Is there?

FINBAR: Sorry?

GRACE: You think anything will change if you throw a brick?

FINBAR: It might.

GRACE: It won't.

FINBAR: How do you know?

GRACE: We march… We make noise.

FINBAR: How do I get you to kiss me again?

GRACE: Don't ask!

FINBAR: I can't figure out any other way to find out.

I can't remember what I did the last time.

GRACE: You looked good. I felt great. It just felt right.

FINBAR: Can I do it again?

GRACE: What?

FINBAR: Can I kiss you again?

GRACE: Okay.

FINBAR: Sorry?

GRACE: Why not?

FINBAR: I can?

GRACE: Sure.

FINBAR: Okay then.

GRACE: Sorry?

FINBAR: I'm going to kiss you.

GRACE: What?

FINBAR: I said I'm going to kiss you.

GRACE: Oh. Okay.

They kiss.

FINBAR: You're right, protests are erotic.

GRACE: They are, aren't they?

FINBAR: My heart is burning.

GRACE: That's good.

FINBAR: I feel really alive.

GRACE: So do I.

They kiss again. The music stops and there's a speech being made. You can't hear any of the words… They speak low.

FINBAR: It's hard to concentrate on the speech. All I can think about is you.

GRACE: If the speech wasn't so boring I'd take that as a compliment.

FINBAR: It feels cheeky to be like this at a march. Shouldn't we be more serious?

GRACE: Nonsense, we need more sex in politics. You can't change anything… unless you get a little… unless you get a little degenerate.

FINBAR: Shhh… He's making an important point.

GRACE: No he's not.

FINBAR: He really isn't.

GRACE: You know what I'd do if I got elected to run this country. First day in the Dáil, with the TD's from the opposition parties scowling at me across the hall…

Opening speech… first order of business, I'd lie across the front bench… I'd put my hand down my knickers… and I'd give myself a long, intense eruption of an orgasm.

FINBAR: Oh man… I shouldn't be in a crowded place.

GRACE: Start with pleasure, then you move on to taxation.

You think I'm vulgar.

FINBAR: That man is trying to make a serious point about housing and you're talking about that.

GRACE: I'm a pagan, is that what frightens you? You want a holy Mary.

FINBAR: I'm not frightened of you.

GRACE: Then what are you?

FINBAR: I am devoted to you.

Everyone claps as the speech ends.

GRACE: You always pick strange words for your feelings.

FINBAR: I would do anything for you.

GRACE: Anything?

FINBAR: Anything.

SCENE 5

2026. The Commemoration Park. GRACE is sitting looking at statue. She has her jacket around her shoulders. The tattoo is half finished.

GRACE: Are you sure they made him taller? He'd love that.

When they do a statue of me I want them to mold my legs directly from a long distance runner. Have them drooling at the commemorations…

Enter BANNION.

BANNION: Do you like the statue?

GRACE: They captured him better than I was expecting... You get a real sense of him.

You never knew him did you?

BANNION: Don't think we ever met. We need to talk...

GRACE: Do we?

BANNION: I've been conferring with some people in the party.

GRACE: About our confidential meeting.

BANNION: Trusted people.

GRACE: Who can we trust? Can I trust you?

BANNION: There is an understanding within the party that negotiations with Gonzi stay within certain parameters.

GRACE: When you say the party, you mean you and your minions.

BANNION: I don't think you understand the seriousness of the situation. European officials have communicated their intentions should we get into power and attempt to implement our programme unilaterally. It's not pretty. We need you to be very clear when you meet him...

GRACE: Remember who is in charge. You only enjoy access to power as long as I allow it.

You can go back to squabbling around with the other parties. I'm sure they'd take you back.

(Pause.) What are their plans?

BANNION: They would collapse our banking system.

GRACE: We know that. That's been their strategy for years.

BANNION: They'd immediately halt funding to the welfare camps. Declare the contracts with the private welfare providers void. OB Enterprises, Crescent Lawns, Hallowed Days... all the companies providing for our pensioners, the homeless, the New Poor, the migrants…they'll all pull out immediately. We're left with hundreds of thousands of people dependent on us and we would have no means of supporting them.

And that's before millions experience the full brunt of food shortages when they introduce import tariffs and water shortages when taps get turned off.

Their weapon is our dependence on them. And they're going to pull the trigger.

The people who will suffer are the people who supported you. The wealthy will look after themselves, it's the ones who have nothing that are in danger. They're the people who are trusting you to act wisely.

GRACE: You're arguing Gonzi's case?

BANNION: I'm providing context for the negotiations.

GRACE: It sounds like you're trying to persuade me.

BANNION: It's the truth.

GRACE: I want to know what the other options are.

BANNION: I don't think we have any. *(Pause.)*

GRACE: That's it?

That's the sum total of your fight.

BANNION: It's a chaotic world.

GRACE: Has it ever been any different?

BANNION: The odds are stacked too high against us. We have to compromise. If we're in power then we might be able to affect some good. It is better than if the others take over.

GRACE: I don't believe you.

BANNION: We are the good guys.

GRACE: It's a lie. You never wanted to do anything else. And what's better, now you've found our moral justification.

BANNION: There's something else…

I've been in contact with my source near the chief of staff of the defense forces. He's been approached by Gonzi through back channels.

He's going to make a statement saying you're threatening our sovereignty by separating us from the mainstream direction of Europe. He is suggesting that if the safety of the country is threatened…

GRACE: A coup?

BANNION: We can't be sure. But there have been communications…

GRACE: You think they'd interfere directly in an election?

BANNION: I'm saying it's a possibility. If we don't let them know our intent to work constructively…

GRACE: These sources of yours… Are you letting me know the threats that I face or are you delivering the message?

BANNION: What are you saying?

GRACE: Have you been working on their side all along?

BANNION: How could you say that?

GRACE: I've never trusted you.

BANNION: You're getting paranoid.

GRACE: What did they offer you? Some cushy job on the Commission? You never make a move unless you're sure there's something in it for you.

BANNION: You're getting emotional now.

GRACE: I am not getting emotional. I promise you. I am starting to see things clearer and clearer.

BANNION: Gonzi will be here in half an hour. I'll consult the party.

GRACE: The people support me.

BANNION: You can't do anything without our agreement.

It's the way it has to be…

EXIT BANNION.

SCENE 6

Protest Camp: 2016.

FINBAR is covered in blood. There is the sound of a helicopter. Protests. Rioting.

He staggers about as if looking for somewhere to hide. He takes out a bottle of water from his rucksack and tries to wash blood off his hands. He retches, and then keeps washing frantically.

GRACE walks into the scene. Her eyes are red and she is disoriented. She's been pepper-sprayed.

FINBAR: Grace…

GRACE: Finbar?

FINBAR: Are you alright?

GRACE: Where are you?

FINBAR: Holy shit.

GRACE: Where are you? I can't see.

FINBAR: That was incredible!

GRACE: I got pepper-sprayed. A tramp of a guard stuck a can straight in my face and sprayed me…

FINBAR: I… I feel light. I feel completely alive.

GRACE: There's going to be trouble… They're going to crack down on us now.

FINBAR: They're going crazy… But we're together against them. Do you feel that?

It feels like the ground is cracking open and the earth's shaking. That energy, I thought I'd be lifted up into another world by it.

GRACE: Finbar… Finbar?

FINBAR: I'm here.

GRACE: Get the vinegar in my backpack.

FINBAR takes the cloth and vinegar out of her backpack and starts dabbing her eyes.

GRACE: They knew we were going to be peaceful. A hundred of them in riot gear. What were they expecting…? The mounted police clopping on the street behind, you could smell the dust in the hair of the horses.

FINBAR: Is that better?

GRACE: It's fine.

I got split off from where the trouble started. Why did they react like that?

FINBAR walks away from her and takes a bottle of water out of his backpack.

GRACE: Did you see it? You know they're going to blame us now. Whatever bunch of idiots started it, they've given them the perfect excuse to evict us and ruin everything.

FINBAR: It was the guards that started it… They were trying to get people off the street. Scuffles started up.

GRACE: Of course they started it. The point is we don't respond.

FINBAR: But it looked like they'd push us back and that would be the end of it.

Giving GRACE the water.

Some people picked up the metal railings. Three or four of us held them along the front of the line of protesters and pushed up against the riot shields. They were jabbing and smacking at our arms with truncheons. There was shouting and the chop of the helicopter hung just over our heads.

GRACE: We need to get on to the lawyers and find out who has been arrested.

FINBAR: The guards were trying to break us in two. They were surging up the middle. You don't think that we should have run away?

GRACE: Don't speak to me like I don't know how this works. We're the ones who have to keep calm.

FINBAR: It felt incredible to be part of that moment. Together... pushing back...

GRACE: You're covered in blood Finbar... Are you hurt?

FINBAR: I've never felt better...

The mounted guards spotted a weak point and four of them turned and cantered straight at us. It was something to see, the two rows of horses beating against us, simply breezing us back with their square chests, their necks lifting and falling, snorting as they strode forward. One of the guards, a huge bastard, was leaning over the side like a Mongol beating anything that moved. I was in a kind of fever.

GRACE: It's not your blood.

FINBAR: Someone shouted that they'd pepper-sprayed you. I tried to move towards you.

I was afraid you would get trampled. I thought they'd run you down. I thought one of the horses was going straight for you. That you'd be really badly hurt.

GRACE: I was fine.

Someone pulled me away and myself and a few others with injuries decided to come back to the camp so they didn't seize it while we were away.

This is a disaster. The people who depend on the camp will be homeless again.

Sound of an explosion from off. FINBAR looks to see what's happening.

FINBAR: People are streaming back into the grounds.

There's hundreds of people. Far more than there were last night. The guards are outside the walls. They're trying to stop people getting in but people are fighting, pushing them back, keeping the gates open.

GRACE: How did you get covered in blood Finbar?

FINBAR: I wanted to get between the police and you.

I must have left the knife in my pocket from earlier. You were lying on the ground with your eyes streaming. I ran towards the horse. It bucked up straight in front of me.

I drove the knife into its neck.

It kicked, and I held onto the handle with two hands, dragging down along its neck, opening it up. It all happened in a second, the guard was thrown, the horse rising up on its hind legs, then falling, a fountain of blood pouring from its neck.

It felt as if the whole city went silent. Even the helicopter seemed to hang there as quiet as a butterfly.

(Pause.)

It collapsed and bled on the ground, trying to get up again but slipping in the pool of its own blood.

The guard on it's back got trapped between it and the ground. It looked like his leg was broken.

The guards waded into the protesters, swinging and clunking heads. They were savage.

I ran.

(Pause.)

Look at all the people pouring in. There's hundreds. Where are they coming from?

Grace?

Grace?

SCENE 7

Commemoration Park: 2026.

LIZARD has stopped working on GRACE's tattoo.

LIZARD: Will we finish this?

GRACE: Not yet. My back aches.

LIZARD: The spine is sensitive.

GRACE: I wonder what my voters would think if they saw me here.

It might not appeal to the middle ground.

LIZARD: Why did you become a politician Grace? You used to turn your nose up at them.

GRACE: I didn't decide to become one. It set in like dry rot.

You think it suits me?

LIZARD: It's a bit disgusting.

GRACE: I turned out to be incredible at it. If I was talentless I
    might still have my integrity.

LIZARD: You can't believe in any of it.

GRACE: I did once.

   The public gatherings we organised at the beginning were
   incredible. We were in every village in the country. The
   party was only getting going but the meetings were packed.
   I remember one, I think it was in Sligo… or Donegal,
   there were about two hundred people squeezed into an
   old community hall. Someone there suggested that we get
   everyone to stand up and say their name and the townland
   they came from.

   People started out nervous. There were whispers down the
   back. Laughing. But as we moved through all those people
   and they spoke their names one by one, the importance of
   it began to sink in.

   A hush fell.

   Name. Place. Name. Place. Name.

   Even the simplest, most ordinary person has to take their
   place in history and speak their voice.

   (Pause.)

LIZARD: I came into wealth recently.

   My family had money. I never had much because my
   father gave me just enough to keep me from ending up on
   the news or in prison.

   He had no other children. No family. Only his money.
   That always seemed enough for him.

   I visited him before he died. I was summoned. He wanted
   to see the son shaped hole his fortune was going to
   disappear down.

All those doctors, all the machines, the nurses. They had been hacking away at him for years, sawing things off, draining things, gluing things on. He threw everything at it but the fact was he was dying. When I arrived they were just sitting around, collecting their wages, waiting for the man to give up.

I walked into the room expecting that old condescension. The contempt. As I walked in the door, my fists were clenched tight, braced for it to hit me as I walked towards him.

But when I saw him there, tiny amongst all the machines, the strangers...

He was looking at me and I knew he was terrified.

He looked like a wild animal.

"I'm going to die," he said.

And after another day he did. I felt something when it happened. I don't know what it was. I wasn't expecting to feel anything...

GRACE: When did he die?

LIZARD: A year ago.

Are you afraid of dying Grace?

When my father died I thought, do you know, I should set my mind to not dying.

GRACE: Wasn't that what your father was trying to do?

LIZARD: No. There's a difference. My father's mistake was he was trying to prolong his life. No matter how successful he was, he was always going to lose eventually. Because he set himself the wrong task. You shouldn't try to stay alive. You should try not to die.

That's when I thought of the tail. Wait...

GRACE: Did you say tail?

LIZARD: It's only a prototype.

LIZARD moves to one of his bags.

He takes a long tail out of the bag. The tail is pristine white, with curved, circular metal scales and two long strips of light that run from end to end...

LIZARD: *(Showing it to GRACE.)* Do you like it?

GRACE: It's lovely.

LIZARD: Do you think so?

Look.

He hold it to his back.

It'll go here.

Is... you don't think that's the right place for it...

GRACE: No. That's perfect.

LIZARD: It looks stupid there.

GRACE: No, it doesn't. Really...

LIZARD: You're just saying that.

GRACE: I'm not... really.

I think it looks beautiful. *(Pause.)*

How are you going to fix it on?

LIZARD: I've held meetings with a surgeon who says he can graft skin from my legs and my back and use the tissue to attach it to my stomach muscles.

At the minute it just trails off my back. But I will be able to flick it.

GRACE: That's amazing Lizard.

LIZARD: Just by thinking. It'll be linked to my mind, like an arm or a leg. I'll be part of it.

GRACE: It's incredible. There's a shine off it.

LIZARD: It was my idea to stitch on the metal scales.

GRACE: I love the detail.

LIZARD: Would you like to see me put it on?

GRACE: Of course. I'd love you to.

LIZARD: Hold that end.

LIZARD hands GRACE the end of the tail. She holds it. He puts it on.

You can let it down on the ground.

LIZARD moves around with the tail trailing after him.

I will be able to flick it.

For the minute you can only sort of… if I swing my hips like this.

The tail flicks pathetically.

The surgeon promises he'll be able to make it work far better.

GRACE: You look amazing. Like it was always meant to be there.

LIZARD: There are sensors built into it. It collects the data of my movements, my eating patterns, the temperature of the rooms I'm in. I can input the thoughts I'm having.

(Pointing to the Lizard mask)

It'll capture every detail of my life, collect every piece of information between now and the moment I die. Store it all up. And then it links to the mask…

LIZARD picks up the mask.

The mask processes all that raw data, my entire collected experiences... it condenses it and creates a mathematical formula from it.

My own equation. Me.

I'm going to become pure eternal consciousness. I won't die.

Look at you. I can see your eyes popping out on stalks and dancing like neutrinos.

This is a new possibility Grace.

I don't have to die.

GRACE: You'll live as a mathematical formula? That doesn't sound like this kind of life.

LIZARD: What's so good about this kind of life? It feels pretty wretched to me..

He tries to swish his tail...

SCENE 8

Protest Camp: 2016

ENTER BANNION. He's got a huge head of hair. He runs his hands through it repeatedly.

BANNION: Big day, big day. Events. All this chaos, it's an opportunity. I was in a meeting in the Dáil when I heard about the riots. It's fantastic. Police brutality. Photogenic protesters covered in blood. A hundred years after nineteen sixteen. All the right mood music. We can make some running out of this. Get in quick, control the narrative. Those kids might have started something big.

Grace! Thank God, you're okay. I was really worried about you.

GRACE: Bannion. What do you want?

BANNION: Were you injured?

GRACE: I'm fine.

BANNION: Are you sure… no bumps, no bruises?

GRACE: I got pepper sprayed.

BANNION: Did you!

> That's brilliant. That's really brilliant. Let me see.
>
> Dry skin… inflamed… no blisters. We could have done with some blisters.

GRACE: I didn't see you at the protest.

BANNION: I was there. You didn't see me?

GRACE: I was looking for you. You weren't there.

BANNION: Damn! We must have missed each other. The crowds…

> It felt like the good old days I have to say, to stand there facing down the guards. It brought me back. Brought me back to my Student Union days. Take the streets! Barricades!
>
> You can't tell can you? That's the genius with pepper spray. It doesn't leave a mark.
>
> I'm just glad you weren't hurt.

GRACE: It doesn't matter what happens to me. It matters that we keep this going. I'm not going to let them arrest us and ignore us. Not this time.

BANNION: Exactly… exactly what I was thinking… You need to get your voice heard don't you?

> I was talking to an old friend of mine in RTE, they're looking for someone to interview… Six O'Clock News.

GRACE: The news?

BANNION: This is history Grace. Sometimes the world opens a little slipstream and if you step into it, there's no knowing where you'll end up…

GRACE: We're all in this together. I don't have any right to speak on other people's behalf.

BANNION: Why are we protesting? Give it to me in one sentence.

GRACE: I can't sum up the entire re-imagining of our social order in a sound bite…

BANNION: If you had to sum it up…

GRACE: But the point is, you can't…

BANNION: If you had to…

GRACE: One: Debt cancellation and redistribution of capital… Two: political reform through direct democratic participation. Three: Environmental…

BANNION: Stop.

Two is enough.

I have one great skill Grace. And that's reading the mood-music. This thing that's coming… We need someone to lead it.

GRACE: I have to get blankets.

BANNION: Send someone else to get the bloody blankets.

It's you Grace. It can't be anyone else. *(Pause.)*

GRACE: I can say what ever I want.

BANNION: We'll keep it simple and focus…

GRACE: I say whatever I want.

BANNION: Of course…

(Pause.)

There is something else…

I've just been at a meeting with a senior Garda. We go way back.

He says they'll let us get in supplies if we hand over those responsible for the violence.

There was an attack. A serious act of violence on the streets of Dublin. You see how that changes things don't you?

GRACE: Tell him we'll hand over those responsible when they charge the Gardai who beat up our protesters.

BANNION: Now, you're smarter than that. That won't help us at all.

They're panicking. The cameras are rolling on them as well.

GRACE: They're looking for a clean way to de-escalate the situation.

BANNION: Exactly. They'll appreciate it if we find a way of working with them. That will help.

Who was it stabbed the police horse Grace?

They're going to want to know. We can use that. We need to get control of how this plays out. It's leverage.

I've heard it was that boy who is always trailing after you. Finbar is his name?

You might be trying to protect him? Maybe your attachment to him is more important than the movement?

GRACE: No. *(Pause.)*

BANNION: Was it Finbar?

GRACE nods.

BANNION: We'll have to choose how to give him up carefully.

We get him out of here... Deny he had anything to do with the camp. The most important thing is you keep well away from him now. Do you hear me Grace? He could drag you down.

This is a big moment for you.

ENTER FINBAR. He has his hood up and is wearing a scarf around his face.

FINBAR: Hello.

BANNION: Finbar...

It is Finbar, isn't it? Grace was just telling me about you. She says you're a fine activist. And a keen mind I'm sure.

FINBAR: Did she say that?

BANNION: You know it does my heart good to see young people show a bit of backbone finally.

I'll tell you this for nothing, you are the future, you young people. You agree?

FINBAR: I...

BANNION: Yes. No doubt about it. I look at you and I see a hopeful future.

FINBAR: Do you?

BANNION: You're who it all depends upon, there's no doubt about that.

You feel free on a day like this don't you, Finbar?

FINBAR: It feels amazing.

BANNION: Of course it does young man.

Remember this day, every moment. You mightn't always have days like this.

FINBAR: Thanks... I think it's important that we...

BANNION claps FINBAR on the arm.

BANNION: Good lad. That's the spirit.

> Grace, I've to make a few phone calls. We'll go over everything… this is going to be huge for you.

EXIT BANNION.

FINBAR: The guards aren't letting people leave the grounds of the asylum. Everyone says there's going to be mass arrests.

> What's stopping them? Why are they waiting?

GRACE: Too much attention at the minute. They know there's not enough tents or sleeping bags. They'll let us spend the night in the cold, see if we've as much zeal in the morning.

FINBAR: People are singing, dancing. It's like a festival.

> I'm afraid Grace. You think I should hand myself in?

GRACE: You were wearing a scarf and hood. They might not be able to identify you from the photographs.

FINBAR: Do you think I'll go to jail?

GRACE: It'll work out.

> We need to get you out of here. You can't be arrested in the camp.

FINBAR: I don't want to leave.

GRACE: We have to smuggle you out of the grounds, get you away from here.

FINBAR: I want to stay with the protest. I want to help you.

GRACE: Finbar you have to stop this. Stop clinging to me.

FINBAR: One moment I feel a connection with you. I know there's something there. The next you look at me like you've forgotten that I exist. What am I doing wrong? Tell me and I'll fix it.

GRACE: You can't fix it.

FINBAR: Do you feel anything for me?

GRACE: I'm your friend.

FINBAR: Are you?

GRACE: Yes.

FINBAR: Well forgive me then for not being able to not want more.

GRACE: You can't force me to feel something for you.

FINBAR: I want to kiss you.

GRACE: Finbar...

FINBAR: It might solve everything.

GRACE: I don't think it will.

FINBAR: It might.

FINBAR kisses GRACE. She struggles away from him.

GRACE: You've got to leave.

FINBAR: Don't talk, let's just...

GRACE: No, I am going to talk.

They're going to arrest you. You're going to jail. That can't be stopped. I can't be seen with you Finbar.

If you want to do one last thing for me. If you do care about me, then make it so I never knew you. If they find you, say you were never here.

(Pause.)

FINBAR: The day we first met, you probably don't remember... you handed me a leaflet about Palestine outside the GPO. I was shaking.

You had an undercut and wore a heavy coat and you were blowing on your hands in the freezing cold. I knew it

449

straight away. Damn it, I thought, I've never seen anyone like this in my whole life.

I can't explain it. I've never had any defenses around you.

GRACE: I'm sorry.

Enter LIZARD in a mask holding a lit flare.

LIZARD: They've broken through. They're firing tear gas and beating anything that moves.

FINBAR: Who have?

LIZARD: The shades, it's like Fallujah! They're making their move. Widescreen, 3-D, big production values. It's awesome!

FINBAR: Are they arresting people?

LIZARD: They'd fucking like to.

GRACE: Go!

EXIT FINBAR.

LIZARD: *(With megaphone.)* Ain't no power like the power of the people, cause the power of the people can't stop…

Come on… I can't fucking hear you…

Banks got bailed out, we got sold out…

Taoiseach in your ivory tower… this is called people power.

Rattle their teeth with your voices! Louder! You have to be louder!

Ain't no power like the power of the people, cause the

power of the people can't stop…

Out! Out! Out! Out! Out! Out! Out! Out! Out! Out! Out! Out! Out! Out! Out! Out! Out!

SCENE 9

Commemoration Park: 2026.

GRACE: I never sensed anything in him that suggested he was capable of doing what he did. There was no sign. It wasn't my fault.

Was there something I missed?

2016. The day before the protests.

ENTER FINBAR with a rucksack and posters.

LIZARD: Where are you Finbar?

FINBAR: It's the day before the protest. Me and Grace have been cycling around for hours. We must have covered every message board and pole in the North Inner city and we've still got more posters. I think they're multiplying on us.

GRACE sits down on a bench looking out at the sea.

We could cycle up by North Wall, I don't think we covered there yet? Or out towards Howth? It's far out but I'm up for it if you are?

GRACE: We've enough done.

FINBAR: Thank God. I'm not sure I can go on any longer.

Something is going to happen this time. Isn't it? I can't face another march where nothing happens. It's starting to feel pointless. Something better happen. Something has to happen.

(Pause.)

What are you looking at?

GRACE: The sea.

FINBAR: *(Pause.)* It's very blue isn't it? *(Pause.)* Or purple… you could say it's purple either. Although the sky is making it a little red now… you could say it's a little red.

I've never really known what people are looking at when they're looking out at the sea.

GRACE takes out a bottle of wine. She takes off the lid and starts slugging from the bottle.

GRACE: Are you going to sit down?

FINBAR: Those posters will be seen by thousands and thousands of people… if only a tenth of those people turned up…

GRACE: It won't make a difference.

FINBAR: What?

GRACE: The same people will turn up that always turn up. Everyone will walk right by the posters and think nothing of them.

FINBAR: What have we been doing then?

GRACE: Maybe we need them to convince ourselves that what we're doing is actually happening.

People won't pay any attention until something really terrible happens. Then they'll pay attention for a short time. Then they'll stop paying attention again until something even worse than the first thing happens.

FINBAR: What would keep their attention?

GRACE: Maybe there's just a tipping point… something all of a sudden that makes everything different. Like when Mohamed Bouazizi set himself on fire in Tunisia. One day this ordinary street vendor walks out into the middle of the road covered in petrol, shouts, "how do you expect me to make a living?" lights up a match, presses it to his cheek and the world changes. Arab Spring.

Human sacrifice.

GRACE laughs.

Maybe it'll change just like that. Something completely unexpected will set it all off.

GRACE passes FINBAR the bottle. She stands up on the bench and holds out her arms.

When I look at the sea I want to just push off into it. Set sail for some distant, incredible place with an unpronounceable name. I want to be overwhelmed.

I think I was Grainne Maol in a past life.

FINBAR: You probably were. It would make sense if you were. *(Pause.)*

GRACE: Have you ever felt like your falling, even though you're really only standing still?

FINBAR: I think so.

GRACE: It feels like I'm falling through the sky and I'm flapping my arms to find out if I have any feathers on them. I might be a bird or I might be a drop of rain, I don't know yet.

FINBAR: You might be a meteorite.

GRACE: What?

FINBAR: You might be a meteorite hitting the earth's atmosphere.

GRACE: I like that.

GRACE sits.

I'm thinking of leaving Ireland for a while.

FINBAR: Where would you go?

GRACE: Anna-Garcia was telling me about a co-operative outside Granada. They live in caves dug into the hills outside the city. The gypsies have been doing it for hundreds of years.

FINBAR: You want to live in a cave?

GRACE: I want to escape. Stop fighting for a while.

Would you go?

FINBAR: Absolutely.

GRACE: You'd live in a cave with me?

FINBAR: Yes.

GRACE: There's no running water.

FINBAR: That would be fine.

GRACE: No toilet. No money.

FINBAR: It sounds perfect.

I'd go anywhere with you Grace.

GRACE looks at FINBAR. She laughs. She kisses him.

FINBAR: I am... besotted... by you.

GRACE: We should get back to the camp.

FINBAR: I've been thinking about this...

GRACE: Please, can we not have a big serious talk. I just want to drink wine.

FINBAR: No. I know. I know. I'm sorry. It's just... you feel that. I'm shaking. Sorry. No, I know. I feel good. This feels good doesn't it?

GRACE: Can I have another drink?

FINBAR hands her the bottle. She takes a drink.

FINBAR: This happened didn't it? Things won't just revert to how they were before. I can't go back to how it was before. Not now. Not when I feel like this.

GRACE: I have to meet Meabh Kelly for a drink later.

FINBAR: Sure. Of course.

GRACE: What I said… It's wrong to sound despondent. It's too easy. The march is going to be huge. It's important that you remember that. We'll get their attention but it's going to take time.

FINBAR: Things are changing Grace… I can feel it.

Exit FINBAR.

SCENE 10

Two weeks after FINBAR's death. 2016: The Protest Camp. The site has a pile of heather around his picture, tributes, a kind of shrine.

ENTER FRANCES.

LIZARD: Who is she?

GRACE: Finbar's mother. Frances. I met her two weeks after it happened. I was leaving flowers where he died.

FRANCES is standing before the shrine.

GRACE walks towards her carrying a bunch of heather.

GRACE: Mrs. Plunkett. I was a friend of Finbar's.

FRANCES: I know who you are. *(Pause.)*

I suppose he's meant to be some class of martyr now…

GRACE: I'm sorry.

FRANCES: Don't apologise… Too many people apologising…

Sorry, sorry, sorry for your troubles, so sorry to hear about your son… What are they all so sorry about? It's not their fault is it?

They didn't know him anyway. Seen some piece of pornography with my son in it and they think they've connected with him. Nonsense.

(Pause.)

GRACE: Did you watch it…?

Of course not… I'm sorry.

FRANCES: What did I just say?

I don't know what these people are wasting their money for.

FRANCES picks up a condolence card.

Listen to this one. This is the worst.

"Dear Finbar, I have been on the edge of despair…"

The edge of despair… do you hear her!

"I've been on the edge of despair for years and have stayed quiet. Buried all my thoughts, swallowed them and struggled on. Lost my job. Lost my house. I felt guilty and alone. What you did has punctured the shame and the silence. I hope you find rest from all your pain."

What pain?

She doesn't know pain. I don't believe her.

GRACE: Some good might come of this.

FRANCES: What good could come of what he did?

GRACE: You must be in grief.

FRANCES: You don't know anything. Don't let on you do.

It's curious how people take on to tell you what you're feeling.

(Pause.)

He didn't leave a letter… No explanation. I suppose there's people who think it was my fault?

I've never believed in molly-coddling anyone.

What had him get involved with you lot? It didn't seem like him at all…

GRACE: He was looking for something. He thought he found it with us.

FRANCES: Well he must have been wrong. If it came to this. *(Pointing at the flower GRACE is still gripping)*

You brought flowers. *(Pause.)*

He came home the night of those riots, let himself into the house without letting me know he was there. That was always his way. So private.

I went up to him. I wanted to know he was alright. I'd been worrying watching the riots on the news, glued to it, trying to pick out his face in the pictures. They were saying there were dangerous people there. I knew Finbar wouldn't be any good around anyone like that.

I rang the guards and they told me that if my son was in the park I'd be able to visit him in his cell once they'd all been arrested. The cheeky bitch. I gave her some earful.

I went into his room and he was bent over on the edge of the bed, just staring at the floor. He was muttering to himself.

He wouldn't answer me. He wasn't making any sense.

If I could have reached out and touched him, if I could have unfurled the fingers of his sadness and shook him…

(Pause.)

What did he have to do this for…

He might have at least been discreet about it. Making a holy show of himself.

GRACE: Some people think what he did matters.

FRANCES: His mind was astray. Don't make this into something it's not.

GRACE: I don't have to, something is already happening.

FRANCES: How? What for?

GRACE: People have taken notice.

FRANCES: This flower business?

GRACE: People are beginning to organise. They're saying what he did was a protest.

FRANCES: You're all mad. You're so mad it hurts me to listen to you. What did you want to achieve here?

GRACE: Another way to live.

FRANCES: Another way to live. Not one of you is fit to imagine a world beyond yourself. A world your grandmother could live in.

There is only this way. *(Pause.)*

This was my son. I raised him, I poured my heart into him and watched him grow. You have no idea what this feels like.

(Pause.)

You asked me did I watch the video of my son's death.

I did. Mother's are infinitely strong, you'll discover that if you ever become one. I watched it. I watched it one morning because I couldn't bear the thought of it. I thought if I watched it I could get rid of the hold it had over me.

I watched it at my kitchen table with a cup of cold tea in my hand.

He was solemn until he dropped the match. When he went on fire he started to do this strange jig. There was something... comic... about it.

Then he fell to his knees as if he was tired, slumped forward on his hands. Something black dripped off the end of his nose. I suppose it was what used to be his face running off.

Finally, he sat back, a dark lump, and was completely still. That's what it was. He died like that. Whatever else you lie about, don't lie about that.

Forget about flowers. They should bring lumps of charcoal instead.

I tried. You might not believe that but I did. In my own way. I did.

(Pause.)

GRACE: He sent me a letter. Before...

FRANCES: Did he mention me?

GRACE shakes her head.

(Pause.)

FRANCES: Are things this bad? They can't be. It can't be worth this...

EXIT FRANCES.

SCENE 11

The Commemoration Park. 2026.

GRACE: He left a note in my things before he ran off.

I still have it.

GRACE is looking back into the site of the old protest camp: 2016

FINBAR has a petrol tank.

He takes out a selfie stick and phone. He starts talking into it.

FINBAR: My name is Finbar Plunkett.

FINBAR jams the stick and video into the ground.

He starts to hum "Wild Mountain Thyme".

GRACE: *(Starting to read the letter.)* Goodbye… I'm sorry. I've let everyone down. I've ruined everything that we were working for.

Being in the camp was something like happiness. I hope the future will be a better place then now. I hope people will stay true. It was great to know you.

I've ruined everything. I understand if you hate me.

Finbar.

FINBAR tips the petrol can over his head.

FINBAR takes out a box of matches.

FINBAR strikes the match.

FINBAR: *(To the camera.)* Bring us your love, it'll be a better…

Bring us your love…

No. What was it… we will make a better… Oh fuck it. Fuck it! FUCK IT!

Grace…

The match burns the tip of FINBAR's finger and he drops the match.

FINBAR bursts into flames.

SCENE 12

2026: The Commemoration Park.

LIZARD, wearing the mask and tail.

GRACE walks to the statue.

She stands in front of it.

LIZARD: What are you going to say about him in your speech?

GRACE: Nothing. I don't own him. I don't have the right to explain or use what he did. But I'll hold him in my mind and remember what he did. After that I'll stay quiet.

GRACE covers the statue of FINBAR with the sheet.

GRACE hears the singing in the distance.

GRACE: They're waiting on the streets. The people. I know what that means now. I used to think it was something abstract or vague. It's not, it's just rare. When it does erupt from whatever deep spring it was gathering in, it is precise and sharp as a blade... capable of almost anything. Terrible. Bracing.

(To LIZARD.)

Will you come to O'Connell Street with me?

LIZARD: I'll stay. It will be nice to sleep here if the rain holds off.

GRACE: You know Lizards have claws?

LIZARD: Claws?

On their fingers?

GRACE: And their feet...

LIZARD: Their feet too?

GRACE: They do. I have to say, I don't think you'll be properly finished without them.

LIZARD: I never thought of claws.

GRACE: I have to go.

LIZARD: Claws…

GRACE: Goodbye Lizard.

LIZARD: I'll input your data into the formula.

When it works everything through, it will take you into account. You'll be a variable.

Stage falls black aside from a single spot on GRACE. She is standing on the podium in O'Connell Street. There are thousands of her supporters gathered on the street.

They begin to sing… "Wild Mountain Thyme"

CROWD: Oh, the summer time is coming/ And the trees are sweetly blooming/ And the wild mountain thyme/ Grows around the blooming heather/ Will you go lassie, go?

The CROWD keeps singing.

ENTER BANNION.

BANNION: Grace. We've prepared your speech. Gonzi has signed off on it. He's seen the polling data and sends his congratulations… He's assured that you're someone he can work with. We'll win other battles Grace. This keeps us in the game.

You've blood on your neck.

GRACE: It's hot.

BANNION: Are you alright?

GRACE: I'm burning up.

GRACE turns and takes off her jacket.

GRACE is wearing a white shirt, soaked through at the back by blood.

BANNION: Grace, your back! Have you been attacked?! Let me look at you.

Blood has seeped through her shirt from the newly cut tattoo down her spine. It spells the word 'traitor'.

BANNION: Grace.

GRACE: I know why you did it.

BANNION: Did what Grace…?

GRACE: I don't blame you.

BANNION: Blame me for what?

GRACE takes the speech and rips in down the middle and drops it on the floor.

BANNION: Hold on a second…

GRACE: Now that I've decided to do this, I can't imagine how I ever thought I could do anything else.

GRACE turns and walks confidently to the front of the podium.

Huge cheers…

GRACE: Friends…

I know you expect me to stand here today and tell you that there is hope. That we will come together to make this country better and overcome all the evils and the fears and the uncertainty that trouble your heart as it troubles mine.

I can't do that. I can't promise you that things will get better. I don't know that it will.

I know… I know you expected me to tell you that if you followed me, that if you voted for me, I would bring back certainty and dignity to your lives. I won't lie to you any longer… It is going to be much, much harder than that.

We are facing into a terrifying future and we have no guide, no certainty. No better life is promised to us.

But it is our task.

It is our life.

We have made mistakes… but we have to control our fears and anxieties and remember what happens if we walk away from our responsibility towards each other.

Things cannot go back to how it was before. I will not betray your trust. There has been too much suffering to let power have its way today. If it wants to extinguish your spirit I will not be the one to do it for them.

Friends, if you will listen, I want to tell you about the things that are happening behind closed doors without your consent. I want to tell you everything I know about the threats that have been made against you, about the efforts that are being made to quash this democratic surge erupting here today.

I want you to know the truth because you have to know how hard this is going to be. I want to give everything I have to you… because I have faith in you…

Lights down on GRACE.

LIZARD is in the Commemoration Park listening to the speech from the distance.

He stomps about. He spits on the ground.

He flicks his tail sadly. He flexes the fingers on his hands.

Light slowly fade, first on the park, then on the statue.